PACIFIC NORTHWEST

TRAVEL✦SMART™ TRIP PLANNER

Richard Harris

John Muir Publications
Santa Fe, New Mexico

Other JMP Books by Richard Harris
American Southwest Travel◆Smart Trip Planner
2 to 22 Days in Florida
2 to 22 Days in Texas
Unique California
Unique Oregon

John Muir Publications, P.O. Box 613, Santa Fe, New Mexico 87504

Printed in the United States of America.
First printing September 1996.

Parts of this book were originally published in *2 to 22 Days in the Pacific Northwest* © 1988, 1991, 1992, 1993, 1994, and 1995 by Black Mesa Production, Inc.

ISSN 1087-3880
ISBN 1-56261-257-3

Cover photo: Unicorn Stock Photos/David Cummings
Back cover photos: *top*—Leo de Wys, Inc./Geoff Butler
                          bottom—Unicorn Stock Photos/Charles E. Schmidt
Maps: American Custom Maps—Albuquerque, NM USA
Editors: Dianna Delling, Peggy Schaefer, Chris Hayhurst, Elizabeth Wolf
Design: Janine Lehmann, Linda Braun
Typesetting: Kathleen Sparkes—White Hart Design
Production: Marie Vigil, Nikki Rooker
Graphics Coordination: Sarah Horowitz, Joanne Jakub
Printing: Publishers Press

Distributed to the book trade by
Publishers Group West
Emeryville, California

PACIFIC NORTHWEST
TRAVEL·SMART™ TRIP PLANNER

HOW TO USE THIS BOOK

This *Pacific Northwest Travel ◆ Smart Trip Planner* is organized in 22 destination chapters, each covering the best sights and activities, restaurants, and lodging available in that specific destination. Thanks to thorough research and experience, the author is able to bring you only the best options, saving you time and money in your travels. The chapters are presented in geographic sequence so you can follow an easy route from one to the next. If you were to visit each destination in chapter order, you'd enjoy a complete tour of the best of the Pacific Northwest.

Each chapter contains:

• User-friendly maps of the area, showing all recommended sights, restaurants, and accommodations.

• "A Perfect Day" description—how the author would spend his time if he had just one day in that destination.

• Sightseeing highlights, each rated by degree of importance: ★★★ Don't miss; ★★ Try hard to see; ★ See if you have time; and No stars—Worth knowing about.

• Selected restaurant, lodging, and camping recommendations to suit a variety of budgets.

• Helpful hints, fitness and recreation ideas, insights, and random tidbits of information to enhance your trip.

The Importance of Planning. Developing an itinerary is the best way to get the most satisfaction from your travels, and this guidebook makes it easy. First, read through the book and choose the places you'd most like to visit. Then, study the color map on the inside cover flap and the mileage chart (page 12) to determine which you can realistically see in the time you have available and at the travel pace you prefer. Using the Planning Map (pages 10–11), map out your route. Finally, use the lodging recommendations to determine your accommodations.

Some Suggested Itineraries. To get you started, five itineraries of varying lengths and based on specific interests follow. Mix and match according to your interests and time constraints, or follow a given itinerary from start to finish. The possibilities are endless. *Happy travels!*

SUGGESTED ITINERARIES

With the *Pacific Northwest Travel✦Smart Trip Planner* you can plan a trip of any length—a one-day excursion, a getaway weekend, or a three-week vacation—around any special interest. To get you started, the following pages contain five suggested itineraries geared toward a variety of interests. For more information, refer to the chapters listed—chapter names are bolded and chapter numbers appear inside black bullets. You can follow a suggested itinerary in its entirety, or shorten, lengthen, or combine parts of each, depending on your starting and ending points.

Discuss alternative routes and schedules with your travel companions—it's a great way to have fun, even before you leave home. And remember: don't hesitate to change your itinerary once you're on the road. Careful study and planning ahead of time will help you make informed decisions as you go, but spontaneity is the extra ingredient that will make your trip memorable.

Nature Lover's Tour

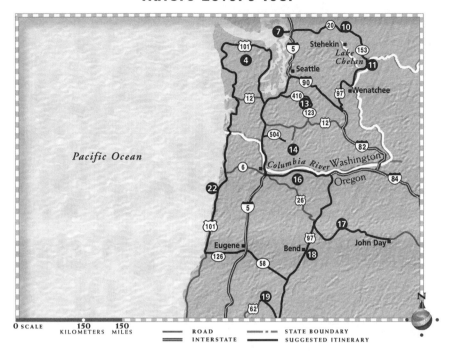

Begin with a ferry trip and orca watching in the San Juan Islands. Travel over the North Cascades Highway to Lake Chelan, returning by way of Mount Rainier National Park and Mount St. Helens. Extend your trip into Oregon by adding the spectacular Columbia River Gorge to your itinerary. Then head south around the back side of Mount Hood and venture to the painted desert of John Day Country, returning by way of Bend and Newberry Crater National Volcanic Monument. Complete the volcanic portion of your trip with a visit to Crater Lake, then return up the Pacific Coast and around the Olympic Peninsula.

- **7** San Juan Island
- **10** North Cascades Highway
- **11** Lake Chelan
- **13** Mount Rainier
- **14** Mount St. Helens
- **16** Columbia Gorge

- **17** John Day Country
- **18** Bend
- **19** Crater Lake
- **22** Northern Oregon Coast
- **4** Olympic National Park

Time needed for this tour: One week for Washington only or Oregon only; at least two weeks for the full tour.

Pacific Northwest in 1 to 3 Weeks

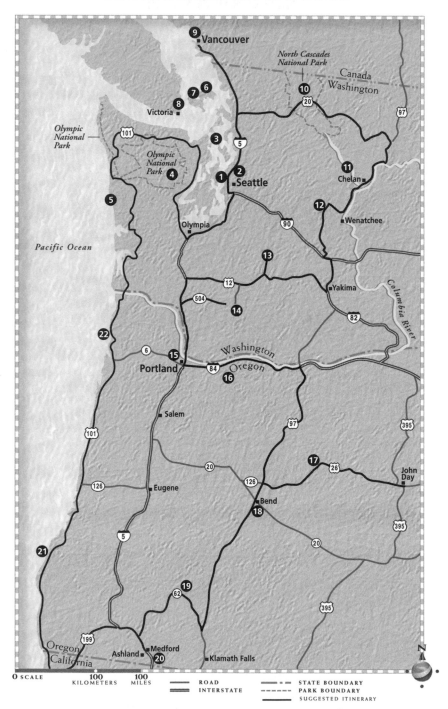

9 Vancouver

North Cascades National Park

Canada
Washington

7 **6**

8
Victoria ■

Olympic National Park

3

10
⑳

㊽

5

11
Chelan ■

Olympic National Park
4

1 **2**
■ Seattle

12

5

Olympia
■

㉚

■ Wenatchee

Pacific Ocean

13

㊻

■ Yakima

Columbia River

⑫
504

14

㊷

22

⑥ **15**
Portland ■

Washington
㊼

Oregon

16

■ Salem

⑨⑦

㊱

㉛

⑳

⑨⑦

17 ㉖

John Day ■

㉕

■ Eugene

㉖
■ Bend

18

㉕

㉛

⑤

21

19
㊽

20
Ashland ■ ■ Medford

■ Klamath Falls

Oregon
California

⑲⑨

N

The tour described is a loop trip. You can start at the most convenient point on the circle. The time required for this itinerary is three weeks. If you have less time to travel, the itinerary breaks up nicely into several shorter trips that make for great weekend to week-long excursions from the Seattle and Portland areas.

Seattle Area (2 days)

- **①** Seattle
- **②** Around Seattle

Puget Sound, San Juan Island, and Vancouver, B.C. (5 days)

- **③** Puget Sound
- **⑥** Orcas Island
- **⑦** San Juan Island
- **⑧** Victoria, B.C.
- **⑨** Vancouver, B.C.

Central Washington (4 days)

- **⑩** North Cascades
- **⑪** Lake Chelan
- **⑫** Apple Country
- **⑬** Mount Rainier

Portland Area (3 days)

- **⑭** Mount St. Helens
- **⑮** Portland
- **⑯** Columbia Gorge

Oregon's Desert and Mountains (3 days)

- **⑰** John Day Country
- **⑱** Bend
- **⑲** Crater Lake
- **⑳** Ashland

Oregon Coast (3 days)

- **㉑** Southern Oregon Coast
- **㉒** Northern Oregon Coast

For a loop trip, Olympic Peninsula is on the return route to Seattle (2 days)

- **④** Olympic National Park
- **⑤** Washington Coast

Arts and Culture Tour

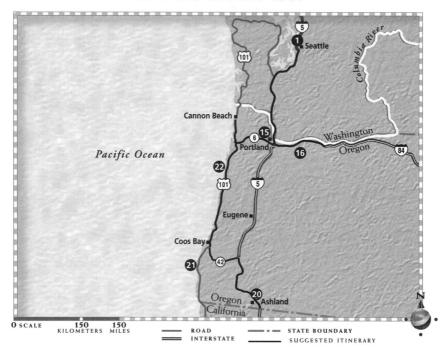

To explore Northwestern arts, first spend at least two days in Seattle, which has the largest art museum in the region as well as two major museums of Asian art and an American Indian arts center, not to mention active popular and classical music, dance, and theater scenes. Portland also has its share of fine arts, ranging from an outstanding art museum to concerts at the zoo.

The arts will also take you by surprise in some of the Northwest's most remote areas. From Portland, take a day trip up the Columbia River to the Maryhill Museum of Art. Then follow the coast south, visiting artists' colonies such as Cannon Beach and outstanding local art museums like the one at Coos Bay, ending up in Ashland for a weekend of world-class theater.

1   **Seattle**
15   **Portland**
16   **Columbia Gorge**
20   **Ashland**
21   **Southern Oregon Coast**
22   **Northern Oregon Coast**

Time needed for this tour: At least eight days.

Hiking, Biking, and Outdoor Sports Tour

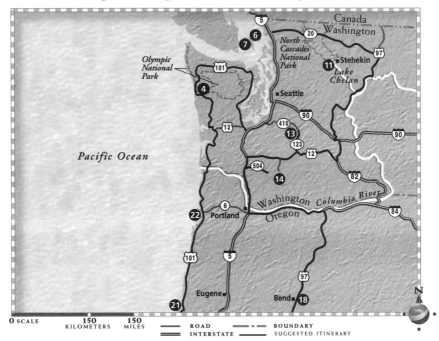

You'll find great hiking and biking just about everywhere you go in the Northwest, including major cities. This itinerary offers maximum outdoor adventure.

6 **Orcas Island** (bike around the island; climb Mount Constitution)

7 **San Juan Island** (sea kayak)

11 **Lake Chelan** (stay in Stehekin, a base for hiking North Cascades National Park)

13 **Mount Rainier** (volcano hiking)

14 **Mount St. Helens** (volcano hiking)

18 **Bend** (bike touring at Newberry Crater, Cascades Lakes; hiking in Crater Lake National Park)

21 **Southern Oregon Coast** (scenic drive)

22 **Northern Oregon Coast** (scenic drive)

4 **Olympic National Park Coast** (backpacking in Hoh Rain Forest and up west side of Mount Olympus)

Time needed for this trip: At least three weeks. Most of these adventures can be done separately in two or three days each.

Family Fun Tour

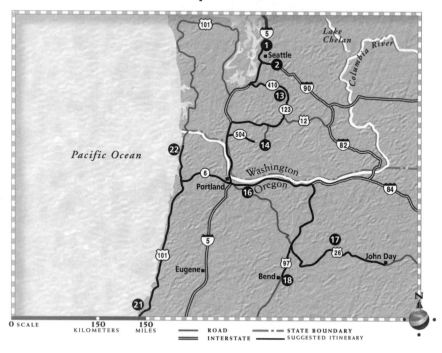

Topping the list of kids' destinations in the Seattle area are the aquarium, the Underground Tour, the monorail, and, of course, Seattle Center with its children's museum, science center, and Fun Forest. While many outdoor itinerary segments covered in this book are fun with children, the most exciting ones include Northwest Trek and Mount St. Helens. If you're visiting during salmon run season, don't miss the spectacle of swarms of salmon climbing the fish ladders over Bonneville Dam. The central Oregon Coast, with its tide pools, sand dunes, and sea lion caves, was made for family fun. If time permits, a trip to the east side of the Cascades means tantalizing young imaginations with more volcanoes in the Bend area and fossils of prehistoric beasts at John Day Fossil Beds.

❶ **Seattle**
❷ **Around Seattle**
⓭ **Mount Rainier** (Northwest Trek)
⓮ **Mount St. Helens**
⓰ **Columbia Gorge** (Bonneville Dam)

㉒ **Northern Oregon Coast**
㉑ **Southern Oregon Coast**
⓲ **Bend**
⓱ **John Day Country**

Time needed for this tour: Nine days.

USING THE PLANNING MAP

A major aspect of itinerary planning is determining your mode of transportation and the route you will follow as you travel from destination to destin ation. The Planning Map on the following pages will allow you to do just that.

First, read through the destination chapters carefully and note the sights that intrigue you. Then, photocopy the Planning Map so you can try out several different routes that will take you to these destinations. (The mileage chart that follows will allow you to calculate your travel distances.) Decide where you will be starting your tour of the Pacific Northwest. Will you fly into Seattle, Portland, or Vancouver, or will you start from somewhere in between? Will you be driving from place to place or flying into major transportation hubs and renting a car for day trips? The answers to these questions will form the basis for your travel route design.

Once you have a firm idea of where your travels will take you, copy your route onto the additional Planning Map in the Appendix. You won't have to worry about where your map is, and the information you need on each destination will always be close at hand.

Planning Map: Pacific Northwest

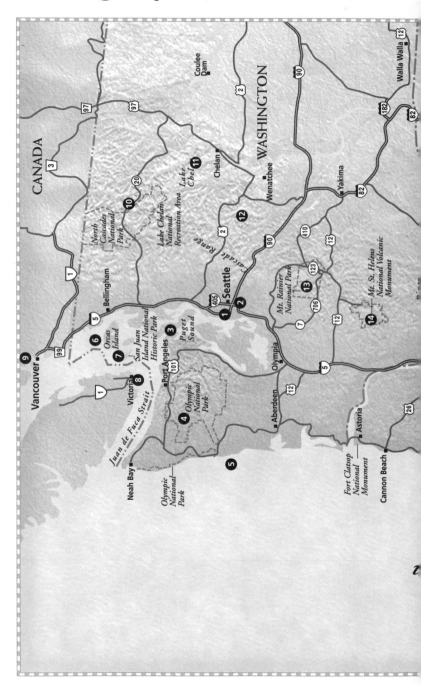

You have permission to photocopy this map.

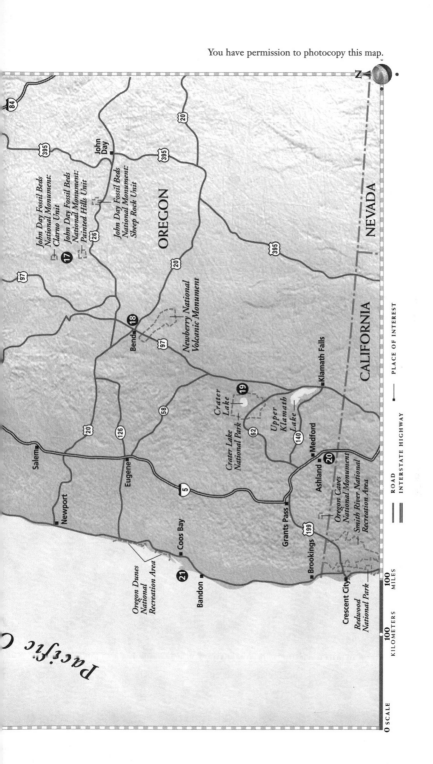

John Day Fossil Beds
National Monument:
Clarno Unit

John Day Fossil Beds
National Monument:
Painted Hills Unit

John Day Fossil Beds
National Monument:
Sheep Rock Unit

John Day

OREGON

Newberry National
Volcanic Monument

Bend

Klamath Falls

Crater
Lake

Upper
Klamath
Lake

Crater Lake
National Park

Salem

Newport

Eugene

Coos Bay

Bandon

Oregon Dunes
National
Recreation Area

Grants Pass

Medford

Ashland

Oregon Caves
National Monument

Smith River National
Recreation Area

Brookings

Crescent City

Redwood
National Park

CALIFORNIA

NEVADA

Pacific O

ROAD
INTERSTATE HIGHWAY
PLACE OF INTEREST

N

0 SCALE

100
KILOMETERS

100
MILES

PACIFIC NORTHWEST MILEAGE CHART

	Seattle	Port Townsend	Vancouver, BC	Concrete	Neah Bay	Port Angeles	Bandon	Ashland	Crater Lake	Bend	John Day	Government Camp	Portland	Astoria	Olympia	Yakima	Wenatchee
Port Townsend	50																
Vancouver, BC	142	122															
Concrete	91	141	128														
Neah Bay	149	122	291	240													
Port Angeles	75	46	183	166	74												
Bandon	411	498	553	502	517	523											
Ashland	460	487	602	551	608	519	182										
Crater Lake	433	460	575	524	587	492	185	85									
Bend	335	362	477	426	489	394	265	200	111								
John Day	410	466	552	501	593	498	401	353	264	153							
Government Camp	230	257	372	321	384	289	324	304	215	104	207						
Portland	175	202	317	266	329	234	236	285	258	160	264	55					
Astoria	175	215	317	266	234	240	283	374	353	255	359	150	95				
Olympia	60	100	202	151	195	121	352	370	374	276	380	171	116	115			
Yakima	142	187	284	296	291	217	421	419	330	219	268	166	185	243	161		
Wenatchee	138	160	237	189	270	196	528	526	437	326	375	273	293	313	188	107	
Chelan	163	188	365	150	298	224	557	555	466	355	408	310	318	338	216	136	37

Orcas Island, San Juan Island, and Victoria can all be reached by ferry.

Port Angeles–Victoria: 23 miles, 1 hour 35 min.; $27 car and driver, $6.50 adult passengers, $3.25 children; Tel. (206) 622-2222.

Seattle—Victoria: 78 miles, 4.5 hours; $46.15 car and driver, $20.80 passenger; Tel. (800) 683-7977 or (360) 625-1880.

Port Townsend–San Juan Islands: 2.5–3 hours; $42.50 RT adults, $30 ages 5–10; Tel. (360) 385-5288.

Washington State Ferries also offers car and passenger transportation. Call for current departures and fares. Tel. (206) 464-6400.

WHY VISIT THE PACIFIC NORTHWEST?

This trip planner guides you on a journey of discovery around a unique, diverse corner of the United States. Along the way you'll wander through wildflower meadows on the slopes of a towering volcano, its fiery soul shrouded in perpetual ice. You'll venture into uninhabited desert where rainbow-hued sands conceal the bones of prehistoric camels and saber-toothed cats. You'll reach out and touch strange living creatures in lava tide pools along sea-swept headlands and, just minutes away, stroll for miles along soft beaches where yours may be the only footprints.

You'll find an exquisite art museum in a French-style château far from civilization, hike through wild woodlands right in the heart of a big city, and sit quietly in an Indian longhouse as ghostly murmurs in an ancient tongue transport you to the dim past. Wildlife, too, abounds in the Pacific Northwest, and you may encounter rare opportunities to watch a bald eagle soaring free, photograph a buffalo or a mountain goat, or glimpse a killer whale. These are just a few of the memorable experiences that await you as you follow the suggestions in this guide to the most fascinating places in Washington and Oregon as well as the major cities of British Columbia.

Variety is the spice of any pleasure trip, and nowhere in the world will you find more vivid contrasts than in the Pacific Northwest. This trip contains more than its share of sudden transitions. You can start your day on the shore of a small misty island, return to the mainland, and drive to the crest of a rugged mountain range in time for lunch. You can wake up in a big city, then travel through luxuriant forests, and find yourself in a vast uninhabited desert the same afternoon.

I sincerely hope that you enjoy your Northwestern trip as much as I've enjoyed gathering this information to share with you. A great sightseeing vacation is a work of art much like a great film or novel. Set in locations more spectacular than any movie, this vacation stars you and your travel companions. The "script" is your personalized trip itinerary. And like any great adventure, your journey of exploration will have a "plot"—a beginning, a climax, and ending, and plenty of exciting developments in between.

HISTORY AND CULTURES

C arbon dating has shown American Indian artifacts found near
Wenatchee, Washington, to be the most ancient ever discovered in
the Western Hemisphere, about 15,000 years old. This evidence has
compelled anthropologists to revise their estimates of when nomadic
humans first migrated to this continent. Exactly what the first human
residents of the Northwest were like is a mystery lost in antiquity's
mists. About all we know for sure is that they used stone-pointed spears
and throwing sticks to hunt the prehistoric elephantlike, camellike, and
horselike creatures whose fossil skeletons have been unearthed by the
thousands in the painted desert country of eastern Oregon.

Through the centuries that followed, some tribes established
coastal communities. Though their homes, tools, and works of art were
made from wood, lasting only a century or two in the damp coastal climate, evidence of thousands of years of human occupation is found in
the huge piles of clam shells, often 15 or 20 feet high, that mark the
sites of long-vanished fishing villages. Meanwhile, nomadic tribes continued to roam the land east of the Cascade Mountains, migrating to
the banks of the Columbia River and its tributaries for the annual
salmon runs. Some of the early people who established lasting settlements along the Columbia but later vanished left behind mysterious
effigies and large heads sculpted from volcanic rock.

The first European explorers to reach the Pacific Northwest came
by sea. In the 1500s the territory that is now Oregon, Washington, and
British Columbia was claimed for Great Britain by privateer Sir
Francis Drake and for Spain by the Aguilar and Vizcaino mapping
expedition. Both claims were hollow, since the Northwest coast was
too remote to colonize. It would be 136 years before another European
ship would anchor along the coast, and that ship would be Russian.
The 1700s would also bring British sea captains James Cook and
George Vancouver to Northwestern shores. Though no Frenchman
had ever set foot there, the territory was also claimed by France, which
sold its interest to the United States in 1803 for $15 million. The U.S.
claim was strengthened when American explorers Lewis and Clark
succeeded in mounting the first overland expedition to cross the west
and reach the Oregon coast. Great Britain continued to claim the
region until 1818, Spain until 1819, and Russia until 1824.

Settlement of the Pacific Northwest got its start in 1829 when

Boston teacher Hall Kelley, inspired by Lewis and Clark's published journals, formed the American Society for Encouraging the Settlement of the Oregon Territory and distributed pamphlets extolling the wealth and beauty of the region—which he had never seen. Years passed before settlers set out in pursuit of Kelley's dream. In 1842 physician Elija White organized the first wagon train, consisting of 120 people and a herd of cattle and other livestock, bound for Oregon's Willamette Valley. The pioneers followed the route mapped earlier in the same year by Lieutenant John Fremont and his guide, mountain man Kit Carson, which would come to be known as the Oregon Trail. Before the completion of the first transcontinental railroad 27 years later, 350,000 pioneers would follow the Oregon Trail—more than all other westward routes combined.

Most Indian tribes in the Pacific Northwest were made up of peace-loving people who put up no resistance to white settlers' intrusion in their domain, even though ranchers in Oregon organized vigilante groups to drive them away to the eastern badlands or exterminate them. The greatest conflict in Oregon was with the Nez Perce, or Saahaptin, people, the most powerful tribe in northeastern Oregon when the first non-Indian settlers arrived. They were moved onto a reservation in Oregon's Wallowa Valley in 1855, but when gold was discovered in the region, they were forced to relocate to a new reservation in Idaho. Some members of the tribe refused to move to the new reservation, touching off the Nez Perce war in 1877. Their leader, Chief Joseph, led 450 refugees on a trek across the Bitterroot Mountains, attempting to reach Canada, but they were captured a few miles before reaching the border. The surviving Nez Perce refugees were sent to Oklahoma but later transferred to a reservation in Washington state. In western Washington, coastal tribes were decimated by epidemics of unfamiliar diseases brought by the white man. Along Puget Sound and in the San Juan Islands, as much as 90 percent of the indigenous population was wiped out by measles within a decade after the first pioneers arrived.

Oregon became a state in 1859, while Washington remained a territory until 1889 before achieving statehood. Then, as now, western Oregon's economy was based on farming as well as timber, while the eastern parts of both states became the private domains of a small number of cattle ranchers. In western Washington, however, virtually all development in the nineteenth century was financed by timber cutting. As Washington's economy diversified with shipbuilding and more recently aerospace industries, timber continued to play a key role in the region through the 1980s, when clearcutting in the national forests reached record levels.

Environmentalists mounted a major campaign to save the northern spotted owl, a threatened species that lives only in ancient forests. Finally, in 1990, a federal district court issued an injunction making more than 3 million acres of ancient forest in the Northwest off-limits to logging. The actual cost to the Northwestern economy of protecting the owl, in terms of lost jobs and the collapse of timber-dependent communities, is not yet known, but there's no doubt that the fluffy little bird with big black eyes has sparked the most heated controversy to hit the region since the days when the United States, England, Spain, and Russia were arguing over ownership of the Pacific Northwest.

THE ARTS

Seattle and Portland boast outstanding performing arts. Seattle, especially, has one of the most active theater scenes on the West Coast, as well as a music scene that ranges from a very popular municipal opera company to dance clubs where dozens of "grunge" rock groups got their starts and later made their way to MTV. The ultimate destination in the Northwest for performing arts buffs, however, is Ashland, Oregon, where the whole town revolves around the oldest Shakespeare Festival in the United States.

The characteristic that most noticeably distinguishes visual arts in western Washington is the use of Northwest Coast Indian motifs, especially Kwakiutl designs. Although the Kwakiutl people live in British Columbia (where you'll find the largest collections of their work in Victoria and Vancouver), their designs are ubiquitous in the Puget Sound area. Contemporary Native American art is created at Daybreak Star Cultural Center, and older indigenous art traditions are being revived at the Makah Indian Cultural Center in Neah Bay and the Yakima Indian Cultural Center in Toppenish.

Both Seattle and Portland have major art museums, as well as more specialized venues that range from Seattle's Asian Art Museum to Portland's American Advertising Museum. However, some of the most interesting art museums are hidden in small Northwestern communities. The most spectacular example is the improbable Maryhill Museum of Art, far away from anyplace on a bluff overlooking a remote stretch of the Columbia River, where you'll find such exhibits as an outstanding Rodin sculpture collection and the Romanian royal furniture.

Washington and Oregon also have two of the most active state film boards in the country and consistently attract major feature films. From *National Lampoon's Animal House* and *Sometimes a Great Notion* to *The River Wild* and *Sleepless in Seattle*, you'll find plenty of previews of your Pacific Northwest adventure in your local video store.

CUISINE

In the Puget Sound area and along the Oregon coast, fresh food is an obsession of many residents. It seems as if every restaurant exudes the tantalizing smell of salmon fillets sizzling over an alder wood fire, and farmers' markets, fish markets, and innumerable small shops sell salmon (fresh and smoked), shark (tastes much better than it sounds, with a texture more like chicken than fish), Dungeness crabs, steamed clams, and a vast assortment of other seafood, as well as some of the healthiest looking farm produce you've ever seen.

Besides fish and shellfish, other Northwestern food specialties include cranberries, fresh forest mushrooms, cheeses, and wines. The coastal Northwest also has more than its share of bakeries and gourmet food shops, and even the typical shopping mall supermarket west of the Cascades offers variety and quality that will amaze visitors from most inland parts of America.

As you travel to the east side of the Cascades in both Washington and Oregon, the food situation changes radically. In some areas exceptional restaurants are hard to come by, and supermarket shopping offers nothing special. Before heading for the "dry side," stock up on foods that will keep for several days (such as smoked, dried, and canned delicacies) so you can be glad you did instead of sorry you didn't. Central Washington does produce an abundance of the red delicious apples for which the state is famous, as well as pears, cherries, and other fruit, and vendors' stands line the roadsides at harvest time. As you move farther south, you'll also find good buys on farm-fresh vegetables. The Yakima Valley, for example, grows more asparagus than any other place in the world.

FLORA AND FAUNA

Among the most spectacular wildlife-watching opportunities in the Pacific Northwest are the largest salmon runs in the world. Thousands of human spectators gather at dams on the Columbia River to watch the salmon swarm up fish ladders. Born in mountain streams, the fish migrate to the ocean where they spend their adulthood. Then after a period of years—apparently following a sense of smell so sharp that it defies imagination—the fish make their way back upriver to precisely the same stream where they were born to spawn and die. Between 700,000 and 1 million adult fish climb up the Columbia River dams each year as they make their way home to mate and die, and from 30 million to 50 million young fish travel down the fish ladders each year on their journey to the ocean. Steelhead run from July through October, and chinook salmon have three separate runs between mid-April and October.

The Oregon and Washington coastline offers boundless opportunities for wildlife watching, from the myriad sea creatures found in tide pools along the rocky shoreline to the whale migrations that draw spectators in the fall and spring. Orcas and dolphins make their homes around the San Juan Islands and other protected areas. Besides whales, the coast offers opportunities to see other seagoing mammals, especially sea lions, black bears, Roosevelt elk, mountain goats, and even moose, while the dry country east of the mountains is the domain of pronghorn antelope, coyotes, and yes, rattlesnakes.

Birds are the most commonly seen wildlife. The Pacific Northwest boasts over 300 species of native birds, including trumpeter swans, wading birds such as great blue herons, raptors such as great horned owls, peregrine falcons, the nation's largest populations of bald eagles, gulls, and other seabirds. In addition, the region is on the migration paths of many bird species, notably Canada and snow geese. You'll quickly discover why the Pacific Northwest is fast becoming the country's top birdwatchers' destination.

When we think of Pacific Northwestern flora, the first thing that comes to mind is the tall, dark, and handsome Douglas firs, Sitka spruce, and other evergreens that reign in the ancient forests on the western slopes of the Cascade Range. Majestic as they are, these forest giants are just part of a rich tapestry of vegetation that includes everything from *Darlingtonia*, a plant that devours insects, to edible mushrooms that are collected in the forest for sale to gourmands and great chefs around the world. The most spectacular Northwestern forest environment is found along the Pacific Coast of Washington's Olympic Peninsula, where narrow valleys support the largest temperate rain forests in the world.

THE LAY OF THE LAND

The principle geographic feature of the Pacific Northwest is the Cascade Range, which contains such large and impressive volcanoes as Mount Rainier, Mount St. Helens, Mount Baker, Mount Adams, Mount Hood, Mount Bachelor and the Three Sisters, and Mount Mazama (Crater Lake). This mountain range traps moisture from the Pacific on the densely forested, foggy and damp "wet side," creating a rain shadow that leaves the "dry side" east of the mountains an arid, though colorful, painted desert.

Across Puget Sound from Seattle, the Olympic Peninsula encompasses a vast area where the mountains, though not nearly as high as the Cascades, appear equally spectacular. The entire peninsula slopes upward to lofty Mount Olympus in its center and encompasses more than 600,000 acres of mountain wilderness that is inaccessible by road.

The Pacific Coast of Washington and Oregon stretches for 632 miles of spectacular beaches, capes, and rocky headlands, considered by many to be the most spectacular shoreline in the United States. And if that's not enough to make your jaw drop with the sheer scenic wonder of it all, take a ferry cruise through the Strait of Juan de Fuca to see the hundreds of misty, often untouchable San Juan Islands.

PRACTICAL TIPS

HOW MUCH WILL IT COST?

I've followed this book chapter-by-chapter on a month-long Northwestern journey, traveling in comfort in a mini-motor home on a $2,000 trip budget. The major expense of the trip is gasoline. Figure 2,500 miles plus the round-trip driving distance from your home to the most convenient point on the tour route, at however many miles per gallon your rig gets.

If you camp and cook your own meals, they'll cost the same as you'd spend eating at home. Public produce and fish markets such as Seattle's Pike Place Market are great places to stock up on camping food and gourmet picnic supplies. But in the Pacific Northwest—on the more populated "wet side," at least—you'll find an irresistible abundance of restaurants. Plan on $7 to $10 per person per meal at a typical "nice" restaurant, more for *really* nice ones. Seattle and Portland have their share of restaurants where dinner for two with wine can set you back $100 or more, but most of them are not mentioned in this book.

I have tried hard to include lodging suggestions in all price ranges when possible. In some places, especially on the less populated "dry side," there are no expensive lodgings. Venture far enough into eastern Oregon and you'll be lucky to find even a budget-basic motel. In other places, especially along the coast and the Columbia River, lodging prices are much higher, and finding any budget-priced accommodations is difficult.

Public campground fees generally run from $6 to $13 a night. National parks charge camping fees of $6 a night plus park admission; national forests usually charge $7. State parks generally fall in the $10 to $13 range in both states, and unlike federal campgrounds, they usually offer RV hookups for water and electricity. National forest roads also offer opportunities for free camping in some areas.

Admission to state parks, national monuments, and national parks is typically $5 per vehicle. A Golden Eagle Pass admits you to all U.S. national parks and monuments.

WHEN TO GO

July and August offer the most consistently beautiful weather in the coastal and mountain areas of the Pacific Northwest. Because the fair weather season is short, travel during these months also means heavy tourist crowds and rigid reservation requirements.

I'd opt for September, the late summer "shoulder season" beginning right after Labor Day. The weather is still fine everywhere, all sightseeing highlights remain open, family tourism magically thins out as school starts, traffic lightens, lodging rates drop, and reservations requirements are forgotten. Wait a few more weeks and you can catch central Washington's apple harvest/Oktoberfest season.

Late May to early June is also a good time to travel. Flowers, both wild and domestic, are everywhere at that time of year. The only drawback is that some mountain areas—notably the road around Crater Lake—are still snowbound.

As for spring . . . I've taken this trip in April, camping all the way in an unheated mini-motor home without suffering uncomfortable cold, and enjoyed it immensely. Several mountain areas still had enough snow to ski on, however, and the North Cascades Highway, the Stevens Canyon/Cayuse Pass Road on Mount Rainier, the forest roads around Mount St. Helens, the Cascade Lakes Highway, and the Crater Lake Rim Drive had not opened for the season yet.

PACIFIC NORTHWEST CLIMATE

Average daily high and low temperatures in degrees Fahrenheit, plus monthly precipitation in inches.

	Ashland	Bend	Portland	Seattle
Jan.	45/30	40/21	45/33	46/37
	2.86	1.83	5.52	5.68
March	55/33	50/25	55/38	53/40
	1.77	.68	3.64	3.51
May	70/42	65/34	67/47	66/49
	1.42	1.13	2.11	1.51
July	87/51	82/44	78/55	75/56
	.30	.40	.57	.73
Sept.	78/46	74/37	74/52	69/53
	.66	.39	1.72	1.88
Nov.	53/34	50/27	52/39	52/42
	1.58	5.47	5.88	5.08

If you're visiting the Pacific Northwest between mid-October and March, 80 percent of this book does not apply. Photocopy the pertinent pages, then put the book aside for another time, or give it to someone you love for Christmas. Your ideal winter itinerary should be built around storm watching (the latest tongue-in-cheek spectator sport on the Oregon coast) and the world's finest cross-country skiing.

TRANSPORTATION

For those traveling by public transportation, Seattle, Victoria, Vancouver, and Portland have excellent local bus systems supplemented with local trains or monorails. Interstate buses tend to stick to interstate highways, but do provide some service to the Oregon coast. Amtrak provides rail service to Grants Pass, Eugene, and Portland, Oregon, to Seattle and Edmonds, Washington, and to Vancouver, British Columbia.

The showpiece of the Pacific Northwest's public transportation network is the Washington State Ferry System. The ferries, which are covered in detail in the applicable chapters of this book, offer inexpensive, wonderfully scenic transportation throughout the Puget Sound area and to the San Juan Islands and Vancouver Island, making it possible to spend days on a series of sea cruises on even the tightest of budgets. In fact, you can build a whole vacation around ferry travel in Washington if you rent a bike (or bring your own); most places the ferries take you are ideal for bike touring. Other ferries serve Victoria and Vancouver, British Columbia, and Lake Chelan to the village of Stehekin, a gateway to North Cascades National Park.

SAN JUAN ISLANDS FERRY AND CANADA TRIP TIPS

The total ferry fares from Anacortes to Victoria with a motor vehicle run just over $40 (about $34 off-season) for car and driver and $7 per additional passenger, and from Victoria to Vancouver, $20.50 for car and driver (more for motor homes) and $4.50 per passenger. The total cost for two people for this four-day ferry cruise is thus about $72. You don't want to take this trip without a vehicle; bicycles (which you can take on the ferry at pedestrian rates) would work fine for sightseeing on Orcas and San Juan islands, but the ferry landings for both Victoria and Vancouver are far outside the cities.

If you didn't obtain a Canadian insurance coverage card from your agent before you left home (or if the terms of your vehicle rental agreement don't let you take it out of the United States), you should skip Victoria and Vancouver or visit them by public transportation. It's unlikely that anyone will actually check whether your vehicular paperwork is in order, but if it's not and you have an accident, the legal entanglements can be long and expensive.

CAMPING, LODGING, AND DINING

Camping allows you maximum flexibility in a tour of the Pacific Northwest. While lodging is available in most areas covered by this itinerary, camping facilities offer a more pleasant environment, usually surrounded by trees and near a lake, river, or seashore. The major exception is the greater Seattle area, where campsites are as scarce as hen's teeth, and a hotel is the best bet even for motor home travelers. Camping can also be a problem at busy times on San Juan Island, which has very few public campsites.

Only public campgrounds—state parks, national parks, and national forests—are recommended in this book. Besides these, most places along your route you'll find private campgrounds and RV parks nearby. As a general rule, private parks have less to offer in the way of natural beauty and cost a bit more (typically $12 a night); they can sometimes be appealing, though, for their shower and laundry facilities. Any KOA-affiliated campground can supply information on other KOAs nationwide, and comprehensive, reliable directories covering private campgrounds and RV parks are published annually by Rand McNally and Woodall. Besides ensuring roadside emergency service in case you need it, the American Automobile Association (AAA) publishes campground directories for its members.

Almost anywhere you go in Washington or Oregon, you'll find a state park campground nearby. Both states provide outstanding camping facilities, including water/electric and sewer hookups at most campsites. Most have coin-operated hot showers. Many state parks have separate areas for tent campers. National forest and national park campgrounds usually do not have hookups or showers.

Nightly camping fees at Oregon state parks are $10 (full hookups) or $8 (tent sites) between Memorial Day and Labor Day, $3 less off-season. Washington state parks charge $8.50 (full hookups) or $6 (tent sites) year-round. National forest campgrounds usually charge $7 a night, and national parks usually charge $6 in addition to the park admission fee.

The most popular state park campgrounds in both Washington and Oregon operate on a reservation system between Memorial Day and Labor Day. Campgrounds recommended in this book that require reservations during the summer are: in Washington—Moran State Park (Orcas Island), Lake Chelan State Park, and Fort Canby State Park (near the mouth of the Columbia River); in Oregon—Honeyman State Park (near Florence) and Fort Stevens State Park (near the mouth of the Columbia River). Reservations, which can only be made by mail, must be prepaid. You can't get a cash refund if you cancel, though you can change reservation dates contingent on space availability. If you are planning to travel during the summer season, these campground reservations call for careful itinerary planning several weeks in advance. Contact the state park system campground hot lines—Washington, (800) 562-0990, within Washington summer only, or (206) 753-2027; Oregon, (800) 452-5687, within Oregon summer only, or (503) 731-3411—to request reservation forms. Campsites that have not been reserved are available on a first-come, first-served basis, but there can be stiff competition for them.

For travelers who don't wish to camp—at least, not every night—I've included suggestions for out-of-the-ordinary accommodations. (On three nights, in central Washington and John Day Country, even run-of-the-mill motel accommodations are few and far between; I'll simply tell you where to look for them.) Lodging recommendations include bed and breakfasts, historic hotels, unusual resorts, national park inns, elegant small hotels, and youth hostels.

National park inns require itinerary planning far in advance, since reservations are almost essential. If you're lucky, you can sometimes get a room there on short notice due to a cancellation if you inquire at the desk around 4:00 p.m., but don't count on it. These inns, most of them Depression-era historic buildings characterized by rustic grandeur, are located in incomparably beautiful natural settings, yours to enjoy after the crowds of daytime visitors have left. A stay at Paradise Inn on the side of Mount Rainier or the lodge on the rim of Crater Lake is particularly memorable and well worth arranging ahead of time.

Bed and breakfasts (B&Bs) also require reservations, though not as far in advance. Most B&Bs recommended in this book are intimate turn-of-the-century places, with fewer than ten guest rooms, where you can get to know your hosts on a first-name basis. For a comprehensive survey of B&Bs in Washington and Oregon (and elsewhere), consult the current edition of Pamela Lanier's *Complete Guide to Bed &*

Breakfasts, Inns and Guesthouses in the United States and Canada, available in fine bookstores.

Hostels, as well as very low cost lodgings that offer private rooms, are mentioned wherever they can be found along this route. Hostels aren't for everybody, but they are inexpensive—$10 or less. They offer clean, attractive, dormitory-type accommodations, usually require an American Youth Hostel (AYH) membership, which you can purchase on the spot for a few dollars, and require that you supply your own bed sheets (or rent them at a small additional fee). Hostels usually close during the middle of the day and observe "lights-out" rules and curfews. If you're willing to put up with these restrictions, hostels provide a roof over your head for about the same price as a campsite. Sometimes called "youth hostels," these places are now popular with budget travelers of all ages, including youthful senior citizens. Hostels attract more than their share of foreign guests and offer the best opportunities to compare impressions of America with European and Asian visitors. If you'd like to meet one or more temporary traveling companions, a hostel is the place to do it: many people who stay there are public transportation travelers eager to share driving expenses for a chance to see places that are only accessible by private vehicle.

I've also recommended a handful of elegant, expensive hotels and resorts along the route, including the finest in Seattle and Portland. These suggestions are not just for the rich. In the matter of lodging, as in all things, variety is the key to maximum vacation pleasure. I recently met a retired couple who travel around America staying in hostels and YMCAs six nights a week and high-priced luxury hotels on the seventh night. Elegance, they told me, is all the more enjoyable when it is a sometime thing, and it costs them less than if they spent every night in a drab budget motel. A luxury hotel can also make for the ultimate "splurge break" from camping. (Hint: If you're wearing camping clothes and a three-day beard stubble, and you walk into a hotel that has a porte-cochere, a uniformed doorman, a concierge with an Oxford accent, and marble columns in the 2-story lobby, it's extremely helpful to have a credit card and confirmed reservations.)

Restaurant suggestions in this book include places I've personally tried and found exceptional, as well as others that have come highly recommended by local residents whose judgment I trust in matters of cuisine. When possible, I've tried to provide restaurant suggestions in all price ranges, focusing on famous local favorites and less known but equally special eating places. While I have not mentioned national fast-food chain locations or good-but-ordinary "family-style" restaurants, an assortment of each can be found in all fair-sized towns in the Northwest. The restaurants listed are only a selective sampling, and no inference should be drawn about the quality of any dining establishment from the fact that I've omitted it.

The availability and selection of picnic foods in most parts of the Northwest, along with the spectacular array of natural settings in which to enjoy them, mean that you could easily and pleasurably spend three weeks touring the region without ever resorting to restaurant fare (although you'd probably want to).

RECOMMENDED READING

Northwesterners like to read a lot, which is probably natural given the long winter months of gray drizzle that make armchairs look more inviting than hiking trails. Both Seattle and Portland have more and bigger bookstores per capita than almost anyplace. You may wish to spend an afternoon browsing in one of the larger ones, such as Seattle's University Bookstore or Portland's truly vast Powell's, said to be the largest bookstore in the world.

There is also an abundance of writers living in the Northwest. Some, like Oregon native Ken Kesey, have tried to capture the unique feel of the Northwestern landscape on paper. Many other novelists live in the region but do not set their books there, though the distinctive climate and natural environment surely affect their work in deeper ways. Famous Northwestern writers that come to mind include prehistoric epic writer Jean Auel, science fiction writer Ursula LeGuin, true crime writer Ann Rule, and the late Bernard Malamud.

One of the most vital pieces of supplementary information for this trip, along with the free Washington State Ferries *Sailing Schedules* and *Fares and Tolls* pamphlets (see Chapter 3), is a tide table. Tides, which rise and fall twice a day by as much as 20 feet, changing the character of the coastline, are an important factor in deciding where to stop and enjoy coastal areas. Beaches are widest at low tide, and the best time to beachcomb or explore tide pools is just before low tide. For photographers, the ocean crashes against rocky shores most dramatically around high tide. The handiest tide tables are calendars that show high and low tides graphically as curves, but these are hard to find. Pocket-sized tide table books costing about $1 are readily available at boating supply shops and many bookstores. Daily high and low tides are also published in the weather reports of all major newspapers. (Northwest-erners assert that this is the only reliable piece of information in the weather forecast.)

The abundance of bird life in the Pacific Northwest is absolutely astonishing. A field guide to western birds (along with a pair of binoculars) will help you appreciate it—and keep children occupied while you drive. I recommend the Peterson guides, with color plates grouped by species to make identification easy for beginning birdwatchers. Nature enthusiasts will also find field guides to wildflowers and marine life useful on this trip.

I've limited hiking suggestions for the most part to trails you can walk in a few hours, barely hinting at the possibilities that exist in Northwestern mountains. Serious hikers should visit a Seattle book-store and pick up one or several of the excellent hiking guides published by The Mountaineers (306 Second Avenue W., Seattle, WA 98119), such as the Footsore series by Harvey Manning (four volumes) and the Trips and Trails series by E. M. Sterling (three volumes). Marge Mueller's *The San Juan Islands Afoot and Afloat*, also published by The Mountaineers, will tell you what's on all the islands where the ferry doesn't stop.

A thoroughly enjoyable look at Seattle's early history is Underground Tours founder Bill Speidel's *Sons of the Profits (or, There's No Business Like Grow Business: The Seattle Story 1851–1901)*. Another of Mr. Speidel's books, *The Wet Side of the Mountains*, is the most detailed and entertainingly practical guide I've seen to the Puget Sound area. Both are from Nettle Creek Publishing Company, available in virtually all Seattle bookstores or from the Underground Tours ticket office at Doc Maynard's in Pioneer Square.

History buffs may want to brush up on the Lewis and Clark expedition before or during this trip. The explorers' journals are published in low-priced editions by Penguin, Bantam, and Mentor.

If you're planning to explore deeper into Oregon, search hard for Ralph Friedman's self-published *Oregon for the Curious*, a remarkably exhaustive, mile-by-mile, "shunpiking" guide to practically every road in the state.

Finally, whether you're traveling with youngsters or just the young at heart, take a look at Rick Steves' *Kidding Around Seattle*, from John Muir Publications. A veteran travel writer from the northern suburbs of Seattle who originated the forerunner of this series in 1985, Rick has rediscovered his hometown in the company of his children.

The result is this deceptively slender and altogether enchanting book, brimming with fresh insights guaranteed to brighten the drizzliest of vacation days. For ordering information, see the catalog pages in the back of this book. John Muir also publishes a pair of fun, illustrated guides for grown-ups—*Unique Washington* by Tom Barr and *Unique Oregon* by . . . well, by me!

RESOURCES

Washington Tourism Division: (360) 586-2088
Washington State Parks and Recreation Commission: (360) 753-2027
Washington State Hotel & Motel Association: (206) 957-4585
Northwest Washington Tourism Association: (360) 671-3990
Southwest Washington Tourism Council: (360) 425-1211
Seattle-King County Convention & Visitors Bureau: (206) 461-5800
Pacific Northwest National Parks and Forests Association: (206) 442-0170
U.S. Forest Service-Pacific Northwest Region: (503) 326-2877
Oregon Tourism Division: (800) 233-3306
Oregon Department of Parks and Recreation: (503) 378-6305
Oregon Motor Hotel Association: (503) 255-5135
Portland Oregon Visitors Association: (800) 962-3700
Tourism British Columbia: (604) 660-2861
Tourism Victoria: (800) 663-3883
Tourism Association of Vancouver Island: (604) 382-3551
Vancouver Tourist Info Centre: (604) 683-2000
Ferries: Washington State Ferries, (800) 843-3779; BC Ferries, (604) 656-0757
Airlines: American Airlines, (800) 433-7300; Horizon Air, (800) 547-9308; Western Pacific, (800) 930-3030; Air Canada, (800) 776-3000
Car Rentals: Avis, (800) 331-1084 in US or (800) 831-2847 in Canada; Hertz, (800) 654-3131 worldwide; National, (800) 227-3876 US and Canada; Xtra Car (Seattle), (800) 227-5397
Bus Lines: Greyhound, (800) 231-2222 in US or (800) 661-8747 in Canada; Green Tortoise, (800) 227-4766
Trains: Amtrak, (800) USA-RAIL; BC Rail, (604) 631-3500; VIA Rail, (800) 561-8630

1
SEATTLE

Seattle's unique features grew out of a brief, boisterous history. The city got its start in 1852, under the name of Duwamps. Although Port Townsend, to the north, was expected to become the region's major port city, transcontinental rail service spurred Seattle's growth: the population leaped to 45,000 in 1890, from 3,500 in 1880. In 1896, Seattle's port became the first U.S. shipping link with Japan; two years later it became the main departure terminal for the Klondike gold rush. By 1910, the city had grown to nearly a quarter of a million, half of its present population.

Within the past few years, Californians and others have moved here in droves, and two satellite cities—Bellevue and Everett—rank among the ten fastest growing cities in the nation. Today, the aerospace industry overshadows shipping in Seattle's economy. Besides Boeing (the area's largest employer), a host of smaller high-tech companies are headquartered here.

Seattle's greatest claim to fame is its rain. Don't tell anybody, but Seattle's weather is actually quite mild. The annual rainfall, 32 inches, is the same as that of Chicago or Atlanta. Temperatures rarely drop below freezing in the winter or reach 80 degrees in the summer. In July, the sun shines almost every day. It's true that spring, fall, and winter weather tends to be gray and drizzly, but don't cancel a minute of your sightseeing plans just because the sky looks dismal in the morning. It commonly clears up after lunch. Seattlites play golf in the rain, go camping, hiking, and fishing in the rain, and drive their sports cars in the rain—convertible top down. Try it—it's only water. ◣

SEATTLE

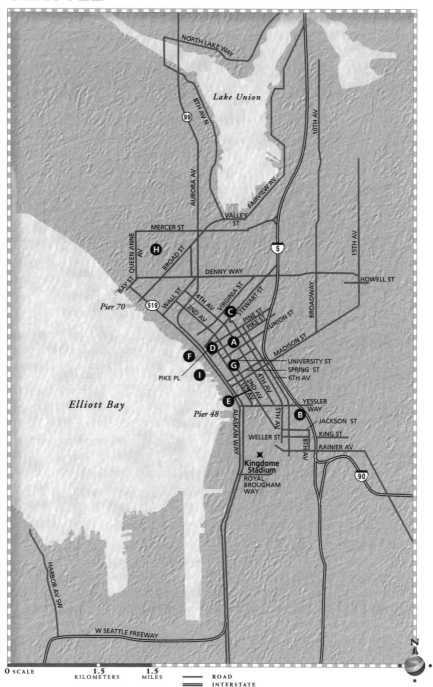

Lake Union

NORTH LAKE WAY

8TH AV N

99

AURORA AV

FAIRVIEW AV

VALLEY ST

10TH AV

15TH AV

5

MERCER ST

BAY ST QUEEN ANNE AV

BROAD ST

H

DENNY WAY

BROADWAY

HOWELL ST

Pier 70

519

WALL ST

4TH AV

VIRGINIA ST

STEWART ST

PINE ST
PIKE ST

UNION ST

2ND AV

C

A

MADISON ST

F

D

UNIVERSITY ST

G

SPRING ST

I

6TH AV

PIKE PL

2ND AV

4TH AV

Elliott Bay

Pier 48

E

1ST AV

5TH AV

YESSLER WAY

B

ALASKAN WAY

JACKSON ST

WELLER ST

KING ST

8TH AV

RAINIER AV

Kingdome
Stadium

ROYAL
BROUGHAM
WAY

90

HARBOR AV SW

W SEATTLE FREEWAY

N

0 SCALE

1.5
KILOMETERS

1.5
MILES

ROAD

INTERSTATE

Sightseeing Highlights

Ⓐ **Downtown**

Ⓑ **International District**

Ⓒ **Monorail**

Ⓓ **Pike Place Market**

Ⓔ **Pioneer Square**

Ⓕ **Seattle Aquarium**

Ⓖ **Seattle Art Museum**

Ⓗ **Seattle Center**

Ⓘ **Seattle Waterfront**

A PERFECT DAY IN SEATTLE

Exploring downtown Seattle on foot is easy. Finding a parking space there is more challenging. I would bypass the parking problem by leaving my car in one of the large pay-parking lots adjacent to Seattle Center, taking the monorail downtown. All the sightseeing highlights in this chapter are within walking distance of the big multilevel transit station where the monorail lets you off. Check out the waterfront in the morning, taking time to enjoy the Seattle Aquarium, then make your way up to Pike Place Market for lunch. Later, head over to Pioneer Square, where an Underground Tour takes you on an urban archaeological adventure through the lost streets of nineteenth-century Seattle. The remainder of the afternoon presents a choice between an array of museums—the Wing Luke Asian Museum in the International District, the Seattle Art Museum in the heart of downtown, or the Pacific Science Center at Seattle Center. If you leave your car at the Seattle Center for the day, you can monorail back just in time to watch the sunset from the Space Needle's observation deck.

SIGHTSEEING HIGHLIGHTS

★★★ **Pike Place Market**—Pike Place started as a farmers' market in 1907. During the market's revival in the early 1970s, arts and crafts people started showing their wares side by side with the vegetable vendors. Today, these artisans complain that they are being displaced by more commercial retailers and rising rents, but many continue to survive and prosper. Pike Place, which has grown beyond its huge three-level building into Post Alley across the street, is firmly established as one of the most fascinating public markets in any U.S. city. Browse among the stalls selling fresh seafood (whole salmon and crabs, baby lobsters, fresh octopus, razor clam meat, and live geoduck—pronounced "gooey duck"—clams), fresh produce ranging from shiitake mushrooms to giant artichokes, gourmet food products, and a plethora of gift items, such as figurines hand-sculpted from Mount St. Helens volcanic ash, Guatemalan weavings, collectible comic books, watercolor paintings "made fresh daily," foreign language magazines and newspapers, and "designer fish" T-shirts. If you've got the urge to shop 'til you drop, this is the place to do it. The market is up the Pike Place Hillclimb stairway, across the street and under the viaduct from the Seattle Aquarium on the waterfront. Hours: Open Monday through Saturday from 9:00 a.m. to 6:00 p.m., Sunday 11:00 a.m. to 5:00 p.m. Address: Pike Street at First Avenue. Phone: (206) 682-7453. (2 hours)

★★★ **Pioneer Square**—Once Seattle's "skid row" (in fact, the term "skid row" derives from the old Skid Road here, now Yesler Way, where Seattle timber baron Henry Yesler slid logs through the mud down to his waterfront lumber mill in the 1880s), the Pioneer Square district underwent historic preservation and then gentrification to become today's downtown historic district, brimming with restaurants, theaters, night spots, and art galleries. The original multiethnic waterfront wino population hangs in there despite the invasion of young urban professionals, making Pioneer Square a people-watcher's paradise.

The *sine qua non* of Pioneer Square sightseeing is the **Underground Tour** that starts at Doc Maynard's in the Pioneer Building on First Avenue facing Pioneer Place Park. When downtown Seattle (today's Pioneer Square district) was devastated by fire in 1889, the ruins were landfilled and the city was rebuilt one story above the former, chronically muddy streets. In the 1960s, while lobbying for historic district status for the area, Pioneer Square Committee Chairman Bill

Speidel revealed the existence of what he called "The Forgotten City Which Lies Beneath Seattle's Modern Streets." Seattlites were electrified by this archaeological discovery in their own basement. The chamber of commerce persuaded Speidel to guide tours into the underground on "Know Your Seattle Day" in May 1965, and 500 people took the tour in 6 hours. Since then, Speidel's tours have become a Seattle institution, acclaimed as the ultimate urban guided tour. Enthusiastic young guides carry on the Speidel tradition: it's not the old brick walls so much as the stories behind them that make this tour outstanding. The charge is $5.50 per adult, $4 for students ages 13 to 17, $4.50 for seniors over age 59, $2.25 for children ages 6 to 12. Times: Eighty- to 90-minute tours are conducted daily at 11:00 a.m., 2:00 p.m., and 4:00 p.m., as well as 1:00 p.m. on Saturdays and Sundays, and 5:00 p.m. Saturdays only. Reservations are recommended. Phone: (206) 682-4646.

Another part of the underground, where you can poke around for free, has been renovated as shops in the **Grand Central Arcade**, entered through an inconspicuous street-level gate on First Street between Main and Washington.

Also adjoining Pioneer Square is the free **Klondike Gold Rush National Historical Park—Seattle Unit**, a small museum run by the National Park Service, with exhibits and movies on Seattle's role as the gateway to the Alaskan gold rush of 1898. Admission is free. Hours: Open daily from 9:00 a.m. to 5:00 p.m. Address: 117 South Main Street. Phone: (206) 553-7220.

At Second Avenue and Yesler Way, on the northeast corner of the Pioneer Square district, the **Smith Tower** was the tallest building in the world outside New York City when it was built in 1914. Today, from its observation deck, you can look up at the modern downtown skyscrapers, some twice as tall, that dwarf it. Admission is $2 for adults, $1 for children under 12. Hours: Open daily from 10:00 a.m. to 10:00 p.m. Address: Second Avenue at Yesler Way. Phone: (206) 622-4004. (1 hour)

★★★ **Seattle Waterfront—The Alaska Way Trolley** can take you up or down the waterfront for 85 cents ($1.10 during rush hour). Buy a trolley token from the vending machine inside the kiosk at any stop; there are also $1 and $5 change machines.

The points of interest along the waterfront are between Pier 70 (a large old warehouse housing arts and crafts and import shops as well as several small restaurants) on the north and Pier 48 (the Alaska Ferry dock) on the south. Pier 69 is the terminal for **Victoria Clippers**,

high-speed luxury catamarans that carry passengers to Victoria and
Vancouver, British Columbia. The Edgewater Inn (see "Lodging,"
below), with its marvelous mural of orca whales on the north wall, is
on Pier 67. Walk south past working ship piers to Pier 59, where the
Seattle Aquarium and Omnidome are located. Across the street, the
Pike Place Hillclimb takes you up to Pike Place Market.

At the **Seattle Aquarium** you'll find a fine collection of sea creatures, both beautiful and bizarre, including African lungfish, Mexican
blind cave fish, electric catfish, a colorful coral reef exhibit complete
with sharks, and a "touch tank" where you can fondle sea snails,
starfish, and crabs. An aviary houses shorebirds and fish of the Puget
Sound area in beach, salt marsh, and rocky shore habitats. Tanks with
sea otters and fur seals permit viewing from both above and below the
water. Schools of fingerling coho salmon are released from the aquarium into Puget Sound each spring. The small fish imprint on the
aquarium's fish ladder and later, as adults, return from the ocean to
spawn, making this the only aquarium anywhere with a direct, living
link to the ocean. Admission is $6.75 for adults, $5.25 for seniors,
$4.25 for ages 6 to 19, $1.75 for ages 3 to 5. Hours: Open daily from
10:00 a.m. to 8:00 p.m. in the summer, until 6:00 p.m. the rest of the
year. Phone: (206) 386-4353. (1½ hours)

The adjoining **Omnidome** shows a movie that depicts the 1980
eruption of Mount St. Helens on a wraparound screen, then contrasts
the devastation with views of the volcano's slopes today. Admission is $6
for adults, $5 for seniors and teens ages 13 to 18, $4 for ages 3 to 12.
Hours: Open daily from 10:00 a.m. to 8:00 p.m. in the summer, until
6:00 p.m. the rest of the year. Phone: (206) 622-1868. (1 hour)

Pier 57, the next one to the south, is the city's **Waterfront Park**
and public fishing pier.

Pier 55 is the dock for **Harbor Tours**. Fares are $11.55 for adults,
$5.30 for ages 5 to 12. The one-hour tours leave at 11:00 a.m. and
12:15, 1:30, 2:45, 4:00, and 5:15 p.m. June through September. In May
and October they leave at 12:15, 1:30, 2:45, and 4:00 p.m., and in April
they operate Friday through Sunday only. For more information, call
(206) 623-4252.

Pier 54 is the home of two venerable Seattle landmarks. **Ivar's
Acre of Clams** was the clam shack that launched the career of the city's
most famous restaurateur, the late Ivar Haglund. Try the steamed clams
or clam nectar and watch the seagulls that flock here in profusion. The
birds will cajole you to buy more clams and feed them. (Clever, Ivar.)

Ivar's Acre of Clams and adjoining Oyster Bar have long, long lines at lunch hour. Pier 54 is also the new location of **Ye Olde Curiosity Shop**. A trading post since the Klondike gold rush, the shop has accumulated so many oddities—Indian and Eskimo art and artifacts, Alaskan furs, exotic seashells, South American shrunken heads, and a mummy from the Gila Desert, to mention just a few—that today it's as much a private museum as a curio shop. Phone: (206) 682-5844.

Pier 53 is where the harbor's two large fireboats park. On summer Saturdays and Sundays, the fireboats pull out into the bay and spray great arcs of water into the air. Why? So you can photograph them, of course! Next door, on Pier 52, is the Washington State Ferries Terminal. Stop in and pick up the current *Sailing Schedules* and *Fares and Tolls*, two tiny brochures that provide essential ferry information. If you can't wait to cruise Puget Sound, hop on one of the frequent ferries to Bremerton, a two-hour round-trip for only $3.50 per walk-on passenger. Ferries also go to Winslow on Bainbridge Island for the same price. Phone: (206) 464-6400 or toll-free (800) 843-3779.

Pier 48 is the Alaska Ferry dock. The boat leaves on Fridays for the three-day cruise up the Inland Passage to Skagway. Near the terminal is Alaska Square Park, with a Tlingit Indian totem pole from Haines, Alaska. Phone: (800) 642-0066. (2 hours)

★★ **Monorail**—Seattle's monorail, constructed as part of the 1962 World's Fair, runs between Seattle Center and downtown every 10 minutes from 10:00 a.m. to 9:00 p.m. (Friday and Saturday until midnight). The fare is 75 cents, and the trip takes just two minutes. If you feel like you do a lot of walking when you're exploring downtown Seattle, think of the poor monorail operator: the monorail doesn't turn around as it changes directions; instead, it has a driver's seat at each end, so every few minutes the operator must walk to the other end of the coach. In the course of a workday he walks farther than the entire length of the monorail track.

The downtown monorail station is in the upper level of the transit station on Pine Street between 3rd and 4th Streets. Below ground level, a 1.3-mile transit tunnel takes Metro buses from other parts of the city to the Pine Street station in the center of downtown. The buses are specially designed to convert from gas to electric power as they enter the underground transit tunnel.

Seattle's major multistory department stores—Nordstrom, Frederick & Nelson, and the Bon Marché—are all within a block of the downtown transit station at Fifth and Pine. From there, if you stroll 3 blocks south on the Fifth Avenue pedestrian mall and a block east on Spring Street to Sixth Avenue, you'll come to Freeway Park, the unique 5.4-acre city park on the concrete roof covering Interstate 5, with gardens, lawns, fountains, waterfalls, and plenty of picnicking downtowners. (1½ hours)

★★ **Seattle Art Museum**—The art museum contains outstanding collections of Asian, African, Northwest Coast Native American, and contemporary art. Admission is $6 for adults, $4 for seniors and students with ID, children under 13 free. Free admission for all on the first Tuesday of each month. Hours: Open Tuesday through Sunday from 10:00 a.m. to 5:00 p.m. (Thursdays until 9:00 p.m.), closed Monday. Address: 100 University Street. Phone: (206) 654-3100. (3 hours)

★★ **Seattle Center**—The site of the 1962 World's Fair has become Seattle's combination town square, playground, and cultural center. Here you'll find the city's most famous landmark, the **Space Needle**, right next to a roller coaster, a laser light show, an opera house, and a collection of international fast-food places. Phone: (206) 684-7200.

An elevator carries sightseers to the observation deck atop the 605-foot Space Needle for the best possible view of Seattle, Puget Sound, Lake Washington, and the surrounding mountains. The cost is $6.50 for adults, $5.75 for seniors, and $4 for children ages 5 to 12. Hours: Operates daily from 9:00 a.m. to 12:00 midnight. Phone: (206) 443-2100. (½ hour)

The Center House, another World's Fair holdover, has 18 fast-food restaurants where you can select anything from Mongolian steak or Vietnamese *banh bao* to Belgian waffles, espresso, barbecued ribs, or even Seattle-style steamed clams. Service is so quick, it puts national chain fast-food places to shame, and complete meals cost $4 to $5. The large pavilion in the Center House hosts all kinds of events. One is a long-standing community tradition: free international folk-dancing lessons (participate or just watch) every Thursday at 6:30 p.m. There is a children's museum downstairs.

The Pacific Science Center, an outstanding teaching museum for children (of all ages!), has hands-on computer exhibits, full-size replicas of spacecraft and a space station, and a reconstructed Salish Indian longhouse called Sea Monster House. An adjoining 8,000-square-foot projection dome offers astronomy presentations and (for a separate admission) 45-minute laser light shows. Admission is $6.50 for adults, $5.50 for seniors and children ages 6 to 13, and $4.50 for children ages 2 to 5; senior citizens are admitted free on Wednesdays. Hours: Exhibit halls are open daily from 10:00 a.m. to 6:00 p.m. during the summer months, Monday through Friday 10:00 a.m. to 5:00 p.m., Saturday and Sunday 10:00 a.m. to 6:00 p.m. the rest of the year. Phone: (206) 443-2001. (2 hours)

Fun Forest amusement park rides include a compact but thrilling Wild Mouse roller coaster, bumper cars, and a Ferris wheel. Ride tickets are 85 cents each, eight for $5.50, 18 for $11. Hours: Rides operate June through August Monday through Thursday from 12:00 noon to 12:00 midnight; Friday and Saturday 12:00 noon to 12:00 midnight; Sunday 12:00 noon to 8:00 p.m., and April, May, September, and October on Friday 7:00 p.m. to 12:00 midnight; Saturday 12:00 noon to 11:00 p.m.; and Sunday from 12:00 noon to 8:00 p.m. Phone: (206) 728-1585. (1–2 hours)

Also at the Seattle Center are the **Seattle Children's Museum** (admission $3.50; open Tuesday through Sunday, from 10:00 a.m. to 5:00 p.m., closed Mondays; phone: 206-728-1585); the Opera House (call 206-447-4711 for current opera information, 206-443-4747 for symphony information); the **Children's Theatre** (call 206-441-1767 for current information); the **Coliseum**, where most Seattle rock concerts are held; and the floodlit, electronically controlled International Fountain.

☆ **International District**—This is Seattle's Asian ethnic neighborhood, where Chinese, Korean, Japanese, Vietnamese, Polynesian, and Filipino influences mingle. On King Street, don't miss Uwajimaya, the largest Japanese supermarket in the United States, where you can shop for bean cakes, sweet Japanese pumpkin, enoki mushrooms, seasoned squid, strange-looking flat fish called mana katsuo, yam paste, fried tangle, 80-pound bags of rice, and other items (many of them pink) so cryptically labeled you can make a game out of guessing what they are. Uwajimaya also has an Asian delicatessen and gift items, including an outstanding selection of Oriental cookbooks, cookware, and tea sets, as well as go boards and other Japanese games. Hours: Open daily from 8:00 a.m. to 9:00 p.m. Address: 519 Sixth Avenue S. Phone: (206) 624-6248.

Up the hill at 414 Eighth Avenue South near the corner of Jackson is the **Wing Luke Asian Museum**, named after the Chinese city councilman who died in a 1965 plane crash in the Cascades. This outstanding Oriental culture museum features special exhibits from Korea, China, and other Asian Pacific nations, as well as permanent displays ranging from firecrackers to medicinal herbs. Admission is $2.50 for adults, $1.50 for seniors and teens ages 13 to 18, and 75 cents for children; free on Thursdays. Hours: Open Tuesday through Friday 11:00 a.m. to 4:30 p.m., Saturday and Sunday 12:00 noon to 4:00 p.m. Address: 407 Seventh Avenue S. Phone: (206) 623-5124. (1½ hours)

FITNESS AND RECREATION

A popular jogging and biking spot downtown is the 1¼-mile paved trail through Myrtle Edwards Park at the north end of the waterfront. Places farther removed from the downtown area, where you can hike, run, and ride for longer distances, are described in the following chapter, "Around Seattle."

FOOD

My top dining recommendation in Seattle, not in the downtown area but worth the drive, is **Ivar's Indian Salmon House** at 401 NE Northlake Way (on the northeast shore of Lake Union under the freeway bridge, south of the University of Washington campus), (206) 632-0767. The specialty is salmon barbecued over alder wood in full view of the clientele. The interior decor replicates a Kwakiutl Indian longhouse. Log canoes hang from the ceiling, and Indian wood carvings, ranging from museum-quality artifacts to contemporary Native American art, are everywhere. There is also a fine collection of turn-of-the-century photographs of the Coast Salish people, the whale-hunting Makah of Neah Bay, and the handsome, nomadic Yakima people. Notice the photograph of Indian canoes on the Seattle waterfront in 1890. Many of the photographs are by the late Edward Curtis, North America's premier photographer of nineteenth-century Indian life. Ivar's Indian Salmon House was designated as a historic landmark just one year after it was built. Wait for a window table and watch the boat traffic on Lake Union while you eat. The restaurant is open daily for lunch and dinner. Reservations are not accepted.

Look for king crab, giant prawns, and great lobster, along with a view of downtown Seattle across the harbor at **Salty's on Alki**, 1936 Harbor Avenue NW, (206) 937-1600. Centrally located on Alki Beach, the moderately priced restaurant is open daily for lunch and dinner and features a seafood Sunday brunch.

The Seattle Center offers two completely different dining experiences. At the international fast-food restaurants in the **Center House** (see "Sightseeing Highlights," above), you can feed a family of five for $25. Considerably higher in both price and elevation is the **Space Needle Restaurant**, open for breakfast in summer only and lunch and dinner year-round. The restaurant revolves once every hour, giving you a 360-degree panorama of Seattle and Puget Sound while you eat. Reservations are essential, and coats and ties are required for men. Phone: (206) 443-2100. A more casual restaurant, somewhat less expensive than the one on top, is the **Emerald Room**, midway up the Space Needle. Reservations are recommended; call (206) 443-2150. The elevator ride and observation deck passes are complimentary with a meal at either restaurant.

Your only problem in finding food around **Pike Place Market** will be choosing among the overwhelming assortment of international restaurants in all price ranges. For instance, you'll find budget-priced Bolivian food at the **Copacabana Cafe**, 1502½ Pike Place, (206) 622-6359; moderately priced French nouveau café cuisine at the **Place Pigalle**, 81 Pike Street, (206) 624-1756; and exquisitely prepared seafood direct from the market at the pricey **Il Bistro**, 93-A Pike Street, (206) 682-3049. Or buy fresh fruits, smoked salmon, steamed clams, and fresh baked goods from the Pike Place Market food vendors and enjoy a picnic lunch at Waterfront Park on Pier 57 behind the market.

Perennial restaurant favorites on the Seattle waterfront include **Ivar's Acre of Clams** and the adjoining **Ivar's Oyster Bar**, Pier 54, inexpensive and unusual for lunch but very crowded during the noon hour.

If liquid refreshment (nonalcoholic) is what you're after, but Ivar's clam nectar isn't exactly your cup of tea, head up Broadway from Pike Place Market to the popular **Gravity Bar**, 415 Broadway E., (206) 325-7186, where you can choose from a selection of wheatgrass cocktails. Though the taste takes some getting used to, it's supposed to be outrageously healthy stuff, sure to leave you bursting with energy for sightseeing.

The moderately priced **Old Spaghetti Factory** at Elliot and Broad Street across from Pier 70 is open for dinner until 9:30 p.m. weeknights, 10:00 p.m. Friday and Saturday, closed Sunday. Reservations are recommended; call (206) 441-7724.

Among the many Asian restaurants in the International District, try the **Nikko Restaurant** (sushi and Japanese-style seafood), 1900 Fifth Ave. (in the Westin) dinner only, Monday through Saturday until

SEATTLE

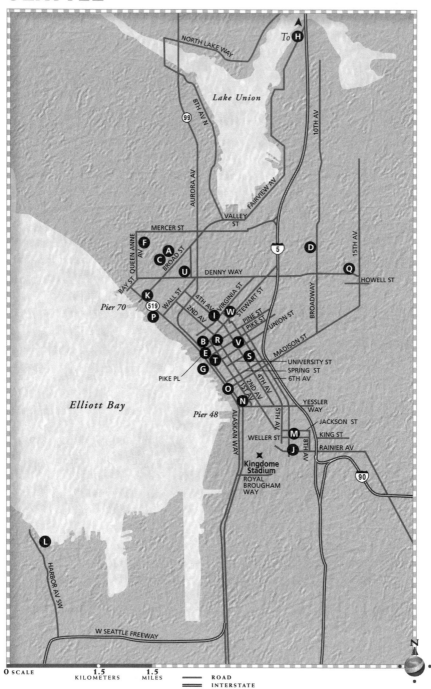

To H

NORTH LAKE WAY

Lake Union

8TH AV N

99

AURORA AV

FAIRVIEW AV

VALLEY ST

MERCER ST

5

15TH AV

10TH AV

BROAD ST

BAY ST QUEEN ANNE AV

F

A

C

U

DENNY WAY

D

Q

HOWELL ST

BROADWAY

K

519

P

Pier 70

WALL ST

4TH AV

VIRGINIA ST

2ND AV

STEWART ST

PINE ST

PIKE ST

UNION ST

I

W

MADISON ST

B

R

V

E

T

S

UNIVERSITY ST

G

4TH AV

SPRING ST

PIKE PL

6TH AV

O

2ND AV

N

5TH AV

YESSLER WAY

Pier 48

JACKSON ST

Elliott Bay

M

KING ST

ALASKAN WAY

WELLER ST

8TH AV

RAINIER AV

J

Kingdome Stadium

ROYAL BROUGHAM WAY

90

L

HARBOR AV SW

W SEATTLE FREEWAY

N

O SCALE
1.5 KILOMETERS
1.5 MILES

ROAD
INTERSTATE

Food

- (A) Center House
- (B) Copacabana Cafe
- (C) Emerald Room
- (D) Gravity Bar
- (E) Il Bistro
- (F) Internet Café
- (G) Ivar's Acre Of Clams
- (H) Ivar's Indian Salmon House
- (G) Ivar's Oyster Bar
- (I) Nikko Restaurant
- (J) Ocean City Restaurant
- (K) Old Spaghetti Factory
- (E) Pike Place Market
- (E) Place Pigalle
- (L) Salty's On Alki
- (C) Space Needle Restaurant
- (M) Tai Tung Restaurant
- (N) Trattoria Mitchelli

Lodging

- (O) Alexis
- (P) Edgewater Inn
- (Q) Gaslight Inn
- (R) Inn at the Market
- (S) Pacific Plaza Hotel
- (T) Seattle International Hostel
- (U) Travelodge by the Space Needle
- (V) YMCA
- (W) YWCA

Note: Items with the same letter are located in the same town or area.

10:00 p.m., moderate to expensive, reservations recommended, (206) 322-4641; **Ocean City Restaurant** (dim sum and Peking duck), 609 South Weller, daily 9:00 a.m. to 1:00 a.m., moderate, (206) 623-2333; or **Tai Tung Restaurant** (Chinese), 659 South King Street, daily 10:00 a.m. to 3:00 a.m., inexpensive, reservations recommended, (206) 622-7372.

The most popular after-theater snack spot in town is **Trattoria Mitchelli**, 84 Yesler Way, (206) 623-3883, half a block from Pioneer Square on Yesler.

Got a craving for cybersnacks? You can surf in Seattle at the **Internet Café**, 1st Street at Mercer Street, (206) 323-7202; http://internetcafe.allyn.com. You can rent a PC by the hour, sip espresso and nibble on homemade muffins while you tell the rest of the world, "Having a wonderful time, wish you were here" via e-mail.

LODGING

The best base for exploring downtown Seattle is the **Edgewater Inn**, 2411 Alaskan Way, (206) 728-7000, on the waterfront at Pier 67. The location is perfect, within easy walking distance of all downtown sightseeing highlights. Rates range from $109 to $195. Completely transformed in 1989, the Edgewater now bills itself as a "mountain lodge" on the edge of Puget Sound. Fishing from the windows is no longer allowed.

Another great downtown location is the **Inn at the Market**, 86 Pine Street, (206) 443-3600, adjacent to Pike Place Market. Rates at this urban version of a French country inn range from $125 to $275 a night.

If money is no object, Seattle's most elegant small hotel is the **Alexis**, 1007 First Avenue, (206) 624-4844. Once a garage, the 1901 building that houses the Alexis is listed on the National Register of Historic Places. Rates start at $185. Executive suites, many with fireplaces, rent for $350 a night.

At the opposite end of the accommodations spectrum is the **Seattle International Hostel** at 84 Union, (206) 622-5443, with 125 $12 beds (bring your own linen or pay extra) in 22 dormitory rooms. AYH or IYHF membership is required and can be purchased upon arrival at the hostel. Desk registration hours are 7:00 to 9:30 a.m. and 5:00 to 10:30 p.m.; the hostel is closed from 10:00 a.m. to 5:00 p.m., and curfew is at midnight. The hostel is at the entrance to Post Alley, near Pike Place Market and within easy walking distance of Pioneer Square and the International District. It's newly opened, relatively undiscovered, and usually not crowded, though that may change. Advance reservations may be made no less than three weeks ahead by mailing a deposit of 50 percent of the charge for your entire stay. Other low-budget downtown accommodations, in the $25 range for private rooms, are the **YMCA**, 909 Fourth Avenue, men and women over 18 only, (206) 382-5000, and the **YWCA**, 1118 Fifth Avenue, women only, (206) 461-4888.

For midrange ($70 to $90) motel accommodations, try the **Travelodge by the Space Needle** at 200 Sixth Avenue North, just a short monorail trip from downtown. For reservations, call (206) 441-7878. Other moderately priced lodging possibilities include the **Pacific Plaza Hotel**, 400 Spring Street, (206) 623-3900, fax (206) 623-2059, a venerable downtown landmark that dates back to 1928 and offers rooms starting under $80; and the **Gaslight Inn**, 1727 15th Avenue, (206) 325-3654, fax (206) 324-3135, a nine-room bed and breakfast in a historic mansion, with lodgings starting at $62.

CAMPING

Camping in Seattle is virtually impossible. While RV travelers could camp outside the city (for example, at Dash Point State Park, 5700 Dash Point Road in Federal Way midway between Seattle and Tacoma, or even at Mount Rainier), taking a hotel room in downtown Seattle and parking your motor home until you're ready to leave town means more sightseeing time and fewer traffic hassles.

NIGHTLIFE

Seattle's nightclub scene keeps getting better and better. Choices range from jazz at **Dimitriou's Jazz Alley** (2033 Sixth Avenue, 206-441-9729) to ballroom dancing at the **Washington Dance Club** (1017 Stewart Street, 206-628-8939). The city is best known, however, for its alternative rock music venues, where performers from golden oldies such as Paul Revere and the Raiders and the late Jimi Hendrix, to Heart, Nirvana, Soundgarden, Pearl Jam, and rapper Sir Mix-A-Lot all got their starts. Top rock clubs today include the **Fenix Café** (111 Yesler Way, 206-447-1514), the **Swan Café and Nightclub** (608 First Avenue, 206-343-5288), **Doc Maynard's** (610 First Avenue, 206-682-4649), and the **Central Café** (207 First Avenue S., 206-622-0209), all at Pioneer Square. Other legendary rock clubs include **The Vogue** (2018 First

Avenue, 206-443-0673), **The Off Ramp** (109 Eastlake Avenue E., 206-628-0232), and **Rockcandy** (1812 Yale, 206-623-0470). Brewpubs have caught on in a big way in Seattle. A standout among the numerous microbrewery night spots is the new **Hart Brewery & Pub** (1201 First Avenue S.; 206-223-1606), featuring live music and fresh-brewed suds.

Seattle is also full of great stand-up comedy clubs. In the Pike Place Market and Pioneer Square area, top venues include the **Comedy Underground** (222 S. Main Street, 206-628-0303), **The Last Laugh Comedy Club** (75 Marion Street, 206-622-JOKE), and the **Seattle Improv** (1426 First Avenue, 206-628-5000).

While municipal performing arts groups—the ballet, the opera, the repertory theater—appear at venues in Seattle Center, most of Seattle's live theater scene centers around Pioneer Square, which is also the city's main art gallery area. Wine-and-cheese opening receptions are held at most galleries in the district on the first Thursday evening of each month. For complete current events listings, consult the "Tempo" insert to the Friday *Seattle Times*. Concert hot-line information is available from radio stations KEZX (folk and new music, 206-547-9890) and KISW (rock, 206-421-5479). Many concerts and events are also posted on the giant bulletin board in Pike Place Market.

HELPFUL HINTS

If you're arriving in Seattle by air, SeaTac Airport is 19 miles south of downtown. You can get from the airport to downtown by city bus. If you have more luggage than you can conveniently carry on the bus, rent a car at the airport: an extra day's car rental won't cost much more than taking a taxi downtown. Simply follow the signs to Interstate 5 and drive north to downtown Seattle. If your plans call for renting an RV in Seattle, avoid traffic aggravation and parking problems by waiting until you're ready to leave the city, then rent a car for these first few days instead. Seattle has hardly any camping facilities.

If you're arriving in Seattle in an RV, you could camp out of town and visit the city as a day trip. Avoid downtown traffic by exiting I-5 at the Seattle Center then ride the monorail downtown. (Even for RV travelers, it's more convenient to spend at least one night in a downtown hotel.)

If you're arriving by Amtrak, the King Street Train Station is at the south end of downtown Seattle, between the International District and Pioneer Square, next to the Kingdome.

2
AROUND SEATTLE

S eattle also offers a lot to see and do away from the downtown area. Whether to go to the beach, take a woodland hike, or visit museums depends on the weather. This chapter features my top suburban Seattle sightseeing highlights. All of these places can be reached by public bus as well as by car, but driving around Seattle is a memorable experience in itself. (See "Helpful Hints," at the end of this chapter, for tips on navigating Seattle's streets.)

While it's easy to get disoriented in the outskirts of Seattle, it's hard to stay lost for very long. Seattle is a long, narrow city, and if you go east or west (taking a street, not an avenue), you're bound to run into a freeway or a shoreline.

Interstate 5, the main north-south freeway, runs right past downtown. Highway 99, a commercial strip and main thoroughfare from the time before freeways were invented, parallels I-5 on the west and becomes the Alaska Way Viaduct above the waterfront. Interstate 405, also north-south, is on the other side of Lake Washington. Highway 520 links the two interstates via the Evergreen Point Floating Bridge, the world's longest (1½ miles).

The fast lanes marked with diamonds on I-5 are for buses and car pools only. If your vehicle contains at least three people, you qualify. ◾

GREATER SEATTLE

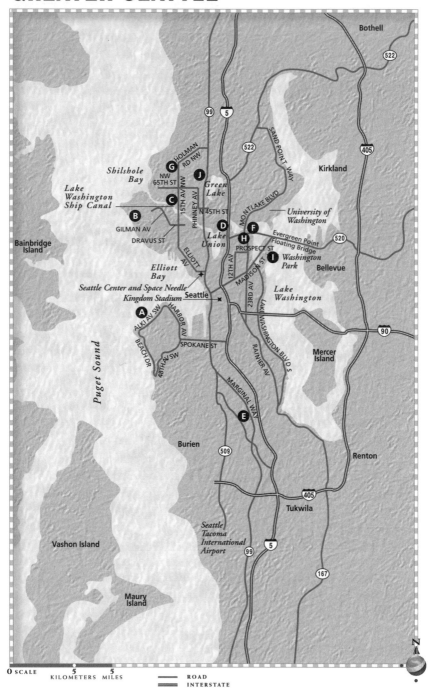

Bothell

522

99 5

522

405

HOLMAN RD NW

Shilshole
Bay

G

NW 65TH ST

J

Green
Lake

Kirkland

Lake
Washington
Ship Canal

C

15TH AV NW

PHINNEY AV

N 45TH ST

SAND POINT WAY

B

GILMAN AV

DRAVUS ST

D

Lake
Union

MONTLAKE BLVD

University of
Washington

F

520

Bainbridge
Island

ELLIOTT AV

H

PROSPECT ST

Evergreen Point
Floating Bridge

I

12TH AV

MADISON ST

Washington
Park

Bellevue

Elliott
Bay

Seattle Center and Space Needle
Kingdom Stadium

Seattle

23RD AV

Lake
Washington

A

ALKI AV SW

HARBOR AV

SPOKANE ST

RAINIER AV

LAKE WASHINGTON BLVD S

Mercer
Island

90

BEACH DR

48TH AV SW

Puget Sound

MARGINAL WAY

E

Renton

Burien

509

405

Tukwila

Vashon Island

Seattle
Tacoma
International
Airport

99

5

167

Maury
Island

N

Sightseeing Highlights

(A) Alki Beach

(B) Daybreak Star Indian Cultural Center

(B) Discovery Park

(C) Hiram M. Chittenden Locks (Ballard Locks)

(D) Maritime Heritage Center

(E) Museum of Flight

(F) Museum of History and Industry

(G) Nordic Heritage Museum

(H) Volunteer Park

(I) Washington Park Arboretum

(J) Woodland Park Zoo

Note: Items with the same letter are located in the same town or area.

A PERFECT DAY AROUND SEATTLE

When planning a perfect day in the greater Seattle area, much depends on the weather. On a sunny day, I can think of few activities more plea-surable than rambling along the foot trails atop the bluffs of Discovery Park, admiring magnificent views of Puget Sound and distant Mount Olympus. But if it's one of those dreary, drizzly days for which Seattle is justly famous, it's a good day to readjust your itinerary and check out some indoor attractions. The Nordic Heritage Museum, for instance, may not be exactly what you came to Seattle planning to see, but sometimes it beats a day at Alki Beach working on your raintan. Pick one (or more) of the unique Seattle sights from the following list and explore the city until you find it.

OUTDOOR SIGHTSEEING HIGHLIGHTS

★★ **Discovery Park and Daybreak Star**—It doesn't sound promising at first: the park, reclaimed from a former military base, adjoins government housing and a sewage treatment plant. Go there and be surprised by 400 acres of forested ravines and broad meadows set aside for hikers only. This is as close to true wilderness as you'll find within Seattle's city limits. The main 2-mile loop trail takes you along Magnolia Bluffs, high sand cliffs that afford a magnificent view of Puget Sound and the Olympic Mountains on a clear day. Side trails lead down to never-crowded beaches on both sides of the point. To get there, take the Seattle Center exit from I-5 and, passing Seattle Center, continue on West Mercer Street, which merges into Elliot Avenue West and turns north to become 15th Avenue West. Just before you reach the Ballard Bridge, turn west on Emerson Place to Gilman Avenue, which becomes Government Way and goes right to the park. Daybreak Star signs will help you find the way. Admission is free. Hours: Open daily from 6:00 a.m. to 11:00 p.m.; visitor's center hours are 8:30 a.m. to 5:00 p.m. daily. Phone: (206) 386-4236. (1 hour)

Also in the park, the **Daybreak Star Indian Cultural Center** has gallery exhibitions of contemporary fine arts by area Native Americans, as well as special events that range from crafts demonstrations to salmon feasts. Admission is free. Hours: Wednesday through Saturday from 10:00 a.m. to 5:00 p.m., Sunday 12:00 noon to 5:00 p.m. Phone: (206) 285-4425. (½ hour)

★★ **Washington Park Arboretum**—Miles of hiking trails lace this 200-acre forest oasis in the middle of the city, south of Union Bay and the University of Washington campus. The 5,500 species of trees and shrubs are a visual feast, though traffic noise is constantly present. Foster Island, on the north end of the arboretum, is a natural wetlands area preserved as a wildlife sanctuary on the shore of Lake Washington, with a soggy nature trail that offers good views of birds and boats. The Foster Island nature trail starts at the lower end of the Museum of History and Industry parking lot and at the other end crosses under the Evergreen Point Floating Bridge freeway to join the main arboretum trails. To get to the arboretum from Interstate 5 (northbound from downtown), take Bellevue-Kirkland exit 168 onto Highway 520, cross Montlake Boulevard to Lake Washington Boulevard E, and follow it into the arboretum. Stop first at the visitor's center and buy a trail map (25 cents). There is a classical Japanese garden at the south end. Admission to the arboretum is free; the Japanese Garden charges $2 for adults and $1 for youths ages 6 to 18 and seniors 65 and over. Hours: Open daily from dawn to dusk. Phone: (206) 543-8800. (1 hour)

★★ **Woodland Park Zoo**—This zoo houses animals in a wide range of simulated habitats, among them African tropical rain forest and savannah, a marsh and swamp, and a Thai jungle complete with elephants. Admission is $7 for adults, $5.25 for seniors, $4.50 for students ages 6 to 17, $2.25 for children ages 2 to 5. Hours: Open daily from 9:30 a.m. to 6:00 p.m. Address: 550 Phinney Avenue N. Phone: (206) 684-4026. (2 hours)

★ **Alki Beach**—Seattle's downtown beach, reached via the West Seattle Freeway just south of downtown, has an early L.A. beachfront ambience, lively on summer days, plus a view of the Space Needle. Don't even think about swimming: the water of Puget Sound is cold enough to cause hypothermia in 15 minutes. Just bask on the sand or flip a frisbee like everybody else. A popular pastime is to bicycle up and down the beachfront, discovering such minor landmarks as the point where Seattle's first European settlers landed and a 6-foot replica of the Statue of Liberty that was presented to the city by the Boy Scouts. (1 hour)

★ **Hiram M. Chittenden Locks (aka Ballard Locks)**—The two locks separate Lake Washington and Lake Union from Puget Sound. The water level of the sound changes with the tide as much as 20 feet daily, while the lake level remains a constant 21 feet above sea level, so the locks are needed to raise and lower boat traffic between the lakes and the sound. A U.S. Army Corps of Engineers visitor's center explains how the process works. The locks are a boat watcher's paradise. About 100,000 vessels pass through them each year, from small pleasure craft to tugboats and barges. Spend an hour or two here and see the proof that Seattle has more boats per capita than any other U.S. city—one for every six residents. A surprising number of salmon and trout also make their way over the locks on fish ladders, especially during the summer months, and visitors can watch them climb through special viewing ports. Admission is free. Hours: The locks are open to the public from 7:00 a.m. to 9:00 p.m. daily. The visitor's center is open mid-June to mid-September daily from 11:00 a.m. to 8:00 p.m., the rest of the year Thursday through Monday 11:00 a.m. to 5:00 p.m. Phone: (206) 783-7059. (½ hour)

INDOOR SIGHTSEEING HIGHLIGHTS

✮✮ **Museum of Flight**—Housed in Boeing's original manufacturing plant, this museum traces the history of aviation from the thirteenth century into the space age. Exhibits include 30 airplanes, many of them suspended from ceiling girders, including a DC-3, a B-7 *Flying Fortress*, and a B-47 *Stratojet*. While the museum understandably emphasizes Boeing's role in realizing mankind's dream of flight, special attention is also given to the little-known contributions of Asian and Pacific Rim nations. To get there, take Interstate 5 exit 158 and go northwest a half-mile. Admission is $6 for adults, $3 for children ages 6 to 15. Hours: Open daily from 10:00 a.m. to 5:00 p.m., Thursdays until 9:00 p.m. Address: 9404 East Marginal Way S. Phone: (206) 764-5720. (1 hour)

✮✮ **Volunteer Park**—Palm trees and cacti in Seattle? You'll find them indoors at the Volunteer Park Conservatory, along with banana trees, giant ferns, and more than 1,500 orchids, in five artificial environments ranging from desert to tropical jungle. Admission is free. Hours: The conservatory is open daily from 10:00 a.m. to 7:00 p.m. mid-May through mid-September, and from 10:00 a.m. to 4:00 p.m. the rest of the year. Address: 1500 East Galer Street. Phone: (206) 684-4743. (1 hour)

Volunteer Park is also the site of the **Seattle Asian Art Museum**, the former location of the Seattle Art Museum and now a branch of the new art museum downtown. Its exhibits of art from China, India, Korea, Japan, Nepal, and Southeast Asia rank among the finest Asian art collections in the world. Admission is $6 for adults, $4 for seniors and students ages 13 through college, free for children under age 13; free admission for all on the first Tuesday of each month; tickets to the Seattle Art Museum downtown will also admit you to the Asian art museum within two days. Hours: Open Tuesday through Saturday from 10:00 a.m. to 5:00 p.m., Thursday until 9:00 p.m. Address: 1400 Prospect Street. Phone: (206) 654-3100. (1 hour)

✮ **Maritime Heritage Center**—This complex on the Lake Union shoreline features a restored shipyard and the **Center for Wooden Boats**, where handmade boats from around the world are exhibited.

Admission is free. It is open Monday through Saturday from 10:00 a.m. to 5:00 p.m., Sundays from noon to 5:00 p.m. during the summer months, and 12:00 noon to 5:00 p.m. daily the rest of the year. Address: 1010 Valley Street. Phone: (206) 382-2628. (½ hour)

Adjoining the Center for Wooden Boats, the 165-foot turn-of-the-century sailing schooner *Wawona* is open to the public for tours. Admission is by donation. Hours: Open daily from 10:00 a.m. to 5:00 p.m. Address: 1002 Valley Street. Phone: (206) 447-9800. (½ hour)

✮ **Museum of History and Industry**—More history than industry (the industry part consists of a vintage Boeing mail plane), MOHAI features changing period costume and decor exhibits, an antique-studded replica of a pioneer-era town's wooden storefronts with photographs recounting Seattle's history, and sailing ship displays. To get there, follow the directions to the Washington Park Arboretum (under "Outdoor Sightseeing Highlights," above), but turn north on Montlake Terrace for 2 blocks. MOHAI is on your right (east) just before you reach the bridge. Admission is $5.50 for adults, $3 for children ages 6 to 12 and seniors over 65, and $1 for children ages 3 to 5. Hours: Open daily from 10:00 a.m. to 5:00 p.m. Address: 2700 24th Avenue E. Phone: (206) 324-1126. (1½ hours)

✮ **Nordic Heritage Museum**—If you're Scandinavian, as many Seattlites are, ja, this one's for you. Exhibits cover fishing, lumbering, and the history of Scandinavian Americans in the Northwest from the eighteenth century to the present. Admission is $3 for adults, $1 for children ages 6 to 16, and $2 for students and seniors. Hours: Open Tuesday through Saturday 10:00 a.m. to 4:00 p.m., Sunday 12:00 noon to 4:00 p.m. Address: 3014 NW 67th Street. Phone: (206) 789-5707. (½ hour)

FITNESS AND RECREATION

A favorite place for bicycling is the **Alki Bike Route**, which borders Seattle's sandiest beach for 6 miles. Bike rentals are available at **Alki Bike Company**, 2722 Alki Avenue SW, (206) 938-3322. Another longer urban bike route, the **Burke-Gilman Trail**, goes from Gasworks Park on Lake Union to Logboom Park on Lake Washington, a 12-mile route that traverses the University of Washington campus. Rent bikes at **The Bicycle Center**, 4529 Sand Point Way NE, (206) 523-8300.

Especially for equestrians, **Bridal Trails State Park** on the east side of the city (take exit 17 from Interstate 405) has nearly 30 miles of trails. Horses are for rent nearby at **Eastside Equestrian Center**; call (206) 827-2992 for reservations.

You can rent a canoe at the **University of Washington Boathouse** (on Boat Street, at the west edge of campus on the north shore of Portage Bay—take NE Pacific Street west from Montlake Boulevard and turn left at the Hospital sign; Boat Street continues past the campus hospital to the boathouse) and paddle through the ship canal to Foster Island and beyond. Rental rates start at $8 per hour. For sailboat rentals contact the Center for Wooden Boats at 1010 Valley, (206) 382-2628.

Look for great urban hiking at the **Washington Park Arboretum** or **Discovery Park**, both described in this chapter.

HELPFUL HINTS

In the Seattle area, suburban streets and avenues are numbered. Streets run east-west, while avenues run north-south. The prefix tells you your direction from downtown, and the street number tells you how many blocks. For example, NE 45th Street, which runs past the University of Washington, is east and 45 blocks north of downtown. Avenues in the same area are also designated "NE," so it's up to you to remember that they're the north-south streets. The system sounds easy enough—and it is, as long as you don't drive far enough to cross a county line (at Edmonds or Lynnwood to the north, Tacoma or Puyallup to the south). Then the frame of reference changes, and ascending "N" numbers become descending "S" numbers. Confusing? You bet. The shoreline and distant mountains aren't much help either, because to the untrained eye, Lake Washington and the Cascade Mountains to the east can look much the same as Puget Sound and the Olympic Mountains to the west, making it easy to convince your-self that you're going in the opposite direction. Don't panic—you're probably not.

3
PUGET SOUND

Take a ferry to the western shore of Puget Sound for the first in a series of minicruises that rank among the Northwest's biggest sightseeing bargains. Washington's ferry network carries 7 million vehicles and 17 million passengers each year. The 22 vessels, traveling eight routes, are vital highway links: without them, driving from one shore of 10-mile-wide Puget Sound to the other would take all day. Every vehicle that uses the highways—commuter traffic, bicycles, motor homes, log trucks, state police cruisers—also uses these boats.

While the total driving distance from Seattle to Anacortes, the departure point for the San Juan Islands Ferry, is less than 70 miles, you'll find enough unusual points of interest on the less-populated side of the sound to keep you occupied until dinner time. Among them are a Salish Indian museum and the longest island in the United States.

The northern part of Puget Sound is as bucolic as metropolitan Seattle is citified. It's a countryside of picture-perfect farms and forests too neatly regrown, like a little piece of coastal New England transplanted 3,000 miles westward. Some towns in the area were among the first permanent non-Indian settlements established in Washington. There's Port Gamble, America's oldest continuously operating lumber company town, and Port Townsend, the largest port on Puget Sound for nearly 40 years in the nineteenth century. ◼

PUGET SOUND

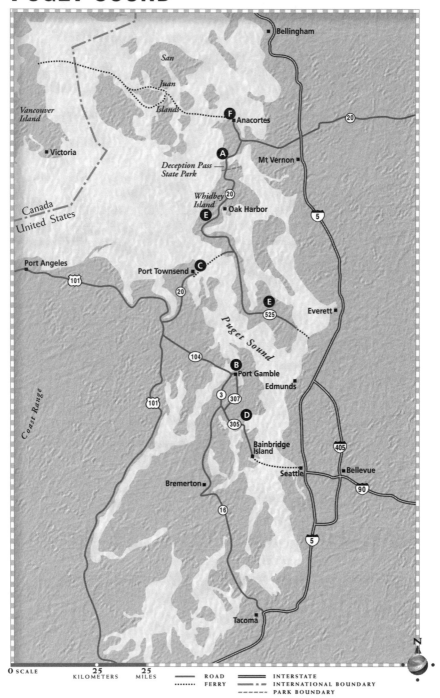

Bellingham

San
Juan
Islands

Vancouver
Island

F■ Anacortes

20

A

Mt Vernon ■

Deception Pass —
State Park

Victoria

Whidbey
Island

20

E ■ Oak Harbor

5

Canada
United States

Port Angeles ■

101

Port Townsend ■ C

20

E

525

Everett ■

Puget Sound

104

101

B
■ Port Gamble

3 307

Edmunds

Coast Range

D

305

Bainbridge
Island

405

Bremerton ■

16

Seattle ■

■ Bellevue

90

5

Tacoma ■

N

0 SCALE 25 KILOMETERS 25 MILES —— ROAD ═══ INTERSTATE
············ FERRY ═ ▪ ═ INTERNATIONAL BOUNDARY
------ PARK BOUNDARY

Sightseeing Highlights

Ⓐ Deception Pass State Park

Ⓑ Port Gamble

Ⓒ Port Townsend

Ⓓ Suquamish Museum

Ⓔ Whidbey Island

Food

Ⓒ Aldrich's

Ⓕ Boomer's Landing

Ⓒ Bread and Roses

Ⓒ Café Piccolo

Ⓒ Elevated Ice Cream Company

Ⓕ Islands Motel

Ⓒ Manresa Castle Restaurant

Lodging

Ⓕ Islands Inn

Ⓒ Manresa Castle

Ⓕ Old Brook Inn

Ⓒ Old Consulate Inn

Camping

Ⓐ Deception Pass State Park

Note: Items with the same letter are located in the same town or area.

A PERFECT DAY ON PUGET SOUND

Start the day by taking the ferry from Seattle's waterfront terminal to Winslow on Bainbridge Island, and drive north on Highway 305 for 6 miles until you reach the Agate Pass Bridge, which links Bainbridge Island with the Kitsap Peninsula. Just over the bridge, turn right and you're in Suquamish.

After visiting the Suquamish Museum, go west for 6 miles on Highway 305, then north for 7 miles on Highway 3. When you reach Highway 104, turn right (east) 1 mile to historic Port Gamble. Upon leaving Port Gamble, go back 1 mile west on Highway 104 and cross the Hood Canal Bridge, the world's longest floating bridge over tidewater, which takes you to the northeastern corner of the Olympic Peninsula. A road to the right just beyond the bridge follows the shoreline all the way to Port Townsend, rejoining the main route, Highway 20, 5 miles from town.

From Port Townsend, the ferry to Keystone on Whidbey Island departs every hour and a half, but only until 5:00 p.m. Departures are later on Fridays, Saturdays, Sundays, and holidays. The fare is about the same as for the one to Kingston. The trip lasts 30 minutes. Arriving in Kingston, stay on Highway 20 (it's the only one) north for 30 miles to Deception Pass. From the park, it's 10 more miles to Anacortes.

SIGHTSEEING HIGHLIGHTS

★★★ **Washington State Ferries**—The key to riding the ferries is a pair of tiny free brochures, *Sailing Schedules* and *Fares and Tolls*. Pick them up the first chance you get—at Seattle's downtown ferry terminal, at a municipal bus schedule rack, upon request at any ferry toll booth, or aboard the ferries—and keep them handy. They are essential! Ferries run more frequently at busy times of day and on certain days of the week. Service on some routes continues until midnight or later, while on others the last boat leaves as early as 5:00 p.m. Fares, which are not always the same in one direction as the other, cost about 20 percent more during the summer months. Fares for vehicles over 18 feet long (including trailer length) cost almost twice as much, and over 28 feet, the fares are still higher. Schedules change seasonally, so the information listed in this book should only be used as a rough guideline. The fares I've listed are basic summer rates, followed by the lower off-season cost in parentheses, for vehicles less than 18 feet long.

Riding the ferry is easy. Drive down to the ferry dock, pay at the toll booth, and proceed to whichever traffic lane you're told to use. If you have a motor home, camper, or travel trailer, federal law requires that you shut off your propane tank before boarding the boat, and the toll-taker will give you a bright orange sticker to paste across the shut-off valve. When the boat arrives, follow the car in front of you on board, turn off your engine, get out, and lock your vehicle. Upstairs, you'll find a snack bar, lounge areas, indoor and outdoor observation decks, and rest rooms. Have coffee and doughnuts, stroll the deck, feed the seagulls, pretend you're on a cruise ship. Return to your vehicle when you see everybody else doing so, just before the boat touches the dock. Then drive off the boat and find yourself in a new place.

From Seattle's State Ferry Terminal, the Winslow ferry departs approximately each hour beginning at 6:20 a.m., $7.00 ($5.90 off-season) per vehicle with driver, plus $3.50 per passenger. Crossing time is 35 minutes. The Kingston ferry is the same price as the Winslow ferry and departs more frequently, 30 minutes crossing time.

Seattle's State Ferry Terminal is at Pier 52 on the waterfront. Address: 801 Alaskan Way. Phone: (800) 843-3779.

★★ **Port Gamble**—As you stroll through this early-day lumber town (founded in 1853), you may feel as if you've been transported to nineteenth-century New England. The town's founder, William Talbot of the Pope and Talbot Lumber Company, patterned Port Gamble after his hometown, East Machias, Maine. Stately elm trees, brought around Cape Horn as seedlings in the mid-nineteenth century, shade a main street lined with New England–style clapboard homes so perfectly preserved that they look as if they'd been built yesterday. While the town feels like a historical park, most of the houses remain private residences. The general store, stocking items aimed more at the tourist trade than the needs of townsfolk, features a fair selection of gourmet foods and Washington wines.

Upstairs you'll find the **Sea and Shore Museum**, a display of more than 14,000 seashells, which is claimed to be the world's largest collection. Admission is free. Hours: Open 11:00 a.m. to 4:00 p.m. Tuesday through Sunday from mid-May through mid-September, weekends only the rest of the year. Phone: (360) 297-2426.

The lower level of the general store houses the **Port Gamble Historic Museum**, which recounts the history of the Pope and Talbot Lumber Company. Even the lumber mill, filling the whole shoreline downhill from the town, has an almost quaint appearance, far different from the heavy-industry ambience of more modern mills you'll see elsewhere in the Northwest. Admission is $1 for adults, 50 cents for students and seniors. Hours: Open daily 10:00 a.m. to 4:00 p.m., summer months only. Phone: (360) 297-3341. (1½ hours)

★ ★ **Suquamish Museum**—This museum, operated by the small neighboring Port Madison Indian Reservation, exhibits artifacts and photographs of the Puget Sound Salish people, as well as quotes from tribal elders. Next to the museum is the grave of Chief Sealth, for

whom the city of Seattle was named. Sealth, the leader of the
Duwamish and Suquamish tribes until his death in 1866, was an elo-
quent orator and spokesman for the Native Americans of the
Northwest. His words upon signing the Port Elliott Treaty in 1855
seem poignant now:

When the last Red Man shall have perished, and the memory of my
tribe shall have become a myth among the White Man, these shores will
swarm with the invisible dead of my tribe, and when your children's children
think themselves alone in the field, the store, the shop, or in the silence of the
pathless woods, they will not be alone. At night, when the streets of your cities
and villages are silent and you think them deserted, they will throng with the
returning hosts that once filled them and still love this beautiful land. The
White Man will never be alone.

Near Chief Sealth's grave is a city park where once stood an
Indian longhouse, burned by federal agents four years after Sealth's
death to discourage communal living. Admission to the museum is
$2.50 for adults, $2 for senior citizens, $1 for children ages 2 to 11.
Hours: Open daily from 10:00 a.m. to 5:00 p.m. during the summer
months, Wednesday through Sunday 11:00 a.m. to 4:00 p.m. the rest
of the year. Address: 15838 Sandy Hook Road, Suquamish. Phone:
(360) 598-3311. (1 hour)

✿ **Port Townsend**—Settled in the 1850s, this town dominated commerce in the Puget Sound region for nearly half a century. Today, with
a population of 6,000, it no longer rivals Seattle as a shipping center,
but its historic district features the finest array of Victorian architecture
(as well as the most bed and breakfasts per capita) in the state.
Panoramic views and beach access can be found at Chetzemolka Park
(Jackson Street at Blaine Street) and Fort Worden State Park on the
north side of the cape. (½ hour)

✿ **Whidbey Island**—This is the longest island in the United States (a
title it gained in 1985 when the U.S. Supreme Court ruled that Long
Island, New York, was actually a peninsula). It's 55 miles long, with
Keystone at the midpoint. A state ferry runs between Port Townsend
and Keystone every 90 minutes ($5.90 for car and driver, $1.75 per passenger, 30 minutes). When you get off the boat, you're still on Highway
20—the same road that took you to Port Townsend. Another ferry con-

nects the southern tip of the island with Mukilteo, a suburb of Everett, on the mainland ($4 for car and driver, $2.30 per passenger, 20 minutes).

FITNESS AND RECREATION

The secondary highways in this area, especially on Whidbey Island, are flat and, on weekdays, relatively traffic-free, making for great road bike touring. Bikes can be rented at **Port Cyclery**, 215 Taylor Street, Port Townsend; (360) 385-6470. (If you're headed for the San Juan Islands and planning to come back the same way, consider renting a bike for the whole trip. The islands are just right for biking, and the savings by not taking a car on the ferry make up for the bike rental charge.)

Deception Pass State Park has a number of hiking trails. Among the most dramatic are the 1¼-mile **Goose Rock Perimeter Trail**, which leads along the rocky edge of Deception Pass with tide waters crashing below, and the 1¼-mile **Goose Rock Summit Trail**, which climbs to the top of a 450-foot-high rock formation for a great view of Whidbey and Fidalgo Islands.

FOOD

Port Townsend is an excellent place for specialty food shopping. You'll find an impressive selection of regional, international, and gourmet picnic fixin's at **Aldrich's**, 940 Lawrence Street. One of the best bakeries in the Northwest is **Bread and Roses** at 230 Quincy Street. At the **Elevated Ice Cream Company**, 627 Water Street, besides fine quality ice cream you'll find espresso, pastries, handmade chocolates, and other irresistibly fattening goodies.

For an elegant dinner in Port Townsend, try the **Manresa Castle Restaurant**, 7th and Sheridan Streets, (360) 385-6221, a dining room with Victorian ambience and a heart-healthy menu emphasizing seafood, open for dinner and Sunday brunch only.

There's quicker and easier eating in Port Townsend at the **Café Piccolo**, 3040 Highway 20, (360) 385-1403. The atmosphere is casual, and the food is pasta and pizza.

For dinner in Anacortes, fresh local seafood is the specialty at **Boomer's Landing**, 209 T Avenue next to Wyman's, with a good waterfront view of Guemes Channel. Prices are in the deluxe range. Open for lunch and dinner daily. Reservations are recommended. Phone: (360) 293-5108.

For European (especially Dutch) cuisine, try the moderately priced, outstanding restaurant in the **Islands Motel**. Dinner only, closed Monday. Reservations are recommended. Phone: (360) 293-4464.

LODGING

Port Townsend has numerous bed and breakfasts. For ambience, none can compete with **Manresa Castle**, 7th and Sheridan Streets, (360) 385-5750 or (800) 732-1281, fax (360) 385-5883. This 40-room mansion on a hilltop above town, built by Port Townsend's first mayor in 1892, was patterned after a castle on the Rhine. It looks like the kind of place where Sleeping Beauty would sleep, and you can too starting at $70 a night (a price range that is typical of most Port Townsend bed and breakfast inns).

Another smaller but ultra-elegant Port Townsend bed and breakfast is the **Old Consulate Inn**, 313 Walker Street, (360) 385-6753 or (800) 300-6753, fax (360) 385-2097, an 1869 Queen Anne Victorian mansion built by Port Townsend founder F. W. Hastings and later occupied by the German embassy when the town was Washington's leading seaport. The six rooms and suites have king-size beds and great views of Puget Sound. Rates start at $80.

Anacortes is the only place to stay if you plan to catch the San Juan Islands Ferry in the morning. There are a lot of motels, mostly in the same price range as Port Townsend bed and breakfasts (budget lodging being almost impossible to find in these parts). Reservations are a must during the summer and on weekends. Try the very Dutch **Islands Inn**, 3401 Commercial Avenue, (360) 293-4644, with rooms for $65 to $95. Reservations are essential at charming bed and breakfasts such as the handsome Cape Cod–style **Old Brook Inn**, 530 Old Brook Lane, (360) 293-4768, where doubles rent for $80 a night.

CAMPING

Deception Pass State Park at the north end of Whidbey Island has an attractive forest campground near Cranberry Lake on the north side of the bridge. The last time I camped there, the racket of jet fighters on the approach path to nearby Whidbey Island Naval Air Station was so deafening that I abandoned my campsite in search of an Anacortes motel room. Area residents assured me, though, that the noise problem is not typical and that Deception Pass is the most popular campground around. Check it out for yourself. Campsites cost $8 a night, no hookups.

4

OLYMPIC NATIONAL PARK

Olympic National Park contains more than 900,000 acres of wilderness in the interior of the Olympic Peninsula and encompasses a variety of environments ranging from seashore and rain forest (covered in the previous chapter) to some of the wildest mountains in Washington. The park was originally conceived as a vast reserve, but this status has been challenged repeatedly. During World War I, large areas of the original park were logged; these areas were later removed from the park as we know it today to form Olympic National Forest, covering the south half of the peninsula. Before 1938 logging and mining interests managed to remove land from park protection on three separate occasions, shrinking the park to less than half its original size. Hunting reduced the population of Roosevelt elk (named for Theodore Roosevelt) nearly to extinction before President Franklin D. Roosevelt passed a law fixing the park's boundaries and prohibiting hunting there. Mountain goats, too, nearly vanished from the park. Today projects are well underway to reintroduce both species.

The lush diversity of flora and fauna you'll find here is due in large part to rainy, though otherwise mild, weather. The summit of Mount Olympus in the center of the park receives more than 220 inches of precipitation a year, making it one of the wettest places on earth. Although temperatures at lower elevations rarely drop below freezing in winter or rise above 80 degrees in summer, the climate in the mountains is another story. Visitors to Hurricane Ridge should prepare for the possibility of abrupt temperature drops of 40 degrees or more at any time of year. ◼

OLYMPIC NATIONAL PARK

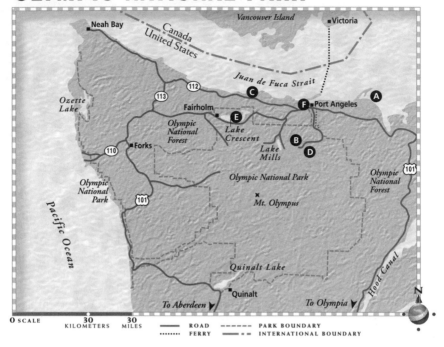

Sightseeing Highlights

Ⓐ **Dungeness Spit**

Ⓑ **Obstruction Point**

Ⓒ **Olympic National Park: Crescent Bay**

Ⓓ **Olympic National Park: Hurricane Ridge**

Ⓔ **Olympic National Park: Lake Crescent**

Ⓕ **Port Angeles Visitor Center and Pioneer Memorial Museum**

A PERFECT DAY IN OLYMPIC NATIONAL PARK

At the eastern tip of Lake Crescent, take the road that turns off along the lake's north shore, goes through the village of Piedmont, then crosses Highway 112 and loops around past Crescent Bay, rejoining Highway 112 in a few miles. Where the highway merges with U.S. 101, turn right (southwest) and drive about 2 miles to the "Heart O' The Hills" road. (This Crescent Bay detour meanders off the beaten path; you can skip it and save about half an hour by driving directly east on U.S. 101 from Lake Crescent to the "Heart O' The Hills" road, just past Elwha.) After about 6 miles the road joins the Hurricane Ridge Highway. Follow it up to Hurricane Ridge. Descending from Hurricane Ridge, stay on the main road, which will take you into downtown Port Angeles.

SIGHTSEEING HIGHLIGHTS

☆☆☆ **Olympic National Park: Hurricane Ridge**—The park's ultimate scenic drive is open (and well traveled) year-round. In the winter and early spring, Hurricane Ridge is a popular snow-play area, with cross-country skis, sleds, and snowshoes for rent at the lodge. Snow reaches a depth of 20 feet and lingers through June. In the summer, the ridge is a wonderland of subalpine meadows, where the wildflowers include several subspecies found nowhere else on earth, such as Plett's violet, Piper's bellflower, and the Olympic mountain daisy. Look for Olympic marmot, Olympic chipmunk, and Olympic snow mole, as well.

The views from 5,200-foot Hurricane Ridge defy comparison. To the north you can see Port Angeles, the Strait of Juan de Fuca, the San Juan Islands, and the Canadian coast—all a mile below you. To the south you can see the immensity of the national park's wilderness interior, more than 600,000 acres of rugged mountain peaks, all inaccessible by road. For the best view, drive the 8-mile Alpine Drive along the ridge-line to **Obstruction Point**.

On the return trip from Hurricane Ridge, stop at Olympic National Park's main visitor's center, the **Port Angeles Visitor Center and Pioneer Memorial Museum**, where the road enters the outskirts of Port Angeles (3002 Mount Angeles Road). Even though you already may have seen the park from several angles in the past few days, it is so vast and complex and changes so much with the weather and the seasons, that the exhibits and audiovisual programs here can add a new dimension of understanding to what you've experienced. Displays feature flora and fauna, geology, history, and Indian culture. Phone for all park units: (360) 452-0330. (3 hours)

✫ **Olympic National Park: Lake Crescent**—Over 600 feet deep and 8½ miles long, this lake is the largest in Olympic National Park. From the Storm King Ranger Station beside U.S. 101 near the midpoint of the lake, a mile-long trail takes you up to 90-foot Marymere Falls. The last part of the trail is quite steep. (1 hour)

✫ **Olympic National Park: Crescent Bay**—In the 1890s, the logging town of Port Crescent, just north of what is now Tongue Point County Park, was one of the largest communities on the peninsula's Juan de Fuca coast. All that's left is the graveyard. Few people come this way any more, and the beach is never crowded. (½ hour)

✫ **Dungeness Spit**—Famed for the Dungeness crabs harvested here, which are a popular gourmet seafood dish around Puget Sound, this 7-mile-long natural sand hook is a national wildlife refuge, a nesting area for waterfowl, and a stopover in the fall and winter for huge flocks of ducks and snow geese. Pay $2 at the entrance in adjoining Dungeness Spit State Park and walk along the sandy beach—with the waters of the Strait of Juan de Fuca on both sides—as far as you want. If you hike the full length of the spit, which few visitors do, you will come to an 1857 lighthouse that is open for touring. (1½ hours)

FITNESS AND RECREATION

The interior of Olympic National Park contains over 600 miles of hiking trails. For breathtaking hiking, leave the crowds behind and follow the trail that goes from **Obstruction Point** east for 2 miles to Elk Mountain. It continues for another 6 miles one way to Deer Park.

Another trail from Obstruction Point follows the ridge-line to the south and then descends steeply to **Grand Lake** and **Moose Lake**, a distance of 3 miles each way. Allow all day for this one. Shorter walking trails are found all along the **Alpine Drive**.

At the end of the Soleduck road off U.S. 101, a short distance past Sol Duc Hot Springs (an old spa resort where there is a campground and privately owned hot springs pools), a lovely 1-mile trail runs from the trailhead to **Soleduck Falls**, a powerful waterfall that crashes through a small gorge. Along the road are several other short trails, including the

OLYMPIC NATIONAL PARK

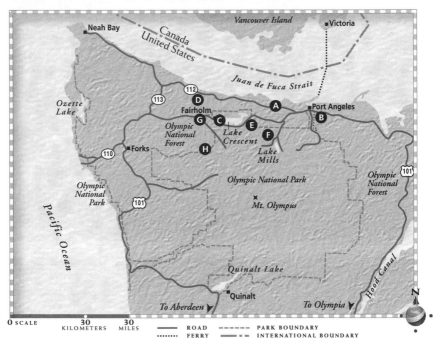

Food

A Café Garden

B C'est Si Bon

A First Street Haven

Lodging

A Bavarian Inn

A Bayton's On-the-Bluff

A Bed and Breakfast
at Our House

C Lake Crescent Lodge

D Log Cabin Resort

Camping

E Altaire Campground

F Elwha Campground

G Fairholm Campground

H Soleduck Campground

Note: Items with the same letter are located in the same town or area.

Salmon Cascades Trail and the **Ancient Groves Nature Trail**. A network of long trails begins near Soleduck Falls and penetrates to the heart of the national park wilderness. One of the trails goes for 17 miles, over a mile-high mountain pass, before joining the trail from the Hoh Rain Forest to the summit of Mount Olympus.

FOOD

A favorite Port Angeles restaurant is the **Café Garden**, 1506 East 1st Street, (360) 457-4611, where specialties include Dungeness crab cakes and excellent stir-fries. Inexpensive breakfasts and lunches, including soups, salads, and sandwiches, can be had at the **First Street Haven**, 107 East 1st Street, (360) 457-0352. If it's time for fabulous classic French cuisine, try **C'est Si Bon**, 2300 Route 101, (360) 452-8888.

LODGING

At **Lake Crescent Lodge** on the lakeshore, rooms and cottages range from $68 to $121 a night. Open May through October; call (360) 928-3211.

Nearby, 3 miles off U.S. 101 via East Beach Road on the northeast end of the lake, is **Log Cabin Resort**, with motel units, cabins, an RV park, a restaurant, and a grocery store. Rates start at $50 a night. For reservations, call (360) 928-3325.

If Lake Crescent Lodge and Log Cabin Resort are full—as they usually are in the summer months unless you made reservations far in advance—you'll find plenty of motels in nearby Port Angeles, as well as a number of good bed and breakfasts. Try **Bayton's On-the-Bluff**, 824 West 4th Street, (360) 457-5569, from $65 per night; **Bavarian Inn**, 1126 East 7th Street, (360) 457-4098 (call after 2:30 p.m.), from $80 per night; or **Bed and Breakfast at Our House**, 218 Whidbey Avenue, (360) 452-6338, $65 per night.

CAMPING

The largest of several national park campgounds near Lake Crescent is **Fairholm Campground** on North Shore Road, with 87 sites. Others nearby are **Altaire Campground** (29 sites) and **Elwha Campground** (41 sites), both a few miles south on Elwha River Road, and **Soleduck Campground** (84 sites), 12 miles south on the Soleduck Road.

5

WASHINGTON COAST

As you continue westward along the Olympic Peninsula's north coast, you will eventually come to the town of Neah Bay, a dreary Makah Indian fishing village where you'll find one of the most fascinating museums in the Pacific Northwest, a must-see for anyone interested in the region's indigenous cultures. From there, your only option is to retrace your route inland before turning south.

Unlike in Oregon, most of the Olympic Peninsula's Pacific coast is inaccessible by road. Highway 101 keeps its distance from the storm-battered coastline, much of which is Indian reservation land. The rest of the peninsula's western shore is the long, slender Coast Unit of Olympic National Park, only a small part of which is close enough to walk to from trailheads along the side of the highway. This side of the peninsula gets five times as much rain as Seattle, which helps explain why it is almost uninhabited—as well as why it boasts North America's only temperate rain forests.

If you continue south along Highway 101 beyond Olympic National Park, you'll find yourself in the midst of the leading commercial timber area in the United States, presently struggling out of the economic depression brought by the decline of logging in the past few years. Fewer log trucks clog the highway than in past years, and ships laden with raw logs no longer set sail for Japan from Aberdeen, formerly the largest timber shipping port in the world. You'll still see clear-cut devastation that looks a lot like the ash-blasted slopes of Mount St. Helens, clearly demonstrating that our endangered ancient forests are not a "renewable resource." ◼

WASHINGTON COAST

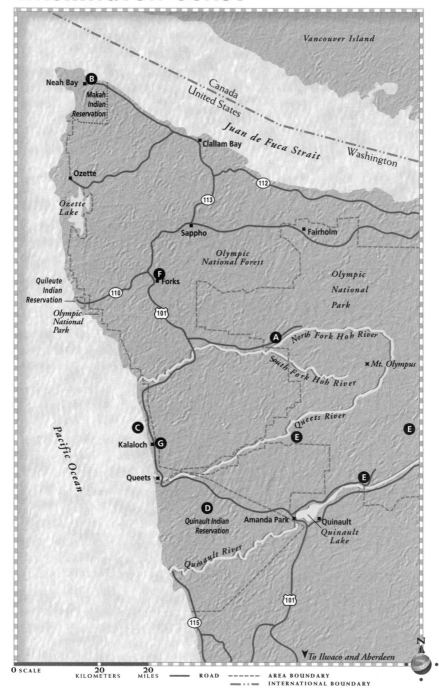

Vancouver Island

Neah Bay **B**

Makah
Indian
Reservation

Canada
United States

Washington

Juan de Fuca Strait

Clallam Bay

Ozette

112

113

Ozette
Lake

Sappho

Fairholm

Olympic
National Forest

Olympic
National
Park

Quileute
Indian
Reservation

110

F Forks

Olympic
National
Park

101

A North Fork Hoh River

South Fork Hoh River

× Mt. Olympus

Queets River

E

E

Pacific Ocean

C

Kalaloch **G**

E

Queets

D

Quinault Indian
Reservation

Amanda Park

Quinault

Quinault
Lake

Quinault River

101

115

To Ilwaco and Aberdeen

N

0 SCALE   20   20
         KILOMETERS MILES   ——— ROAD   -------- AREA BOUNDARY
                                      ——-—-— INTERNATIONAL BOUNDARY

Sightseeing Highlights

Ⓐ Hoh Rain Forest

Ⓑ Makah Museum, Neah Bay Cultural and Research Center

Ⓒ Olympic National Park: Coast Unit

Ⓓ Quinault Indian Reservation

Ⓔ Quinault and Queets Rain Forests

Lodging

Ⓕ Forks Motel

Ⓖ Kalaloch Lodge

Ⓕ Manitou Lodge

Ⓑ Thunderbird Resort

Ⓑ Tyee Motel & RV Park

Camping

Ⓐ Hoh Rain Forest

Ⓑ Tyee RV Park

Note: Items with the same letter are located in the same town or area.

A PERFECT DAY ON WASHINGTON'S PACIFIC COAST

U.S. 101 will bring you to the turnoff on your right for the 19-mile drive to Hoh Rain Forest. After visiting the Hoh Rain Forest, return to U.S. 101, turn right, and drive north for 25 miles to the little town of Sappho. Turn left on the road marked to Neah Bay. Ten more miles will bring you to the intersection with State Highway 112. Turn left (west), and in 6 miles you'll reach the northern coastline of the Olympic Peninsula at Clallam Bay. It's 20 more slow miles along the narrow, winding road, always in sight of the seashore with views 15 miles across the Strait of Juan de Fuca to Vancouver Island in Canada. As you enter the poor but honest Indian fishing village of Neah Bay on the Makah Indian Reservation, watch for the Neah Bay Cultural and Research Center on your left.

SIGHTSEEING HIGHLIGHTS

✦✦✦ **Olympic National Park: Hoh Rain Forest**—You may already have seen a wide variety of forests on your Pacific Northwestern tour—ancient forests, second-growth forests, industrial fir forests, dry-side pine forests, California redwood forests—but you'll never find another one like the Hoh Rain Forest. This and similar areas in the Quinault and Queets river valleys not far to the south make up one of only three temperate-zone rain forests in the world. (The others are in New Zealand and southern Chile.) The Hoh Valley receives an average of 145 inches of rain a year—more than four times as much as Seattle. As a result, every square inch of ground is covered with vegetation. Ferns and sorrel form such a thick carpet on the forest floor that tree seedlings have a hard time taking root, so trees grow in neat rows from older trees that have fallen and decayed. Moss drips from branches, and licorice ferns grow from the sides of living trees without ever touching the earth. Sitka spruce reach 300 feet in height and 23 feet in diameter (considerably larger than they grow in Sitka, Alaska, for which they are named, and about the same height as California's giant redwoods). Black-tailed deer wander the forest without fear, and Roosevelt elk descend from the mountains to graze here in autumn. Colorful harlequin ducks are also a common sight. Admission, which covers all units of Olympic National Park for seven days, is $5 per vehicle. About 12 miles north of where U.S. 101 leaves the coast unit of the national park (see page 75), watch for the road that exits on your right (east) to the Hoh Rain Forest. The road into the rain forest is 19 miles long. Phone: (360) 956-2400. (3 hours)

✦✦✦ **Makah Museum, Neah Bay Cultural and Research Center**— This is the most unusual and rewarding Native American museum in the Pacific Northwest. It houses the artifacts excavated from the 500-year-old village at Ozette, 15 miles south along the Pacific coast. Excavations at the Ozette site have been completed, and the site has been reburied to protect any remaining artifacts. There's little to attract visitors—except for one of the peninsula's largest lakes and a 3-mile hike to the coastline at the northern end of Olympic National Park's coastal unit.

While dampness has rotted and destroyed most Northwest Coast Indian artifacts, the village of Ozette was buried in a mudslide and preserved in perfect condition for five centuries, until its discovery in 1970. Beautifully displayed under tribal supervision at the Makah Museum, the items unearthed at Ozette evoke a vivid picture of these people who harpooned whales from canoes, cultivated potatoes that somehow got here from Peru, and made tools of metal fragments washed ashore from the wreckage of Asian sailing vessels. A profound sense of mystery surrounds these articles of everyday life from a forgotten time. When you've viewed all the exhibits, sit and meditate for a while inside the longhouse replica, where recorded voices murmur softly in the Makah language. Although the Makah people clung to their traditional way of life until the beginning of the twentieth century, their descendants today don't remember much more about it than you'll know after visiting this one-of-a-kind museum. The gift shop carries American Indian arts and crafts as well as books on Indian subjects.

Admission is $4 for adults, $3 for full-time students and senior citizens, free for children under age 4. Hours: Open daily from 10:00 a.m. to 5:00 p.m., closed Mondays and Tuesdays from mid-September through May. Phone: (360) 645-2711. (2 hours)

★★ **Olympic National Park: Coast Unit**—Beginning 2 miles north of Queets, the seashore wilderness strip of Olympic National Park extends for 57 miles to the north, interrupted only by three very small coastal Indian reservations, Hoh, Quillayute, and Ozette. Only the south 14 miles are accessible by road, along the stretch of U.S. 101 known as the Kalaloch-Ruby Beach Highway. For most of the drive, you can't see the ocean or beach from the highway. Stop at any (or all) of seven pullouts, where short trails lead down to the beach. This coastline feels wild and untouched; wander it and dream. Watch for tracks of raccoons, otters, and even bears in the wet sand. If the lure of this coastline captures your imagination, and the weather is fair, you can walk for many miles north of Ruby Beach and the Hoh reservation without seeing another human being. Before undertaking a long hike, stop at the little National Park Service information station across the highway near Kalaloch (pronounced "CLAY-lock") Lodge and pick up the *Strip of Wilderness* brochure that tells you how to circumvent treacherous headlands on overland trails. There is no admission charge for this unit of the national park. (2 hours)

★ **Quinault Indian Reservation**—From Lake Quinault to the coast, U.S. 101 follows the northern boundary of the largest Indian reservation on the Olympic Peninsula. Most of the tribe's 1,000 people live far from the highway, near the river, where travel is prohibited unless you have tribal permission, which is difficult to obtain. The Quinaults make their living fishing for salmon and processing it in the tribal cannery, thanks to a landmark court decision that restored their fishing rights under a treaty that had long been ignored. The tribe is also known for its decision to ban non-Indians from a once-popular beach in the coastal town of Queets. White men, they said, leave too much trash. The chief of this small tribe spends much of his time in Washington, D.C., where he is the nation's foremost lobbyist for American Indian rights. (1 hour)

✿ **Quinault and Queets Rain Forests**—North of the Quinault reservation, two roads run east from the main highway to trailheads in a remote corner of Olympic National Park. They provide access to two other pockets of temperate rain forest much like the Hoh Rain Forest (see above). The difference is, these two less-known areas do not have national park visitor's centers, rangers on duty, admission booths at the entrance, or hordes of visitors. The Quinault Rain Forest can be reached from the road on either the north or south shore of Lake Quinault, just east of the main highway. The roads pass through a lakeside summer homes area and then continue as an unpaved road to a campground and a forest trailhead into the national park wilderness area. The Queets Rain Forest, reached by a shorter side road about 20 miles farther north on U.S. 101, has a 3-mile nature trail through the forest as well as a longer trail that leads along the Queets River deep into the national park. (1½ hours for either forest)

FITNESS AND RECREATION

In the Hoh Rain Forest, walk the 1-mile **Hall of Mosses Trail**. It's beautiful but short. For more, take the 1.3-mile **Spruce Nature Trail**. These are the only two short trails in the rain forest. If they're not enough to satisfy your fascination with this damp verdant wonderland, hike part of the **Hoh River Trail**. This 17-mile trail goes up to the base of the glaciers on Mount Olympus and is the shortest route for mountaineers climbing Olympic National Park's highest mountain (7,965 feet). The first 12½ miles are through rain forest. You must first obtain a free wilderness permit at the visitor's center.

Beyond Neah Bay the only paved road ends at an Air Force Station. From there, a dirt road leads northwest for about 5 miles to the **Cape Flattery Trailhead**. A short (½-mile, half-hour each way) trail through the woods takes you to Cape Flattery, where you can stand on the northwesternmost point in the Lower 48.

For a longer hike, take the dirt road that goes south from the Air Force Station across the Waatch River Bridge. It goes 7 miles, past Hobuck and Sooes Beaches, to the **Shi-Shi Beach Trailhead**. A 3-mile hike (allow 90 minutes each way) will bring you to Shi-Shi Beach, a wild and virtually untouched beach where yours will be the only footprints. There are tide pools and huge rocks that lean at improbable angles. Nearby, old shipwrecks lie offshore.

LODGING

There is no lodging at the Hoh Rain Forest. The best plan for visitors to the west side of Olympic National Park who do not wish to camp is to stay at **Kalaloch Lodge** overlooking the ocean, on U.S. 101, 26 miles south of the turnoff to the Hoh Rain Forest. Check in first, then drive to the rain forest for the afternoon, and return to the lodge for dinner. Rooms start around $125 in season (June through October) and on weekends year-round, $60 off-season. Private cabins cost more. For reservations, contact Kalaloch Lodge, H.S. 80, Box 1100, Forks, WA 98331, or call (360) 962-2271.

Lower-priced lodging as well as some newly built resort facilities and several restaurants can be found at Forks, on U.S. 101, 14 miles north of the turnoff to the Hoh Rain Forest. The **Forks Motel** on U.S. 101, (360) 374-6243, has large guest units starting at $38 a night. The **Manitou Lodge** offers peaceful bed and breakfast accommodations starting at $57 per night double. Call (360) 374-6295. Reservations are essential on the west coast of the Olympic Peninsula during the summer months, since the fledgling lodging industry has not caught up with the rapid growth of tourism in the area.

In Neah Bay, your best motel bets are **Thunderbird Resort**, (360) 645-2450, and **Tyee Motel & RV Park**, (360) 645-2223. Rooms cost about $40 a night at both places.

CAMPING

The Hoh Rain Forest has a 95-site national park campground with a dumping station but no hookups. The fee is $6. There is also a larger national park campground, with comparable facilities and rates, near the ocean at Kalaloch.

6
ORCAS ISLAND

Misty, remote, forested, and wild, the cluster of islands at the northern end of Puget Sound will tug at your imagination as you glide among them on the San Juan ferry, one of America's best cruise bargains.

Though just about 65 miles straight-line distance from downtown Seattle, the San Juan Islands are a world apart from the freeways, suburbs, and shopping malls of the mainland. The number of islands in the San Juans is variously estimated at anywhere from 172 to over 700, depending on where the line is drawn between an "island" and a "rock." Most of the islands can only be reached by small boat. They include privately owned islands, many with luxurious vacation homes, as well as state parks, federal wildlife refuges, and lighthouse reserves. Annual rainfall in the San Juans is 29 inches, significantly less than in Seattle.

The ferry trip through the San Juans is the most scenic cruise of the Washington State Ferry System. The islands are a popular summer tourist destination, and on weekends and holidays from Memorial Day to Labor Day motorists may wait in line for several hours to board a ferry, then spend the rest of the day searching for a room or campsite. For this reason, I suggest visiting the islands during the middle of the week and leaving Anacortes as early in the morning as possible, breakfasting on the ferry. ◪

ORCAS ISLAND

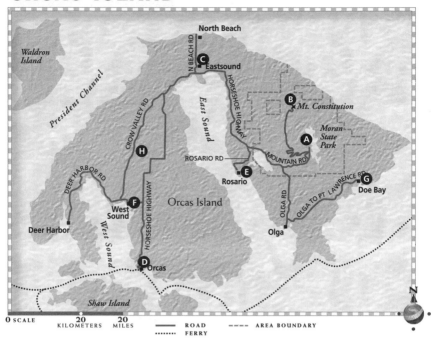

Sightseeing Highlights

- **A** Moran State Park
- **B** Mount Constitution

Food

- **C** Bilbo's Festivo
- **C** Christina's
- **D** grocery store
- **C** La Famiglia Ristorante
- **D** Orcas Hotel
- **E** Rosario Resort
- **C** Ship Bay Oyster House
- **F** Westsound Store

Lodging

- **G** Doe Bay Village
- **D** Orcas Hotel
- **E** Rosario Resort
- **H** Turtleback Farm Inn

Camping

- **A** Moran State Park

Note: Items with the same letter are located in the same town or area.

A PERFECT DAY ON ORCAS ISLAND

At Anacortes, board the San Juan Islands ferry for Orcas Island. Unless you have lodging reservations on Orcas Island, be at the ferry dock early to make sure you get a space on the next boat—particularly on summer weekends, when it's much busier than any other Washington State ferry ever is, even during rush hours. At those times, a wait of three hours in line is common.

Arriving at the little port of Orcas, drive (or bike or ride a rented moped) to Moran State Park. Get a campsite (usually difficult in season unless you have made advance reservations) or check into your island accommodations, then picnic in the park. Spend the afternoon experiencing the park's majestic forest and waterfalls and the panoramic view from the summit of Mount Constitution.

SIGHTSEEING HIGHLIGHTS

★★★ **Ferry to Orcas Island**—Nationalities can be confusing around Anacortes, which exists primarily as the mainland connection for the San Juans and Canada's Vancouver Island. Anacortes adjoins the largest tulip-growing area outside the Netherlands and has a substantial Dutch population, though which came first—the tulips or the Dutch—is unclear. The town's name—pronounced "anna-CORT-is"—is a stylized version of "Anna Curtis," the wife of an early real estate promoter who felt that the Fidalgo Island gateway to the San Juan Islands and the Strait of Juan de Fuca ought to have a Spanish-looking name. (Incidentally, the sea captain responsible for the other Spanish names in the area was actually a Greek, Apostolos Valerianos, who adopted the alias "Juan de Fuca" to get a job sailing for the king of Spain.) (½ hour)

Eight ferries go daily to Orcas Island; plan to take an early one— 6:35, 7:20, or 8:50 a.m. After the 8:50 a.m. departure, there isn't another ferry to Orcas until 11:15 a.m. The fare is $16.60 ($13.85 off-season) for the car and driver, plus $4.65 per passenger. Crossing time from Anacortes to Orcas is one hour. (Earlier ferries, but not the 8:50, stop at Lopez and Shaw islands, 20 minutes and ten minutes before arriving on Orcas.) *Note:* All San Juan Islands/Sidney, B.C., ferries run Monday through Saturday only.

Because the line for this ferry can be impossibly long in the summer, if you are going all the way to Sidney you can make reservations at least 24 hours in advance by calling (206) 464-6400. If you're planning to stop at Orcas and/or San Juan Island en route to Sidney, reservations are mandatory.

Most tourists bypass this mainly agricultural Lopez Island. There are two public parks on Lopez—Odlin County Park and Spencer Spit State Park. Both are on the north shore of the island, near the ferry dock, and both have campsites. Persistent rumors, confirmed by occasional newspaper reports of big busts, suggest that Lopez Island is the marijuana-growing capital of Washington. Visitors to the island will find no evidence of this low-key greenhouse farming, but minding one's own business is wise around here.

Shaw Island, the smallest of the four islands you can reach by ferry has 100 residents, a combined general store and post office, a little red schoolhouse on the National Register of Historic Places, and a small county park on the south shore.

★★★ **Orcas Island**—The largest of the San Juans is almost two separate islands, linked only by a narrow neck where Eastsound, the largest town, is situated. From the tiny port village of Orcas on the western half of the island, where you get off the ferry, it's an 8½-mile drive to Eastsound on the main road, known as the Horseshoe Highway. Then the road turns back south across the eastern half of the island, 4½ miles more to the entrance of **Moran State Park**. Following the signs to the park, you can't get lost. Ignoring the signs, you can't get very lost anyway—it's a small island.

Moran State Park, the largest park in the San Juan Islands, and the largest state park in Washington, was a gift to the public from Seattle industrialist, shipbuilder, and ex-mayor Robert Moran. In 1905, suffering from exhaustion, Moran was told by doctors that he had only six months to live. He retired to Orcas Island to spend his remaining days—and lived there for the next 38 years. Moran bought most of the eastern half of the island, built the luxurious Rosario Resort on a portion of it, and donated the remaining 13 square miles of land to the state of Washington.

The easy way to reach the top of 2,160-foot **Mount Constitution** is to drive up the steep, narrow, paved road. Whether you hike or drive, don't miss the trip to the summit, where you'll find the best possible bird's-eye view of the San Juan Islands. You can also see the mainland coastline, the Cascade Mountains, Whidbey and Fidalgo Islands, Vancouver Island, and, on an exceptionally clear day, Mount Rainier and the Olympic Mountains far to the south. The tower at the summit is a replica of a twelfth-century Eastern European watchtower. It was built in 1935–36 by the Civilian Conservation Corps, using stone that was quarried on another island, brought to Orcas Island by boat, and hauled all the way up the mountain.

While in Moran State Park, watch carefully and constantly for bald eagles. Most Americans never have a chance to see this endangered bird, our nation's symbol, flying free. More likely than not, you will spot one if you look here or on San Juan Island. The San Juan Islands are home to the highest permanent concentration of bald eagles in the world: at least 30 of these magnificent birds are known to live here year-round. Admission to Moran State Park is free. Hours: Open daily from 6:00 a.m.; closed after dusk except to campers. Phone: (360) 376-2326. (4 hours)

FITNESS AND RECREATION

Moran State Park has two large lakes (Cascade Lake and Mountain Lake), the highest mountain in the San Juans (Mount Constitution), and 26 miles of hiking trails. The 2½-mile **Cascade Loop Trail** around the far side of Cascade Lake leaves from the roadside at either end of the lake and takes about 1½ hours to walk. A quarter-mile downhill walk, from the pullout on your right about a half-mile up the Mount Constitution road from where it leaves the main highway, takes you through lush ancient forest to Cascade Falls and a series of other small waterfalls. A long lakeside hike is the 4-mile **Mountain Lake Loop Trail**, which starts from the ranger's cabin near Mountain Lake Campground; allow three hours.

The ultimate hike in the park, only for the ambitious, is the **Twin Lakes Trail**, which branches off the Mountain Lake Loop at the north end of the lake, leads 2 miles to a pair of small secluded lakes (passing an abandoned cabin said to have been a hideout for draft dodgers from the Civil War), and then climbs another 4 miles to the 2,160-foot summit of Mount Constitution. Allow all day for this long hike, or five to six hours one-way if you can arrange to have someone drive to the summit and pick you up there.

The island is good for bike touring, though some roads in Moran State Park are steep enough to pose a real challenge. Bicycles are for rent on Orcas Island at **Orcas Bicycle Company**, Orcas, (360) 376-4517, right at the ferry dock, and at **Wildlife Cycles**, Eastsound, (360) 376-4708.

FOOD

The dining rooms at **Rosario Resort**, (800) 562-8820, and the **Orcas Hotel**, (360) 376-4300, both serving moderate to expensive breakfasts, lunches, and dinners daily, are among the island's top restaurants.

Christina's, on Horseshoe Highway in Eastsound, is the most famous restaurant on the island—open daily for dinner, (360) 376-4904. The fare is seafood with a continental flair. Another great Eastsound restaurant, the **Ship Bay Oyster House**, Horseshoe Highway, (360) 376-5886, serves fresh-caught seafood specials in an early-day sea captain's home, open daily for dinner. Prices at both restaurants are moderate to expensive.

Bilbo's Festivo on North Beach Road has a reputation as one of Washington's best Mexican restaurants, open for dinner only, closed Monday, (360) 376-4728; and **La Famiglia Ristorante** is a popular Italian restaurant, open 11:30 a.m. to 2:30 p.m. and 5:00 to 9:00 p.m., closed Sunday, (360) 376-2335. Both are moderately priced.

The country-style **grocery store** in Orcas, a block down the hill from the ferry dock ramp, has a good selection of picnic and camping food, from simple staples to gourmet treats. **Westsound Store**, on Crow Valley Road in Westsound, has a great delicatessen.

LODGING

Located near the Moran State Park entrance, **Rosario Resort** was built by the man who created the park. Rosario has waterfront views, tennis courts, a beach, and a spa, as well as bike and moped rentals. Its villas surround Robert Moran's original 1906 mansion. Rooms range from $63 ($95 on weekends) to $195 single or double. Phone: (360) 376-2222.

A different kind of Orcas Island resort is **Doe Bay Village**, on the southeast shore beyond Moran State Park and Olga. Cottages start at $45, and there is also a hostel dormitory ($11.50 for AYH members, $14.50 for nonmembers) and a campground (sites $10.50 per night). Best of all are the hot mineral baths and steam sauna ($3 for guests, $5 for nonguests). Reservations are essential for both cottages and the hostel. Write Doe Bay Village, Star Route, Box 86, Olga, Orcas Island, WA 98279, or call (360) 376-2291 or 376-4755. Guided kayak trips ($25) to the national wildlife refuge provide a special experience. The

60-acre facility also has a natural foods café and a general store leaning toward health foods.

Near the ferry dock in Orcas is the historic Victorian **Orcas Hotel**. Famed for its fine restaurant, it operates as a bed and breakfast with rooms starting at $69 double. For reservations, write P.O. Box 155, Orcas, WA 98280, or call (360) 376-4300.

Among the other Orcas Island bed and breakfasts, I recommend **Turtleback Farm Inn**, an 1890s farmhouse at Route 1, Box 650, Eastsound, WA 98245, (360) 376-4914, located 4 miles from Eastsound on Crow Valley Road. Rates range from $75 to $155 a night.

CAMPING

Moran State Park has a total of 136 campsites (no hookups) in several campgrounds at Cascade Lake and one at Mountain Lake. This is one of the few Washington State Parks camping areas where you can (and should) make reservations if you'll be visiting between May 1 and Labor Day. Reservation applications are available from the Washington State Parks and Recreation Commission, 7150 Clearwater Lane, KY-11, Olympia, WA 98504, (360) 753-2027. Without an application form, you can make a reservation by sending your name, address, and phone number, number of people in your party, arrival date, number of nights you will stay, and the type and size of your camping unit, along with a $4 reservation fee and $8 first night's camping fee, to Moran State Park, Star Route, Box 22, Eastsound, WA 98245-9603. If you are hoping to camp at the park without a reservation during the summer months, call the state parks campground hot line, (800) 562-0990, to check on availability before leaving the mainland. At any time of year, plan to arrive early and locate a campsite first thing upon arrival.

7

SAN JUAN ISLAND

When you hop from Orcas to Friday Harbor, you'll quickly discover that while the two largest islands in the San Juans are only a few miles apart, they're as different as can be. Among the experiences today holds in store for you are a visit to a whale museum, a whale-watching picnic lunch, and a stroll on the site of one of the longest—and quietest—"wars" in U.S. history.

Situated midway between the United States and Canada, San Juan Island got its chance to become a historical footnote in 1859, when American farmer Lyman Cutlar shot a British pig from the Hudson's Bay Post that was rooting in his potato patch. It was the first crime ever committed on the island. When British authorities came to bring Cutlar to Victoria and justice, they touched off a 12-year dispute over whether the San Juans belonged to Canada or the United States. Opposite ends of the island were occupied by 461 U.S. Marines and more than 2,000 British soldiers. A sign at English Camp says the confrontation "brought England and the United States to the brink of war," though the only shot fired was the one that killed the pig. Acting as mediator, Kaiser Wilhelm I of Germany, Queen Victoria's cousin, proved his impartiality by deciding that the island was U.S. territory—which is why you don't have to exchange currency here. ◣

SAN JUAN ISLAND

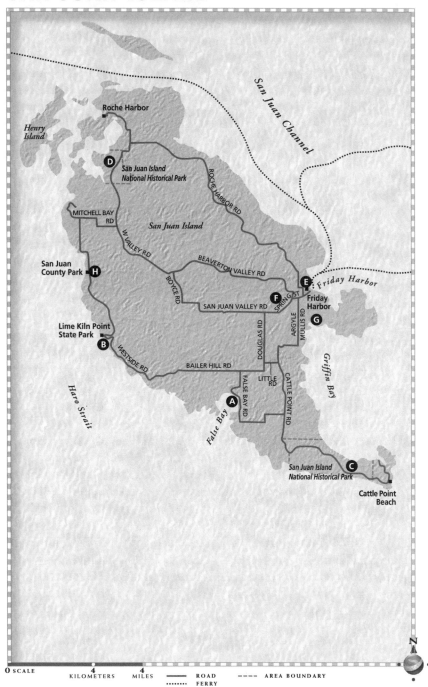

San Juan Channel

Roche Harbor

Henry Island

D

San Juan Island
National Historical Park

MITCHELL BAY RD

San Juan Island

ROCHE HARBOR RD

W VALLEY RD

BEAVERTON VALLEY RD

San Juan
County Park **H**

BOYCE RD

E Friday Harbor

F

SAN JUAN VALLEY RD

SPRING ST

Friday
Harbor

ARGYLE

MULLIS RD

G

Lime Kiln Point
State Park

B

WESTSIDE RD

Griffin Bay

DOUGLAS RD

Haro Strait

BAILER HILL RD

LITTLE RD

CATTLE POINT RD

A

FALSE BAY RD

False Bay

San Juan Island
National Historical Park

C

Cattle Point
Beach

N

0 SCALE   4   4
KILOMETERS   MILES   ROAD   - - - - - AREA BOUNDARY
.... FERRY

Sightseeing Highlights

Ⓐ False Bay

Ⓑ Lime Kiln Point State Park

Ⓒ San Juan Island National
Historical Park - American
Camp

Ⓓ San Juan Island National
Historical Park - English Camp

Ⓔ San Juan Island National
Historical Park - Visitor's
Center

Ⓔ Whale Museum

Food

Ⓔ Friday Harbor Bistro

Ⓕ Down Riggers

Ⓖ Springtree Café

Lodging

Ⓔ Friday's Bed & Breakfast

Ⓔ Hillside House Bed &

Ⓔ Breakfast
San Juan Inn

Ⓔ Trumpeter Inn

Ⓔ Tucker House

Camping

Ⓗ San Juan County Park

Note: Items with the same letter are located in the same town or area.

A PERFECT DAY ON SAN JUAN ISLAND

Assuming you spent the night on Orcas Island, return to the Orcas ferry dock early to board the 7:35 or 8:35 a.m. ferry to San Juan Island, an incomparably pretty 35-minute trip. Upon arriving at Friday Harbor, drive or bike out to visit English Camp and then watch for orcas at Lime Kiln State Park. Later, visit American Camp and return to Friday Harbor to visit the Whale Museum. If you have a place to stay on the island, the best way to spend the afternoon is on a *Western Prince* wildlife watching cruise.

Ferries from San Juan Island to Vancouver Island, B.C., only run in the afternoon. If you're continuing to Canada today, board the ferry at 3:30 and find yourself in Victoria by nightfall.

SIGHTSEEING HIGHLIGHTS

✸✸✸ **Ferry from Orcas to San Juan Island**—Ferries leave Orcas for Friday Harbor on San Juan Island at 7:35 a.m., 8:35 a.m., 10:20 a.m., and three other times in the afternoon and evening. Take the earliest ferry you can, since camping and other accommodations are a problem on San Juan Island. The interisland fare is $7.75 ($6.50 off-season) per vehicle, no additional charge for passengers. The crossing time is approximately 40 minutes. Toll-taking is a relaxed affair at Orcas; on slow days, instead of paying at the gate, you may have to buy a ferry ticket at the state liquor store, a block down the hill and across the street from the grocery store. (Evening ferries from Friday Harbor to Anacortes leave at 6:50, 7:55, and 10:00 p.m.)

✸✸ **San Juan Island National Historical Park**—The historic park has three units—a visitor's center in Friday Harbor that tells the story of San Juan Island's "Pig War" and the sites of the English and American military encampments from the conflict, located on opposite sides of the island. Admission to all the park units is free. Hours: Open daily from 8:00 a.m. to 6:00 p.m. during the summer months, Thursday through Sunday from 8:00 a.m. to 4:30 p.m. the rest of the year. Visitor's center address: 125 Spring Street, Friday Harbor. Phone: (360) 378-2240.

   English Camp—On lovely Westcott Bay at the west side of the island, reached by following Beaverton Valley Road (the main cross-island road from Friday Harbor), this site has three restored buildings from the British occupation on 530 landscaped acres. One building contains an interpretive center. Park rangers tend the formal English gardens originally cultivated by officers' wives and, on summer weekends, don nineteenth-century uniforms for historical presentations. There are no camping facilities. (½ hour)

   American Camp—On Cattle Point at the southeastern tip of the island, this site is twice as large as English Camp. There's little left in the way of historical structures, but along a ¾-mile walking trail you'll find a series of signs recounting the story of the Pig War and get a feel for what U.S. soldiers must have experienced as they defended this lonely little corner of the country—and, in so doing, completely missed the Civil War. (½ hour)

✸✸ **Whale Museum**—Whale watching has become big business all along the U.S. coastline in the past decade, proving that helping tourists look at the earth's largest creatures is more lucrative than killing whales ever was. If the appeal of waiting for hours for the chance to see a cetacean surface and breathe has been lost on you up to now, this casual museum located a couple of blocks from the ferry dock is likely to convert you. It is probably the most comprehensive museum in the world devoted entirely to whales. Exhibits include whale skeletons, whale art, whale migration maps, whale videos, whale voice recordings, and lots more. A reading area contains a collection of articles and books on whales that you could spend the rest of your life perusing. On one wall, a chart traces the genealogy of every pod (family) of orcas (killer whales) that swims in the Strait of Juan de Fuca, with photographs that identify each individual orca by its unique fin markings. Admission is $3 for adults, $2.50 for students and seniors, $1.50 for children ages 6 to 11. Hours: Open daily from 10:00 a.m. to 5:00 p.m. Memorial Day weekend through September, 11:00 a.m. to 4:00 p.m. the rest of the year. Address: 62 First Street, Friday Harbor. Phone: (360) 378-4710. (1 hour)

If you have extra time, the Whale Museum operates wildlife and whale-watching cruises from May through September on the *Western Prince* tour boat to see harbor seals, bald eagles, and sea birds and search for orcas, minke whales, and porpoises. The cost is $43 per adult, $31 for children ages 4 to 12, and includes admission to the Whale Museum. Four-hour cruises leave daily except Tuesday at 2:00 p.m. during the summer months, 1:00 p.m. May and September. Phone: (360) 378-5315 or (800) 757-6722. (4 hours)

✸ **False Bay**—On the west shore, beyond Lime Kiln State Park, toward American Camp, follow False Bay Road to this shallow, circular bay, which becomes a mud flat at low tide, revealing a weird and wondrous assortment of marine life, including clingfish, bright orange ribbon worms, and purple crabs. The bay is a biological study area owned by the University of Washington, but you're welcome to don galoshes or squishy sneakers and slog around to your heart's content; just don't remove or kill anything living there. (½ hour)

✸ **Lime Kiln Point State Park**—On the west side of the island, midway between English Camp and American Camp, Lime Kiln Point State Park is reputed to be the best place to watch for orcas. On the average, one sighting is reported each day. The orca's large dorsal fin (up to 6 feet tall) makes it easier to spot than most other whales, and its loud breathing can be heard for a great distance. Orcas, as well as minke whales, are spotted here throughout the year since they do not migrate, but summer is the peak time to watch for them. Orcas travel in pods, so if you spot one, keep looking and you're likely to glimpse the rest of the family. (½ hour)

FITNESS AND RECREATION

Level terrain and limited motor vehicle traffic make the paved roads of San Juan Island perfect for bicycle touring. Bikes can be rented at **Island Bicycles**, 380 Argyle, Friday Harbor; (360) 378-4941.

Hiking trails are found only in San Juan Island National Historical Park. The 1-mile **Lagoon Trail** at American Camp takes visitors through the woods to a hidden beach. The 1½-mile **Bell Point Trail** at English Camp leads to an observation deck that presents a striking view of many small islands in the strait.

FOOD

Picnicking is your best bet on San Juan Island. English Camp, San Juan County Park, and American Camp are all good picnic spots, but I'd choose Lime Kiln Point State Park, where you can whale-watch while you eat.

Down Riggers, 10 Front Street, (360) 378-2700, is a good steak and seafood restaurant with a waterfront view, open for lunch and dinner. Or how about pizza at the **Friday Harbor Bistro**? It's in the Friday's Bed & Breakfast, along with the youth hostel, but not cheap. It's open 10:00 a.m. to 9:00 p.m., (360) 378-3076.

The Springtree Café, 310 Spring Street, (360) 378-4848, is a health-conscious midpriced restaurant that offers a full range of seafood and vegetarian options. The restaurant is moderately priced and open for lunch and dinner.

LODGING

What San Juan Island lacks in camping facilities is more than compensated for by its fine selection of bed and breakfasts. You need advance reservations at any of them. Friday Harbor B&Bs include the **Tucker House**, $85 and up ($10 less October–May), 260 B Street, and the **San Juan Inn**, about $80 a night, P.O. Box 776. Elsewhere on the island are the **Trumpeter Inn**, $90 to $100, 420 Trumpeter Way, Friday Harbor, (360) 378-3884; and the **Hillside House Bed & Breakfast**, $85 to $155, children over age 10 welcome, no pets, 365 Carter Avenue, Friday Harbor, (360) 378-4730. Friday Harbor also has an AYH youth hostel in the historic **Friday's Bed & Breakfast**, 35 First Street, (360) 378-5555. Dormitory beds cost $7.50 for members, $9 for nonmembers. The old hotel also has a few private rooms at $30.

CAMPING

During the summer season, even if you are equipped for camping, it's best to reserve a room in advance if you plan to spend the night on San Juan Island. The island has just one tiny public campground, 14 units at **San Juan County Park** on the west side of the island at Smallpox Bay (so named because it was the site of a tragedy that destroyed the island's Indian population when they plunged into the frigid water to cool the smallpox fever—and died of pneumonia instead; nevertheless, the bay is beautiful). To get there, take Beaverton Valley Road across the island from Friday Harbor, turn left on West Side Road, and follow it around several corners to the park. Camping costs $10. The park sometimes closes due to water short-ages during the peak of the summer tourist season.

8

VICTORIA

The capital of British Columbia, Victoria (pop. 350,000) got its start in 1843 as the western headquarters of the Hudson's Bay Company. Originally called Fort Camosun, in 1849 its name was changed to Victoria in honor of the British queen when Vancouver Island became a crown colony. Twenty-two years later, when British Columbia was declared a province of Canada, Victoria—then the largest settlement on the West Coast—was made the provincial capital. Climate was then, as it is now, a Victoria virtue: sheltered by the mountains of the Olympic Peninsula, the city receives only 27 inches of rainfall a year—less than Seattle and less than half as much as Vancouver.

Through the twentieth century, Victoria has existed in the economic shadow of its much larger neighbor, Vancouver, across the Strait of Georgia. In many ways, the island capital seems bound by British colonial tradition and bypassed by time. In fact, many residents proudly claim that Victoria is more British than Great Britain. Victoria capitalizes on its quaintness, and the tourist trade rivals government and explains the plethora of tea shops and double-deckers, bagpipers and horse-drawn carriages, formal gardens and stately Tudor mansions. Commercial attractions have sprung up in profusion, among them Undersea Gardens, Sealand of the Pacific, Fable Cottage Estate, the Classic Car Museum, and the Royal London Wax Museum (yes, Chuck and Di are represented there). You won't run out of sights to marvel at in this unique city. It's like prewar London—with totem poles. ◼

VICTORIA

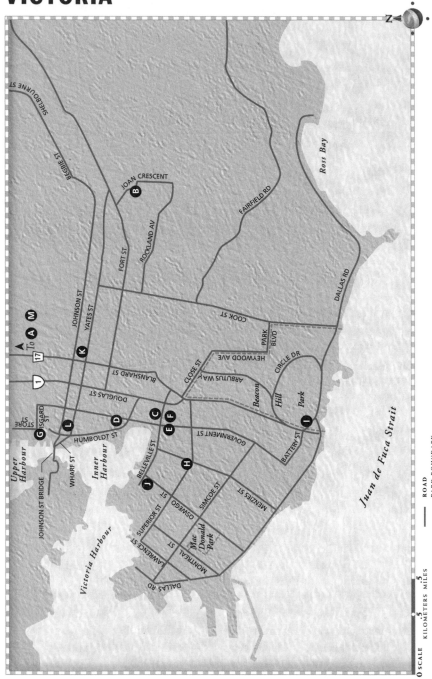

0 SCALE
.5
KILOMETERS MILES

ROAD
PARK BOUNDARY

Sightseeing Highlights

Ⓐ Butchart Gardens

Ⓑ Craigdarroch Castle

Ⓒ Empress Hotel

Ⓓ Maritime Museum of British Columbia

Ⓔ Parliament

Ⓕ Royal British Columbia Museum

Food

Ⓐ Butchart Gardens

Ⓒ Empress Hotel

Ⓖ Fogg n' Suds

Ⓗ James Bay Tearoom

Ⓒ Rattenbury's

Lodging

Ⓘ Battery Street Guest House

Ⓙ Captain's Palace Inn

Ⓚ Dominion Hotel

Ⓒ Empress Hotel

Ⓗ James Bay Inn

Ⓛ Victoria Hostel

Camping

Ⓜ McDonald Provincial Park

Note: Items with the same letter are located in the same town or area.

A PERFECT DAY IN VICTORIA

If you're traveling from the San Juan Islands, you'll arrive on Vancouver Island around 5:00 in the afternoon, making the following day perhaps one of the most relaxing days of your vacation. In the morning, enjoy a leisurely breakfast and call Butchart Gardens for lunch reservations. Then take a stroll around downtown Victoria, stopping in at such landmarks as the Empress Hotel and Parliament. At noon, drive, taxi, or bus (take municipal bus #74) to Butchart Gardens. Have lunch and stroll through the gardens.

Around midafternoon, return downtown to visit the Royal British Columbian Museum and nearby Thunderbird Park. On a warm summer evening, you may want to take a walk to Craigdarroch Castle for a tour before dinner.

ENTERING CANADA

The boundary between the United States and Canada is the longest undefended border on earth. Normally, crossing it is easy, especially when entry points are busy, as they are at the Vancouver Island ferry dock and on the interstate highway that links the two largest cities in the Pacific Northwest. Unless you're so suspicious-looking that you are routinely detained for interrogation at airport security checks, you will be waved through after a few quick questions about your citizenship, the purpose of your visit, and whether you are carrying any alcohol, tobacco, fruit, vegetables, or firearms. Vehicle or baggage searches are uncommon, and you probably will not be required to show any documents. Still, it's a good idea to have the legally required paperwork in your possession.

U.S. citizens do not need a passport, visa, or tourist card to enter Canada. Citizens of other nations must have a valid passport unless they are permanent legal residents of the United States, in which case a green card will do. Naturalized U.S. citizens should carry birth certificates or other proof of citizenship. A voter registration card is acceptable. If you are traveling with a dog or cat, you must have a current rabies vaccination certificate (not just the collar tag) for the animal.

Besides your vehicle registration (and, if it is not registered in your name, written permission from the owner to use the vehicle in Canada), you must have a Canadian Non-Resident Inter-Provincial Motor Vehicle Liability Insurance Card. Get one from your insurance agent before leaving home.

While there are very few restrictions on personal effects you can bring into Canada, you are limited to one carton of cigarettes and either 40 ounces of liquor or wine or 24 cans of beer per person. Crossing into Canada with illegal drugs in your possession, including any amount of marijuana, means prison if you're caught. If you smoke cigarettes, it's a good idea to bring a supply along from the United States instead of planning to buy them in Canada, where they cost at least twice as much—often $5 Canadian (US$3.50) a pack.

You can exchange currency at any bank or, for a slightly less favorable rate, at most hotels. A Canadian dollar is worth about 70 U.S. cents; a U.S. dollar is worth about $1.40 Canadian. Since the North American Free Trade Agreement went into effect, practically any business in Victoria or Vancouver will accept U.S. currency at approximately the official exchange rate. Don't exchange more money than you expect to spend. Back on the U.S. side of the border, few businesses will accept Canadian money, and you can only exchange it back at a bank or major airport.

The border check upon reentering the United States from Canada is equally easy. If you have spent at least 48 hours in Canada, you can bring back up to $400 per person worth of goods you bought there without paying import duties. However, if you were in Canada less than 48 hours, you can only bring back $25 worth of purchases per person without being taxed. (Since there is no document to show when you entered Canada, the U.S. officer will take your word for how long you were there.) The kinds of contraband that you cannot legally bring into the United States are numerous and well known: drugs, endangered species products, pornography, subversive publications, switchblade knives, and so on; but such items are generally harder to find in Canada than in the United States anyway. The most common item readily available in Canada and illegal to bring back is Cuban cigars.

Because the only ferry from Friday Harbor to Vancouver Island runs in midafternoon, most visitors will find it more convenient to stop for a few hours on San Juan Island, then continue on to Canada and spend the night in Victoria. The ferry leaves Friday Harbor at 3:30 p.m. (*Note:* Another ferry leaves Anacortes at 8:00 a.m. and Orcas at 9:15 a.m. but bypasses San Juan Island to arrive at Sidney at 11:00 a.m.) The fare is $15.90 ($13.25 off-season) for vehicle and driver, plus $2.25 per passenger. Sailing time from Friday Harbor to Sidney is about 1 hour 25 minutes. Reservations are mandatory for passengers who wish to board the ferry to Sidney from Orcas or San Juan Island. Call (206) 464-6400 at least 24 hours in advance.

San Juan Island, in the United States, is actually north of the city of Victoria, British Columbia. The ferry, traveling just about due west, lands at the tiny port town of Sidney, about 18 miles north of the city on a peninsula. Follow Highway 17 south, and it will take you directly into downtown Victoria as Blanshard Street. You'll find convenient parking just north of the Empress Hotel.

To visit Victoria's premier sightseeing attraction, Butchart Gardens, on your way into the city (most other sights are located in the downtown area), turn off Highway 17 on either McTavish Road or Mt. Newton Cross Road and drive across the peninsula to Highway 17A (West Saanich Road), which takes you to Benvenuto Road and Butchart Gardens. Upon leaving the gardens, continue south on Highway 17A. It joins Highway 17 a few miles north of downtown.

A private car ferry, the Black Ball Transport, leaves Port Angeles on the Olympic Peninsula for Victoria daily at 8:20 a.m. Call (360) 475-4491 in the U.S. or (604) 386-2202 in Canada for current rates. Get in line at least 90 minutes early—there are no advance reservations.

BC Ferries operates car ferries between Tsawwassen, a Vancouver suburb, and Swartz Bay, north of Victoria, every two hours. Fares (in Canadian dollars) are $22.75 per car, $6.50 per passenger, including the driver. There is a large surcharge for campers and motorhomes.

SIGHTSEEING HIGHLIGHTS

★★★ **Butchart Gardens**—Thanks to the mild climate and bountiful rainfall, the Pacific Northwest boasts more than its share of the finest formal gardens in North America, and no other is as large, elegant, or world-famous as Butchart Gardens. Strangely, this 50-acre horticultural wonder got its start as an industrial cement quarry. In 1904, when the quarry was abandoned, Jenny Butchart, the owner's wife, decided to start reclaiming the eyesore by hauling in topsoil in a horse-drawn wagon and landscaping it. The original garden is now known as the Sunken Garden. Over the next two decades, Jenny added a Japanese garden, an English rose garden, and an Italian garden, enhancing them with fountains, ponds, and waterfalls and introducing waterfowl and peacocks. As word of her gardens spread, the Butcharts abandoned the cement business and devoted their full efforts to developing the tourist attraction. Today, nearly a century later, the gardens are owned and maintained by the Butcharts' grandson. Butchart Gardens contain over 1 million plants, including 700 varieties of flowers that bloom from March through October. Leaf color changes prolong the display through autumn, and a large greenhouse ensures plenty of bright colors even in the depths of winter.

Admission is $11 for adults, $5.75 for students ages 13 to 17, and

$1.50 for children ages 5 to 12. Hours: Open daily from 9:00 a.m. to 11:00 p.m. in July and August (with spectacular lighting at night and fireworks on Saturday nights); 9:00 a.m. to 9:00 p.m. in June and September; 9:00 a.m. to 5:00 p.m. in March, April, May, and October; 9:00 a.m. to 8:00 p.m. in December; and 9:00 a.m. to 4:00 p.m. the rest of the year. Address: Highway 17, Brentwood. Phone: (604) 652-4422. (3 hours)

✮✮✮ **Royal British Columbia Museum**—Besides a collection of Northwest Coast Indian artifacts only barely surpassed by that of the UBC Museum of Anthropology (see Chapter 6, "Sightseeing Highlights"), and dioramas and multimedia displays revealing the Indians' myths and traditional way of life, the provincial museum also features elaborate natural history exhibits showing the flora and fauna of the seacoast, the river delta, and the coastal rain forest. Historical re-creations let you walk backward through time, decade by decade, experiencing sights, sounds, and smells from the 1920s to Captain George Vancouver's first landing on the island in 1792. This outstanding museum is located downtown at 675 Belleville Street, next door to the Parliament buildings. Admission is $7 for adults, $5 for senior citizens and students ages 13 to 18, and $3 for children ages 6 to 12, with a maximum family rate of $15. Hours: Open daily from 9:30 a.m. to 7:00 p.m. May through August, 10:00 a.m. to 5:30 p.m. the rest of the year. Address: 675 Belleville Street. Phone: (604) 387-3701 or (800) 661-5411. (3 hours)

Thunderbird Park, adjoining the museum, features a collection of totem poles, most of which depict the thunderbird, the native people's symbol for the overwhelming power of nature. Here is your opportunity to photograph Victoria's unique character: Indian totem poles in the foreground and the Old World, elegant Empress Hotel in the background.

Also in Thunderbird Park is the Helmcken House, one of British Columbia's first pioneer homes, built in 1852 by a Hudson's Bay Company doctor. Displays include original furnishings and medical equipment. Admission is $3.75 for adults, $2.75 for students, $1.75 for children ages 6 to 11. Hours: Open mid-June to mid-December daily 10:00 a.m. to 5:00 p.m.; in September, Thursday through Monday 10:00 a.m. to 5:00 p.m. Closed off-season. Phone: (604) 387-4697. (1 hour)

✮✮ **Empress Hotel**—Even if you aren't planning to spend the night here (rooms start at over $150 a night during the summer months), be sure to take a look at this magnificent hotel, which has been Victoria's most recognizable landmark since it opened in 1908. The greatest accomplishment of architect Francis Rattenbury, who also designed the Parliament buildings, the Empress has hosted the rich and famous from Rudyard Kipling to John Wayne. Newly renovated in 1989, this twentieth-century castle is as elegant as hotels get. The Empress is across Belleville Street from the Royal British Columbia Museum and Thunderbird Park. Address: 721 Government Street. Phone: (604) 384-8111. (½ hour)

In the hotel basement is one of Victoria's most unusual commercial tourist attractions, **Miniature World**. For the past 25 years, circus performers Don and Honey Ray have collected miniatures from all over the world to assemble this fantastic "Greatest Little Show on Earth." Sixty exhibits include a complete, animated miniature circus, the world's largest miniature electric train layout, the world's smallest operating sawmill, two of the world's largest doll houses, the world of Charles Dickens, and a battle between animated toy soldiers. Admission is $6.75 for adults, $5.75 for students ages 12 to 17, and $4.75 for children ages 5 to 11. Hours: Open Monday through Friday from 9:00 a.m. to 5:30 p.m., Saturday and Sunday from 9:00 a.m. to 9:00 p.m. May through October, daily from 9:00 a.m. to 5:30 p.m. the rest of the year. Phone: (604) 385-9731. (1 hour)

✹ **Craigdarroch Castle**—Robert Dunsmuir, a Scottish immigrant who built railroads, owned coal mines, and eventually became the richest man on Vancouver Island, lured his wife away from Scotland with a promise to build her a castle grander than any in the old country. This is it. Dunsmuir died before the castle was completed in 1889, but his wife lived there for 19 years. Since then, it has served as a World War I veterans' convalescent home, a college, and a conservatory of music. In 1979, the castle was restored as a museum. It contains period furniture, artwork, and decor, including many of Dunsmuir's original furnishings, and features changing exhibits on Victorian lifestyles. The castle is located 1 mile east of the harbor via Fort Street. Admission is $6 for adults, $5 for students ages 12 to 17 and senior citizens, and $2 for children under 12. Hours: Open daily from 9:00 a.m. to 9:00 p.m. mid-June through August, 9:00 a.m. to 7:00 p.m. the rest of the year. Address: 1050 Joan Crescent. Phone: (604) 592-5323. (1 hour)

✹ **Maritime Museum of British Columbia**—Five blocks north on Government Street from the Empress Hotel, at 28 Bastion Square, the

Maritime Museum is packed with sailors' gear, nautical tools, figure-heads, and model ships. The item most likely to capture your imagination is the *Tilikum*, a 36-foot-long Northwest Coast Indian dugout canoe fitted with sails, which sailed around the world from Victoria to England 1901–1904. Admission is $5 for adults, $4 for senior citizens, $3 for students ages 12 to 17, and $2 for children ages 6 to 11. Hours: Open daily from 9:30 a.m. to 4:30 p.m. Address: 28 Bastion Square. Phone: (604) 385-4222. (1 hour)

☆ **Parliament**—Intricate hand-carved facades, fountains, and statuary grace the exterior, which is illuminated after dark by more than 3,000 lights. Inside you'll find murals, wood carvings, stained-glass windows, rotundas, and British Columbian legislators. This Parliament operates by the same rules and ceremonies as Great Britain's House of Commons (there is no House of Lords, since Canada has no titled aristocracy), and it's worth watching from the galleries during sessions. Guided tours, available on weekdays and summer weekends, help visitors marvel at the architecture. The Parliament buildings were constructed entirely of British Columbian materials—except for the copper used in the domes. Today copper is one of the province's major natural resources, but it hadn't been discovered when the Parliament buildings were unveiled in 1897 to commemorate the sixtieth year of the British queen's reign. Admission is free. Hours: Open daily during the summer months, Monday through Friday the rest of the year, from 9:00 a.m. to 5:00 p.m. Phone: (604) 387-3046. (½ hour)

FITNESS AND RECREATION

Victoria has a well-developed and exceptionally beautiful system of urban walking and jogging trails. The 2-mile **Songhees Trail** follows the shoreline of the harbor in the downtown area. In Thetis Lake Municipal Park, more than 3 miles of trails loop around the park's two lakes and follow pretty little Craigflower Creek. The park is located 5 miles northwest of the city on Highway 1. One of the most popular trails on Vancouver Island, despite the admission charge you must pay to access it at the Butchart Gardens end, the 6-mile **John Dean Trail** leads through pastoral farmlands, meadows, and stately groves of trees. The most ambitious hike in the Victoria vicinity is the 3-mile climb to the top of **Mount Douglas**, a thousand-foot summit overlooking Haro Strait on the east side of the island. The trailhead is at Mount Douglas Municipal Park, 5 miles northeast of the city on Highway 17.

Unfortunately, most of the foot trails around Victoria are off-limits to bicycles, leaving cyclists with little alternative to braving the often heavy traffic on the streets and highways. Nonetheless, bicycle rentals, as well as mopeds and motor scooters, are available at several shops around town. Try **Sports Rent**, 3084 Blanshard Street, (604) 385-7368.

Sea kayaking provides an increasingly popular way to explore the shoreline of Vancouver Island on your own. For kayak rentals and information on the best places to go, contact **Ocean River Sports**, 1437 Store Street, (604) 381-4233.

FOOD

Your best bet for a memorable lunch in Victoria is at **Butchart Gardens** (see "Sightseeing Highlights," above), (604) 652-4422, where meals are served in several price ranges: a gourmet dining room, a moderately priced greenhouse restaurant, and in the summer months an outdoor coffee bar.

For elegant (and expensive) dining this evening, you might try the main dining room at the **Empress Hotel**. Call (604) 384-8111 for reservations. The hotel also has a more casual and moderately priced coffee shop. Behind the Empress, in a wing of the Crystal Garden (a tropical rain forest greenhouse complete with monkeys and exotic birds that operates as a commercial tourist attraction), is **Rattenbury's**, a moderately priced steak and seafood restaurant with both indoor and outdoor tables, open daily for lunch and dinner. Call (604) 381-1333 for reservations.

The **James Bay Tearoom**, behind the Parliament buildings at 322 Menzies Street, offers reasonably priced, traditional English fare daily for breakfast, lunch, and supper. Afternoon tea is served Monday through Saturday from 1:00 to 5:00 p.m., with high tea Sunday from 2:00 to 5:00 p.m. The decor consists of innumerable photos of Great Britain's royal family along with some royal wedding mementos. Call (604) 382-8282 for dinner reservations.

Or dine quite affordably at **Fogg n' Suds**, 1630 Store St., one of a chain of popular pub-style restaurants opening throughout the Greater Vancouver-Victoria area. The "Fogg" part of the name is for Phileas Fogg, hero of Jules Verne's *Around the World in 80 Days*, and reflects the menu choices, each representing a different nationality.

The "Suds" part is for beer—your choice of more than 250 different brands. Open daily for lunch and dinner.

LODGING

The **Empress Hotel** (see "Sightseeing Highlights," above) offers antique-furnished rooms, some with harbor views, from about $220 to $250 a night mid-May to mid-September, as low as $135 a night off-season. For reservations, call (604) 384-8111 or toll-free (800) 828-7447 from the United States, (800) 268-9420 from Canada.

A more affordable historic lodging is the **Dominion Hotel**, at the corner of Yates and Blanshard a couple of blocks west of the Maritime Museum. Dating back to 1876, the Dominion is Victoria's oldest hotel and has an antique-filled lobby and modern guest rooms. Rates are $95 to $115 during the summer months, in the $50 range off-season. Call (604) 384-4136 or toll-free (800) 663-6101.

Victoria has a wealth of English-style bed-and-breakfast inns, many in historic houses. Typical rates are in the $100-a-night range. Try the **Battery Street Guest House**, 670 Battery Street, Victoria, BC V8V 1E5, (604) 385-4632, or the **Captain's Palace Inn**, 309 Belleville Street, Victoria, BC V8V 1X2, (604) 388-9191. For other bed and breakfast possibilities, contact the **All Season Bed & Breakfast Agency**, Box 5511, Station B, Victoria, BC V8R 6S4, (604) 595-2337.

Simple budget accommodations can be found downtown at the **James Bay Inn**, 332 Menzies Street, (604) 384-7151. The inn is a converted 1907 mansion that was once the home of Victoria's best-known painter, Emily Carr. Rates are $30 to $40 a night with shared bath, about $50 a night with private bath. The inn is at the corner of Government Way and Toronto Street, a few blocks south of Thunderbird Park.

The **Victoria Hostel** (IYH), at 516 Yates Street, (604) 385-4511, offers dormitory accommodations near the waterfront at $10 per person including kitchen privileges, a TV room and library, and laundry facilities.

CAMPING

The most convenient public campground on Vancouver Island, about 18 miles from town but midway between the Sidney and Swartz Bay ferry docks, is **McDonald Provincial Park**, off Highway 17. There are no hookups or showers. Camping costs $8 a night.

NIGHTLIFE

Rock 'n' roll is scarce in this sedate, dignified city, so plan an English traditional evening instead. Discover the fun of an evening at the pub. The **Pig & Whistle**, next to the Empress Hotel at 634 Humboldt Street, is a little on the touristy side (the doorman dresses like a British bobbie) but lively with music hall acts and sing-alongs. For a more authentic pub experience, seek out **Spinnaker's** at 308 Catherine Street, across the Johnson Street Bridge off Esquimalt Road, where the beer is homemade and the crowd is a curious mix of local yuppies and crusty old waterfront characters.

The top venue in Victoria for contemporary dance music is **Harpo's** on Bastion Square near the waterfront and the Maritime Museum. Call (604) 385-5333 for current playbill and cover charge information. Or get into the old-fashioned spirit with an evening of ballroom dancing in the conservatory at **Crystal Gardens**.

Victoria also has a few low-key gaming casinos. (See Chapter 7's "Nightlife" section for more on British Columbia's new, limited gambling laws.) You'll find one, the **Casino Victoria**, downtown at 716 Courtney Street. Don't expect Las Vegas–style glitz and clatter, or you'll be disappointed. Dress up, take your place at the roulette table, and pretend you're James Bond.

9
VANCOUVER

B ritish Columbia is larger in area than Washington, Oregon, and
California combined. Yet three-fourths of the province's popula-
tion lives in Vancouver and its suburbs. In sharp contrast to Victoria's
British ambience, Vancouver feels thoroughly international. Only 40
percent of the city's residents are of English descent. Besides its large
Chinese population, major ethnic groups in Vancouver include Italian,
Greek, Japanese, Sikh, and Pakistani.

Younger than Seattle, Portland, or Victoria, the city of Vancouver
was founded in 1886 when Canada's transcontinental railroad reached
the Pacific Coast. Within five years, it had become the major shipping
port linking Canada with Asia. In 1915, when the opening of the
Panama Canal made it practical to ship lumber from the West Coast to
Europe, Vancouver's economy boomed, and the city grew larger than
Seattle and Portland combined. Today forest products remain the leading industry, and Vancouver is still the largest city in the Pacific
Northwest and the third largest in Canada.

One main reason most British Columbians live in the greater
Vancouver area is that the climate there is much milder than in the rest
of this subarctic province. Winter temperatures in Vancouver rarely
drop much below freezing. However, it is very wet, with an average
annual rainfall of 57 inches—nearly twice as much as Seattle. Seventy-
five percent of the days are sunless. When the sun *does* come out, at
least half the days in July, August, and September, Vancouverites take
to the streets, parks, and beaches in droves. But don't wait for sunshine
to begin your Vancouver exploration. Sogginess is an essential element
of any authentic Pacific Northwestern adventure. ◼

VANCOUVER

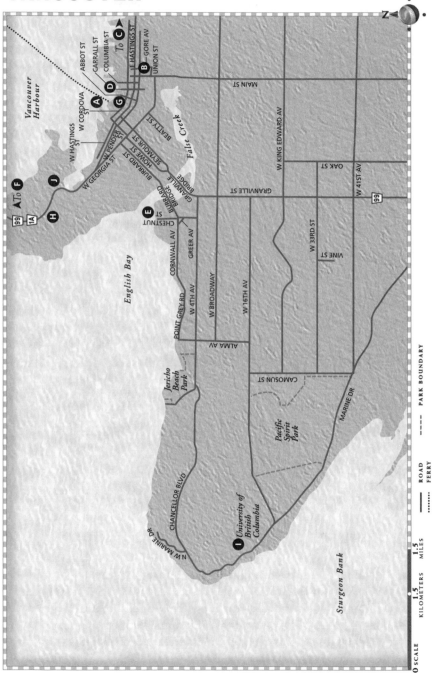

Vancouver Harbour

English Bay

False Creek

Sturgeon Bank

Vancouver Harbour

ABBOT ST
CARRALL ST
COLUMBIA ST
E HASTINGS ST
GORE AV
UNION ST
W CORDOVA ST
W HASTINGS ST
W PENDER ST
BURRARD ST
HOWE ST
SEYMOUR ST
BEATTY ST
W GEORGIA ST
GRANVILLE BRIDGE
BURRARD BRIDGE
CHESTNUT ST
CORNWALL AV
GREER AV
POINT GREY RD
W 4TH AV
W BROADWAY
ALMA AV
W 16TH AV
CAMOSUN ST
CHANCELLOR BLVD
N W MARINE DR
MARINE DR
VINE ST
W 33RD ST
W KING EDWARD AV
MAIN ST
GRANVILLE ST
OAK ST
W 41ST AV

To C
To F

99
1A
99

Jericho Beach Park

Pacific Spirit Park

University of British Columbia

A B C D E F G H I J

0 SCALE

1.5 KILOMETERS
1.5 MILES

ROAD
FERRY
---- PARK BOUNDARY

Sightseeing Highlights

Ⓐ Canada Place

Ⓑ Chinatown

Ⓒ Exhibition Park

Ⓓ Gastown

Ⓔ H. R. MacMillan Planetarium and Vancouver Museum

Ⓕ Lynn Canyon Park

Ⓖ Sky Train and Terminals Sea Bus

Ⓗ Stanley Park

Ⓘ UBC Museum of Anthropology

Ⓙ Vancouver Aquarium

Ⓙ Vancouver Zoo

Note: Items with the same letter are located in the same town or area.

A PERFECT DAY IN VANCOUVER

After a round-trip orientation ride on the Sky Train, walk around Gastown and Chinatown, stopping for lunch along the way. Later, drive to the University of British Columbia for a visit to the UBC Museum of Anthropology. The evening is for dining and nightlife in this vibrant, modern, mildly foreign city.

SIGHTSEEING HIGHLIGHTS

✮✮✮ **UBC Museum of Anthropology**—Here is your best opportunity to learn more about the Haida, Kwakiutl, Tsimshian, and other native peoples of British Columbia's coast whose totem designs are seen everywhere in the Pacific Northwest. They wove their stylized bird and animal motifs into tapestries and hats, painted them on house facades, and carved them on poles, masks, canoe prows, and ceremonial bowls. The Northwest Coast Indians (called "First Americans" in Canada) based their economy on gift giving (and the obligation to reciprocate), which not only built a sophisticated system for distributing resources but also created a need for all sorts of decorative items. Contact with European whalers, merchants, and colonists, who based their business dealings on something other than generosity, destroyed the native way of life in an ironic way: as villages grew prosperous through trade, they held more and more lavish potlatches (gift-giving feasts) that bankrupted many. Foreign diseases killed more than 90 percent of the Northwest Coast Indians by the early twentieth century. Today the only remaining native people on the British Columbia coast who live in the traditional ways are the Haida, who sparsely inhabit the remote Queen Charlotte Islands, only accessible by ferry from the port of Prince Rupert, about 300 miles northwest of Vancouver. It's 850 miles by the shortest road.

The Museum of Anthropology at the University of British Columbia houses the world's finest collection of Northwest Coast Indian artifacts, from a replica Haida village and a large totem pole collection to hundreds of pull-out display drawers full of jewelry, pipes, fetishes, and other small objects. There are also contemporary Northwest Coast Indian wood sculptures as well as international archaeology exhibits. The museum is near the tip of the peninsula. To get there from Granville Street, just south of the Granville Bridge turn west onto 47th Avenue and go about 4 miles. Turn left onto NW Marine Drive, which curves around through the UBC campus. You can also reach the university from downtown by taking municipal bus #10; return on bus #14; bus fares are the same as those for the Sky Train and Sea Bus (see above) and are covered by the same daily pass. Admission is $5 for adults, $2.50 for students and senior citizens, and free for children under age 6; free admission for everybody on Tuesdays. Hours: Open daily from 11:00 a.m. to 5:00 p.m., Tuesdays until 9:00 p.m. during the summer months, closed Mondays off-season. Address: 6393 NW Marine Drive. Phone: (604) 822-3825. (2 hours)

✩✩ **Canada Place**—Like Seattle, Vancouver has hosted a World's Fair. Unlike Seattle Center, though, Vancouver's fairgrounds from 1986 have not been preserved intact. Much of the main fair site has been rebuilt as offices and public housing. The huge Canada Pavilion remains on the waterfront near the end of Granville Street. Now called Canada Place, it features a 17-story geodesic sphere and five 80-foot-tall fiberglass "sails" designed to suggest a clipper ship in the harbor. Primarily a trade center and convention complex with an expensive hotel and restaurant, as well as a cruise ship terminal, there are international fast-food places and an exhibit of totem poles and native quilts.

An Imax theater at Canada Place shows various films on a 40-foot-tall wraparound screen. Admission is $6.50 daytime/$10 at night for adults, $5.50/$9 for senior citizens and students ages 13 to 17, and $4.50/$8 for children ages 3 to 12. Hours: Showings hourly from 12:00 noon to 10:00 p.m. Phone: (604) 682-4629.

You can learn about Vancouver's history from dozens of information plaques along the outdoor **Promenade Into History** around Canada Place. Guide yourself or take one of the free tours that depart frequently from the information booth on the downtown side of Canada Place. (1 hour)

✹✹ **Chinatown**—One-fourth of Vancouver's population is of Chinese descent, and this minority group is growing as tens of thousands of people from Hong Kong buy property in Vancouver each year to gain landed immigrant status and a new home in Canada before Hong Kong becomes part of the People's Republic of China in 1997. Already Vancouver's Chinese-American community rivals San Francisco's in numbers. With immigration from Hong Kong, it is expected to become the largest in the Western Hemisphere any day now. Vancouver's Chinatown is less tourist-oriented than San Francisco's, but you'll find plenty of shops offering gift items of jade and silk, as well as other shops and sidewalk market stalls displaying exotic vegetables, mysterious-looking herbs and elixirs, and smoked ducks hung by their heels. It's enough to make you forget which side of the Pacific you're on.

The heart of Chinatown is within walking distance of Gastown. From Maple Tree Square, follow Carrall Street south to Pender Street. At the intersection, the **Chinese Cultural Center** shows free changing exhibits on local history and culture and has a bookstore where you can buy a detailed walking tour map of Chinatown. Pender Street east of Carrall is Chinatown's main business street. (2 hours)

Dr. Sun Yat-sen Park and Classical Chinese Garden is a block south of the cultural center on Carrall. The $6 million garden is patterned after gardens in the Chinese city of Suzhou that date back to the Ming dynasty (fourteenth to seventeenth centuries). Most of its architectural elements are antiques brought from China. Admission is

$4.50 for adults, $3 for children ages 6 to 11 and seniors over 65, maximum $10 for families. Hours: Open daily from 10:00 a.m. to 7:30 p.m. Address: 578 Carrall Street. Phone: (604) 662-3207.

☆☆ **Gastown**—Nineteen years before Vancouver was founded, a colorful pioneer entrepreneur by the name of John "Gassy Jack" Deighton opened the area's first saloon, catering to lumberjacks from nearby logging camps and sawmills, on the site that is now Maple Tree Square—the intersection of Carrall, Powell, Walter, and Alexander Streets, 6 blocks southeast of Granville Street and Canada Place. The story of Gassy Jack is a dismal one: the saloon owner married a 12-year-old girl, was cuckolded, raised a son who was not his own as his only heir, lived to see his bar and the neighborhood around it destroyed by fire in 1896, and drank himself to death. Always the "bad part of town," Gastown declined during the Great Depression to become perhaps the most decrepit and disreputable waterfront slum on the West Coast.

Refurbishment of this historic district began in the 1960s, and today Gastown is Vancouver's showpiece historic district, packed with galleries, boutiques, craft shops, night clubs, and restaurants, all aimed at the tourist trade. A big bronze statue of Gassy Jack, posthumously vindicated as a man of foresight and a local hero, stands atop a bronze whiskey barrel in Maple Tree Square. Nearby, at the corner of Cambie and Water Streets, North America's only steam-powered clock chimes every 15 minutes. Walk around and explore the district's notorious past and artsy-cutesy present in side passageways with names like Gaoler's Mews and Blood Alley. (2 hours)

☆☆ **H. R. MacMillan Planetarium and Vancouver Museum**—One of the largest and best-equipped planetariums in North America, H. R. MacMillan boasts a $1 million Zeiss star projector and hundreds of computer-controlled special effects projectors as well as a sophisticated laser imaging system. The most spectacular special effects can be seen in the planetarium's laser light shows with rock music sound tracks (Pink Floyd shows have been a perennial favorite here for more than 15 years). Admission to the astronomy shows is $5.50 for adults and $3.75 for children under age 17 and senior citizens, with a $14 maximum family rate; admission to laser shows is $7.50 for everybody. Hours: Astronomy shows are presented during July and August daily at 1:00, 2:30, 4:00, and 7:00 p.m.; the rest of the year Tuesday through Sunday at 2:30 and 7:00 p.m., with additional shows at 1:00 p.m. on Friday and 1:00 and 4:00 p.m. on Saturday and Sunday; closed Mondays September through June. Laser light shows are presented Tuesday through Sunday at 8:30 p.m. as well as Friday and Saturday at 9:45 p.m. Address: 1100 Chestnut Street. Phone: (604) 736-4431. (1 hour)

The planetarium is in the same cone-shaped building as the Vancouver Museum which contains dioramas of nineteenth-century life in British Columbia, including replicas of a pioneer trading post, an Edwardian home, and a railroad car. Other features are natural history exhibits and Northwest Coast Indian artifacts. The planetarium and museum are situated in Vanier Park overlooking Sunset Beach. To get there, take Burrard Street (2 blocks west of Granville) south from downtown. Vanier Park is just over the Burrard Bridge. Admission is $5 per adult, $2.50 for children ages 6 to 18 and senior citizens, with a $10 maximum family rate. Hours: Open daily from 10:00 a.m. to 9:00 p.m. during July and August, 10:00 a.m. to 5:00 p.m. Tuesday through Sunday the rest of the year. Address: 1100 Chestnut Street. Phone: (604) 736-7736. (1 hour)

★★ The Sky Train and the Sea Bus—The computer-operated, magnetically driven, elevated Sky Train starts from the station 2 blocks east of Canada Place on Cordova Street and runs 16 miles east to suburban Burnaby, Westminster, and Surrey. A round-trip is a great way to get an overview of the greater Vancouver area. You don't need to ride the whole route (the fare is higher if you go beyond the Vancouver city limits); just hop off at any station and catch the next train back. Fares range from $1.50 to $3, depending on how many zones you cross. Sky trains run every five minutes from 5:30 a.m. to 1:00 a.m. Phone: (604) 521-0400.

The Sea Bus passenger ferry starts at its terminal just across Canada Place from the Sky Train station and runs across Burrard Inlet to North Vancouver, providing a fine view of the waterfront. One-way fares on both the Sky Train and the Sea Bus are $1.50 for adults, 75 cents for children ages 5 to 13 and seniors 65 and older. Fares are higher during rush hours. You can buy a one-day unlimited travel pass valid on both the Sky Train and the Sea Bus as well as municipal buses for $4.50, a money-saver if you want to ride both the train and the ferry. Exact change, Canadian money only, is required. Hours: The Sea Bus operates weekdays from 6:15 a.m. to 1:00 a.m., Saturdays from 6:30 a.m. to 1:00 a.m., and Sundays from 8:30 a.m. to 11:30 p.m. Departures are every 15 minutes from 6:15 a.m. to 7:15 p.m. weekdays and 10:15 a.m. to 7:15 p.m. Saturdays, every half-hour the rest of the time. Phone: (604) 521-0400.

✸ **Exhibition Park**—The attraction that makes this public park worth the drive is a giant relief map—76 feet by 80 feet—of the entire province of British Columbia. It is located in the B.C. Pavilion, which also houses the British Columbia Sports Hall of Fame. Exhibition Park is several miles east of downtown via East Hastings Street, between Renfrew and Cassiar Streets. Admission is $5 for adults, $3 for students. Hours: Open Wednesday through Sunday from 10:00 a.m. to 5:00 p.m. Phone: (604) 253-2311. (1 hour)

Also in Exhibition Park is **Playland Amusement Park**, a traditional amusement park featuring the biggest wooden roller coaster in Canada. An all-day ride pass costs $12.95 if you're under 4 feet tall, otherwise $15.95. Phone: (604) 255-5161. Hours: Open Sunday through Thursday from 11:00 a.m. to 10:00 p.m., Friday and Saturday from 11:00 a.m. to 11:00 p.m. during the summer months; weekends only the rest of the year with shorter hours. Phone: (604) 255-5161. (1 hour)

✸ **Lynn Canyon Park**—The main attraction at this 200-acre park is a suspension footbridge that stretches across a 240-foot-deep gorge, which visitors can walk across if they dare. There are also nature trails and a visitor's center with environmental exhibits. Admission is free. Hours: Open daily from 8:00 a.m. to 5:00 p.m. Address: 3663 Park Road, North Vancouver. Phone: (604) 987-5922. (1½ hours)

✸ **Stanley Park**—This 1,000-acre park, just a 15-minute walk or a five-minute drive north of downtown Vancouver via Georgia Street, is one of the finest natural city parks in North America. Much of Stanley Park is wooded with fir and cedar, providing a home for abundant wildlife within sight of the city skyscrapers. You can walk for miles along forest trails, beaches, or the seawall promenade. Within the park, in addition to cricket fields, lawn bowling greens, a golf course, tennis courts, a rose garden, a totem pole display, and an open-air theater, are the **Vancouver Zoo** (admission $2 per adult, 95 cents for children under age 13 and senior citizens; open during daylight hours; phone: 604-257-8531) and the excellent **Vancouver Aquarium** (admission $9.50 per adult, $8.25 for students ages 13 to 18 and senior citizens, $6.25 for children ages 5 to 12; open 9:30 a.m.

to 8:00 p.m. during the summer, 10:00 a.m. to 5:30 p.m. the rest of the year; phone: 604-682-1118). (2 hours)

FITNESS AND RECREATION

As a jogging and biking town, Vancouver leaves a lot to be desired. The city's peninsular layout does not lend itself to the development of greenbelt trails. However, you'll find about 10 miles of good paved trails with lots of cyclists and joggers on them starting at **Stanley Park**. There is even a convenient bike rental shop, **Stanley Park Rentals**, 1798 West Georgia, (604) 681-5581.

For hiking, it's hard to beat **Pacific Spirit Park**, a 15-minute drive from downtown Vancouver at 4915 West 16th Avenue, (604) 224-5739. The park has 30 miles of trails through misty fir forests.

Near the Museum of Anthropology is a half-mile trail that descends very steeply down the Point Grey cliffs to **Wreck Beach**. The cliff climb puts this beach beyond the reach of law enforcement and Anglo-Canadian prudery. It is Vancouver's only nude beach, popular on those rare days when the sun shines. The trail can be hazardous in the rain.

FOOD

Situated under the sails at Canada Place, **The Prow**, (604) 684-1339, is a contemporary Vancouver landmark where you can dine with a view of Burrard Inlet or the cruise ship terminal. The cuisine is expensive and extraordinary, with a focus on fresh fish and seafood. The Prow is open daily for lunch and dinner.

Among the dozens of restaurants in Chinatown, a good bet is the **New Diamond Restaurant**, 555 Gore Avenue between Pender and Keefer, (604) 685-0727, open daily except Wednesdays for breakfast, lunch, and dinner. You can also dine affordably and well from sidewalk vendors' dim sum carts along the main streets of Chinatown.

Noodle Makers, one of the best Chinese restaurants around, is not in Chinatown but in neighboring Gastown at 122 Powell Street, (604) 253-4316. Inside you'll find traditional decor, including nineteenth-century Chinese-American antiques, as well as a goldfish pool and a waterfall. Entrées, each served on a bed of fresh handmade noodles, include imaginative salmon, crab, oyster, and shrimp dishes. Prices are moderate. The restaurant is open for lunch on weekdays only and for dinner nightly.

VANCOUVER

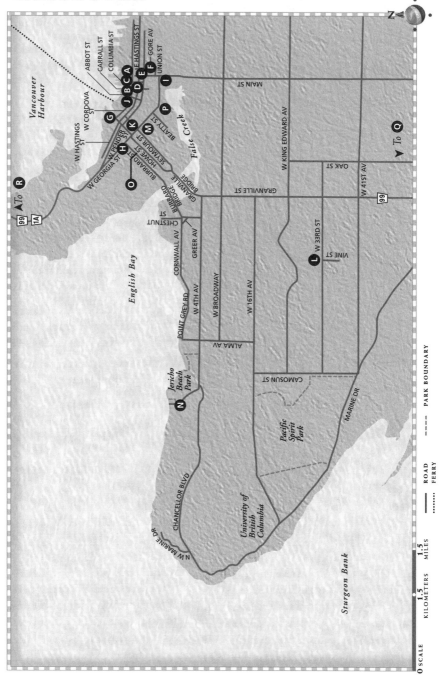

Vancouver Harbour

Vancouver Harbour

ABBOT ST
CARRALL ST
COLUMBIA ST
E HASTINGS ST
GORE AV
UNION ST

W CORDOVA ST

W HASTINGS ST

MAIN ST

W PENDER ST

W GEORGIA ST

BURRARD ST

HOWE ST

SEYMOUR ST

BEATTY ST

False Creek

W KING EDWARD AV

GRANVILLE ST

OAK ST

W 41ST AV

99

BURRARD BRIDGE

GRANVILLE BRIDGE

CHESTNUT ST

CORNWALL AV

GREER AV

POINT GREY RD

W 4TH AV

W BROADWAY

W 16TH AV

ALMA AV

W 33RD ST

VINE ST

English Bay

Jericho Beach Park

CAMOSUN ST

MARINE DR

Pacific Spirit Park

CHANCELLOR BLVD

N W MARINE DR

University of British Columbia

Sturgeon Bank

To Q

To R

99
1A

0 SCALE

1.5 KILOMETERS

1.5 MILES

ROAD
FERRY

PARK BOUNDARY

Food

Ⓐ Al Forno

Ⓑ India Village

Ⓒ Kilimanjaro

Ⓓ Le Railcar

Ⓔ New Diamond Restaurant

Ⓕ Phnom Penh Restaurant

Ⓖ The Prow

Lodging

Ⓗ Abbotsford Hotel

Ⓘ Backpackers Youth Hostel

Ⓙ Dominion Hotel

Ⓚ Hotel Vancouver

Ⓛ Johnson House

Ⓜ Niagara Hotel

Ⓝ Vancouver Hostel

Ⓞ YMCA

Ⓟ YWCA

Camping

Ⓠ Park Canada Recreational Vehicle Inn

Ⓡ Porteau Cove Provincial Park

You can find a truly international mix of restaurants in Gastown. Consider **India Village** (East Indian) at 308 Water Street (604) 681-0678, open daily for lunch and dinner; **Phnom Penh Restaurant** (Cambodian) at 244 East Georgia Street, (604) 682-5777, open daily except Tuesday for lunch and dinner; **Le Railcar** (French) at 106 Carrall, (604) 669-5422, open for lunch on weekdays only and for dinner nightly, closed Sundays off-season; **Kilimanjaro** (East African) at 322 Water Street, (604) 681-9913, open for lunch on weekdays only and for dinner daily; or **Al Forno** (Italian—great pizzas!) at Columbia and Water Streets, (604) 684-2838, open for lunch Sunday and Tuesday through Friday and for dinner nightly except Monday.

LODGING

The grandest old hotel in downtown Vancouver is the **Hotel Vancouver** at 900 West Georgia Street, (604) 684-3131 or toll-free (800) 828-7447 from the United States and (800) 268-9411 from Canada. King George VI of England stayed here shortly after the hotel opened in 1939, and as a guest today you'll feel like royalty too. Edwardian elegance pervades the hotel lobby with its marble columns and crystal chandeliers; the rooms are modern, quiet, and spacious. Room rates are steep, ranging from about $215 to $315 Canadian from April through October, about $40 less during the winter months, with lavish suites running as much as $1,250 a night. Even so, rates are equally high at several of the contemporary luxury hotels downtown.

A more moderately priced classic hotel downtown is the art deco-style **Abbotsford Hotel** at 921 West Pender Street, (604) 681-4335 or toll-free (800) 663-1700. Room rates are about $80 a night during tourist season, $50 during the winter months.

One of Vancouver's nicest small bed and breakfasts is the **Johnson House**, located at 34th and Vine Streets in the Kerrisdale district, a residential neighborhood out toward the University of British Columbia. This antique-filled home features a lovely rock garden and decor accented by wooden carousel animals. Rates range from $50 to $90 a night. For reservations, call (604) 266-4175.

Look in Gastown for low-priced lodging. The turn-of-the-century **Dominion Hotel** at the corner of Abbot and Water Streets, (604) 681-6666, offers clean, simple rooms and a lobby full of Victorian antiques at around $50 a night; there are a couple of drawbacks, though. There's no elevator, so you reach your room by climbing the kind of giant staircase they don't make any more, and the dance club downstairs features LOUD bands until 1:30 in the morning. Budget-priced, spartan rooms can be found at the **Niagara Hotel**, 435 West Pender Street, (604) 688-7574, where doubles run $30 to $40 a night. In the same price range, downtown but not in Gastown, are the **YMCA**, 955 Burrard Street, (604) 681-0221, open to both men and women, and the **YWCA**, 733 Beatty, (604) 895-5830, for women, couples, and families but not single men; both offer private rooms with shared baths.

Dormitory accommodations cost as little as $8 per person at the **Vancouver Hostel** (IYH), Canada's largest youth hostel, west of downtown at 1515 Discovery Street, (604) 224-3208, closed 10:00 a.m. to 4:00 p.m., and the **Backpackers Youth Hostel** (unaffiliated) near Chinatown at 927 Main Street, (604) 682-2441, no closed hours or curfew.

CAMPING

There are no public campgrounds in the greater Vancouver area. The closest is at **Porteau Cove Provincial Park**, about 21 miles north of the city via Highway 99, with a swimming beach but no hookups. To get the most out of a visit to the city, even confirmed campers should consider taking a downtown hotel room tonight. For those who wish to see Vancouver as a day trip, the **Park Canada Recreational Vehicle Inn**, about 2 miles east of the ferry terminal at Tsawwassen, offers full hookups and amenities for $18 a night. If you're entering Canada via Interstate 5/Highway 99, the KOA Vancouver, 8 miles north of the border crossing, charges $16.50 a night.

NIGHTLIFE

Vancouver is a good city for live theater. Most nights there are about a dozen plays in performance, ranging from repertory standards and touring company productions of recent Broadway hits to works by Canada's best contemporary playwrights. Check the daily papers or the weekly *Georgia Straight* arts and entertainment publication for current playbills. The most offbeat of Vancouver stage venues is the improvisational **Back Alley Theatre** at Georgia and Thurlow Streets, (604) 688-7013.

Gastown is a good place for nightclub hopping. Look for jazz in an Irish pub atmosphere at the **Blarney Stone**, 216 Carrall Street,

(604) 687-4322; disco at Amnesia, 99 Powell Street, (604) 682-2211; or rock at the **Town Pump**, 66 Water Street, (604) 683-6695.

Casino gambling is legal in Vancouver, with certain restrictions. Casinos are limited in size to 15 tables, craps and other dice games are prohibited, and the maximum bet is $5. Perhaps the most intriguing gambling house in town, because of its multicultural clientele, is the **Vancouver Casino** on the edge of Chinatown at Main and East Georgia Streets, (604) 253-4263. Alongside the roulette and blackjack tables you'll find the Chinese favorite, sicbo.

HELPFUL HINTS

There are a couple of ways to enter Vancouver. Arriving by ferry from Swartz Bay on Vancouver Island, you'll reach the mainland at Tsawwassen, about 20 miles south of downtown. From there, Highway 17 takes you to Highway 99, the main north-south freeway leading to downtown Vancouver.

If you are coming into Canada by car from the U.S. border, Interstate 5 becomes Highway 99 as it enters Canada and points you straight toward downtown Vancouver.

Either way, after crossing under the South Arm of the Fraser River via the George Massey Tunnel and over the North Arm via the Oak Street Bridge, Highway 99 becomes a congested city street. Turn west (left) to Granville Street, then north (right). Granville leads you into the heart of downtown and ends at Canada Place, a good place to park.

While satellite cities in the greater Vancouver area—West Vancouver, Coquitlam, Westminster, Langley, Delta, and Richmond—sprawl across four peninsulas and several islands linked by commuter ferries, bridges, and one of the most confusing freeway systems ever built, the city of Vancouver itself nestles on a single arm of land bound by Burrard Inlet on the north and the north arm of the Fraser River on the south. Downtown Vancouver, including Canada Place, Gastown, Chinatown, and Stanley Park, is on a spit of land jutting into Burrard Inlet midway along the north side of the peninsula. The University of British Columbia is on the western tip of the peninsula.

10
NORTH CASCADES HIGHWAY

The North Cascades Highway lets you cross the mountains from Interstate 5 south of the Canadian border crossing or from the Anacortes area into central Washington without returning to the heavy traffic of the greater Seattle area. This route is said by many to be the most scenic route in Washington, on a busy summer weekend you may find a paradox there: bumper-to-bumper seekers of wilderness solitude. Much of the time, though—especially on weekdays—heavy traffic is not a problem.

The highway runs through Ross Lake National Recreation Area, a narrow strip that divides the two halves of North Cascades National Park. The national park itself is wilderness area, accessible only on foot or horseback. The same National Park Service office that administers North Cascades National Park also administers Ross Lake National Recreation Area, as well as Lake Chelan National Recreation Area, so in effect all three areas form a single national park.

In the North Cascades, you will not find the visitor's amenities or commercial concessions that characterize many U.S. national parks. In fact, beyond Newhalem you won't find gas, food, or lodging for 75 miles. What you will find is some of the most spectacular mountain scenery in the United States.

(*Note:* The North Cascades Highway is closed until early May. Off-season travelers, see "Helpful Hints" at the end of this chapter.) ◧

NORTH CASCADES HIGHWAY

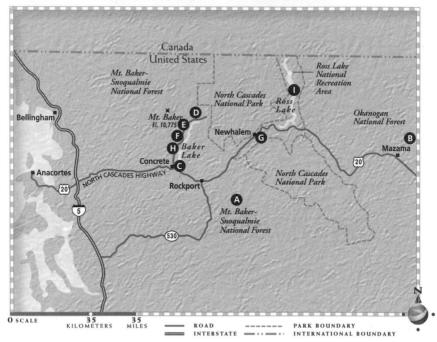

Sightseeing Highlights

Ⓐ Mount Baker-Snoqualmie National Forest

Ⓑ Pacific Crest Trail

Food

Ⓒ North Cascades Inn

Lodging

Ⓓ Baker Lake Resort

Camping

Ⓔ Boulder Creek Campground

Ⓕ Horseshoe Cove Campground

Ⓖ Newhalem Creek Campground

Ⓗ Panorama Point Campground

Ⓘ Ross Lake National Recreation Area

A PERFECT DAY IN THE NORTH CASCADES

Here's an all-day, 269-mile scenic drive that will take you from
Vancouver across the border and the northern Cascade Range, bring-
ing you to Lake Chelan in central Washington by dinner time. From
downtown Vancouver, go south across the Granville Bridge and follow
Highway 99 south. Drive 31 miles and you'll reach the border, where
you clear U.S. Customs and the highway becomes Interstate 5.
Continue south for 49 miles, passing through the small city of
Burlington, and exit east on Highway 20. Take Highway 20 through
Sedro Wooley, Lyman, and Concrete, where a road turns off to the
north for Mount Baker Recreation Area, a winter sports area.

Continue on Highway 20 past the lower dam of Baker Lake,
through Rockport, Marblemount, and Newhalem to Ross Lake. It is 67
miles from I-5 to Newhalem, the last town before the high mountains.

You'll crest Rainy Pass 30 miles beyond Newhalem. Here and at
Washington Pass, 5 miles farther, overlooks afford spectacular views of
the rugged North Cascades to the north, south, and west. A segment
of the Pacific Crest Trail parallels the road for about a mile near Rainy
Pass, where you can hike if the Hart's Pass Road is closed by snow or
sounds too ambitious. From Washington Pass, it's 17 miles to Mazama,
where you turn off to reach Hart's Pass.

After your Pacific Crest hike, continue on Highway 20 for 27
miles, through the towns of Winthrop and Twisp. About 3 miles past
Twisp, Highway 153 forks off to the right. Follow Highway 153 south
to the U.S. 97 junction, a distance of 31 miles. Turn right (south) on
U.S. 97, and another 17 miles will bring you into Chelan.

SIGHTSEEING HIGHLIGHTS

★★ **Mount Baker-Snoqualmie National Forest**—The North Cascades route takes you through a portion of this 2½ million-acre national
forest, which extends down the west side of the Cascade Range from the
border to Mount Rainier. Mount Baker (10,778 feet) has been showing
signs of volcanic activity since 1975, and some experts believe it will be
the next Cascades volcano to blow its top—but probably not today.
Since the early 1980s, Mount Baker-Snoqualmie National Forest has
seen disturbances of a different sort as the epicenter of the Northern
Spotted Owl War between conservationists and the forest products
industry. Your chances of actually seeing one of these elusive, nocturnal

birds are only slightly better than your chances of spotting Sasquatch, or "Bigfoot," but on today's drive you will see in the distance vast expanses of coniferous forests, some of which have never been touched by lumberjacks. And you'll have an opportunity to ponder (not for the last time on this tour of the Northwest) the devastation caused by excessive clearcutting of the national forests during the past decade. As this book goes to press, the federal courts have banned logging in virtually all Northwestern ancient forests, a hard-won (though perhaps temporary) environmental victory that has left loggers out of work and in a state of rage. Remember, the forests you'll see on today's trip belong to you.

★★ **The Pacific Crest Trail**—The United States' longest and most famous National Scenic Trail runs all the way from the Canadian border to the Mexican border along the Cascade and Sierra Nevada mountain ranges. You will intersect it three more times later in this tour: at Cascade Locks where it crosses the Columbia River; on the south slope of Mount Hood; and in Crater Lake National Park. To hike the whole Pacific Crest Trail takes several months, but you can try a tiny sample of the experience and imagine the rest on a short detour from the North Cascades Highway. Here's how.

One mile beyond the Early Winters Forest Service Information Station, turn off the highway into Mazama, then turn right on Hart's Pass Road. (Snow closes this unpaved road in the winter, sometimes until mid-June, and trailers are not allowed past Ballard Campground.) The road twists and climbs switchbacks for 13 miles from Mazama to the 6,197-foot crest of the North Cascades. Just beyond Meadows Campground, you can hike on the Pacific Crest Trail as far as you want in either direction from the trailhead. Afterward return to the main highway the same way you came. (4 hours)

FITNESS AND RECREATION

Besides the Pacific Crest Trail (see above), there are hundreds of other hiking and horse trails through Mount Baker-Snoqualmie National Forest and North Cascades National Park. Hikers can take their choice from signs that mark trailheads every few miles along the North Cascades Highway. One of the most spectacular routes is the 7-mile (each way) **Cascade Pass Trail**, which climbs southeast from the Marblemount vicinity to the top of the roadless pass that was the only route to the isolated town of Stehekin (see the Lake Chelan chapter) before the creation of Lake Chelan made ferry service possible. Another popular hike, the 3-mile (each way) **Coleman Glacier Trail** makes its way up the forested slopes of Mount Baker to the edge of a massive glacier.

Most trails in the North Cascades are equally suitable for horse pack trips as well as backpacking. Because the area is so undeveloped, however, riding stables where you can rent horses are few and far between. Try the stable at **Sun Mountain Lodge** in Winthrop, (509) 966-2211, west of the park. They rent horses to the general public by the hour or overnight.

The North Cascades Highway is both challenging and spectacular by bicycle, with extra-wide shoulders to accommodate the cyclists who often seem to outnumber cars on this route. Although the highway is suitable for road touring bikes, a mountain bike lets you take side trips on the logging roads west of the national park area. Unfortunately, there are no commercial bike rental shops nearby, so if you didn't bring your own, the best plan is to rent one, perhaps in Seattle, for this trip.

FOOD

Visitors who don't expect to find fancy restaurants along the North Cascades Highway won't be disappointed. Budget-priced and rustic, the **North Cascades Inn**, 4284 Highway 20, Concrete, (360) 853-8771, dominates the local dining scene with its stick-to-your-ribs meat-and-potatoes meals and homemade pies.

LODGING

Several small lodgings are located in the Concrete area, south of Mount Baker and west of North Cascades National Park. **Baker Lake Resort**, Baker Lake Road (360) 853-8325, offers seven basic log cabins on the lake shore about 20 miles north of Concrete. The cabins, which cost about $50 a night, have private baths and fully equipped kitchenettes, but guests are asked to provide their own sheets and towels.

CAMPING

What the area lacks in terms of restaurants and hotels, it makes up for with an abundance of public campgrounds. North of Concrete on forest roads that branch off the Baker Lake Road, the **Horseshoe**

Cove and **Panorama Point** national forest campgrounds together have 50 campsites for tents and RVs on the shores of the lake. Camping fees are $7 per night. On the same road but not on the water, the **Boulder Creek Campground** has ten free campsites but no drinking water.

The **Newhalem Creek Campground** adjoining North Cascades National Park at the west end of the town of Newhalem has 115 RV sites (no hookups) and a tent camping loop. Fees are $7 per night.

You'll also find upwards of 300 more campsites in three campgrounds operated by the National Park Service at **Ross Lake National Recreation Area**, west of Newhalem. Camping fees range from free to $7 a night.

HELPFUL HINTS

The tour described in this and the next three chapters can be done only in the summer. The North Cascades Highway is closed until early May. The Lake Chelan cruise operates on a limited schedule year-round, but from November through April you can only get to Chelan from the west side of the mountains via the Stevens Pass Highway, U.S. 2 east, which exits I-5 at Everett. The back way into Mount Rainier National Park is also closed in winter, though the park itself is open to Paradise and can be reached from Seattle or Tacoma in less than two hours' drive.

11

LAKE CHELAN

More than 1,500 feet deep (the lake bottom is below sea level), Lake Chelan is among the world's deepest lakes. In the United States, only Crater Lake is deeper. As you travel up the lake by boat, its narrowness makes it seem more like a great river: 55 miles in length, it is only about 2 miles across at its widest point and, in other places, only half a mile across. Some visitors mistakenly assume that Lake Chelan is man-made; certainly, it appears similar to Franklin Roosevelt Lake to the west, formed by Grand Coulee Dam, and a dam at the south end of the lake raises the water level by 21 feet. In fact, Lake Chelan is a natural phenomenon. The glacier that gouged this deep canyon, or coulee, through the North Cascades during the last ice age pushed ahead of it a massive wall of mud and rocks that formed a natural dam at the lower end of the coulee.

While the lower end of the lake is a busy dry-side resort area where many Seattlites come to escape rainy weather, Lake Chelan thrusts northward deep into the heart of the North Cascades, providing a navigable waterway through the Sawtooth and Glacier Peak wilderness areas, which are inaccessible by road. You can glide through the wilderness, between sheer cliffs at the foot of glacier-clad peaks, on the *Lady of the Lake* ferry. ◼

LAKE CHELAN

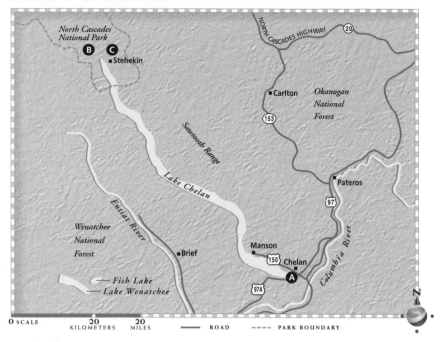

Sightseeing Highlights

Ⓐ *Lady of the Lake* Cruise

Ⓑ North Cascades National Park

Ⓒ Stehekin

A PERFECT DAY ON LAKE CHELAN

Board the *Lady of the Lake* before 8:30 a.m. for a cruise up Lake Chelan
to the mountain hideaway of Stehekin. The rest of the day will take
care of itself.

SIGHTSEEING HIGHLIGHTS

★★★ *Lady of the Lake* **Cruise**—Originally a private ferry serving
small communities at the north end of Lake Chelan, today it is a popular excursion cruise and the only way for backpackers to reach the
south boundary of **North Cascades National Park**. Mile for mile, the
Lady of the Lake may be the best cruise bargain in the United States. It
is undoubtedly one of the most scenic: even the San Juan Islands ferry
trip pales by comparison!

The *Lady of the Lake* ferry leaves the Lake Chelan Boat Company dock at the south end of the lake, a short distance west of the
town center on U.S. 97, daily from April 15 through October 15, at
8:30 a.m. The *Lady of the Lake* is a different boat at different times of
year—a sleek, modern 90-passenger excursion boat in the summer
peak season or, at slower times of year, a comfortable, lovingly cared
for older craft that carries up to two dozen passengers. Reservations
are not taken. Be at the dock soon after 8:00 a.m. If the office is
open, buy your tickets; otherwise, simply board the boat and a crew
member will take your fare sometime during the northbound cruise.
Address: Lake Chelan Boat Company, P.O. Box 186, Chelan, WA
98816. Phone: (509) 682-4584.

The first hour of the cruise takes you past seemingly endless lakefront vacation cottages. Then you pass beyond the reach of civilization,
between 8,000-foot mountains where small streams tumble as much as
a half-mile down sheer cliff faces. Watch carefully with binoculars
handy: you're likely to see mountain goats traversing the cliffs. After a
brief stop at Lucerne, the port for Holden, a well-preserved historic
mining town and wilderness trailhead, you'll arrive at noon in
Stehekin, the village at the north end of the lake.

The round-trip fare for this all-day cruise is $21 per adult, half-
price for children ages 6 to 11. No pets are allowed on board during
the busy summer season. For those visitors who are on a tight schedule
or are easily bored by long boat trips, the Lake Chelan Boat Company
has recently added a new, faster boat called the *Lady Express* which cuts

the round-trip time from Chelan to Stehekin in half. The *Lady Express* leaves at 8:30 a.m., arrives in Stehekin at 10:30 a.m., leaves Stehekin at 11:55 a.m., and arrives back in Chelan at 1:30 p.m. The round-trip fare is $39 for adults, half-price for children ages 2 through 11. In the summer you can ride one way on the *Lady Express* and return on the *Lady of the Lake*, allowing yourself 3½ hours in Stehekin, for $30. Off-season, the *Lady Express* makes the trip Monday, Wednesday, and Friday year-round, as well as Sundays from mid-February to mid-April.

The most spectacular way to see Lake Chelan is to take a sight-seeing flight one way to Stehekin on Chelan Airways ($40 per person, reservations recommended, call 509-682-5555) and take the boat back (one-way fare is $14 per person). (full day)

★★ **Stehekin**—*Stehekin* is a Native American word meaning "the way through." For both Indians and early pioneers, a main route from inland Washington through the Cascade Mountains to the coast was to canoe up Lake Chelan and the Stehekin River, climb 5,400-foot Cascade Pass, and follow the Cascade River west. This route brought them out of the mountains at Marblemount, where the North Cascades Highway starts into the mountains going east. At Stehekin, you are only about 11 miles straight-line distance from Rainy Pass on the North Cascades Highway; if you're planning to walk there, allow two days.

In Stehekin, the **North Cascades National Park visitor's center** is in a converted 1920s resort hotel. A few other small hotels are still in operation, including one where you can eat lunch. There are also some rustic private homes and a historic homestead with interpretive signs about pioneer life. Since Stehekin cannot be reached by road, you may be surprised at the number of old, beat-up automobiles in the village. Brought on barges, the cars take local residents up and down the 22-mile road between the ferry dock and homesteads in the valley.

FITNESS AND RECREATION

If you choose to spend the night (or longer) in Stehekin, you can arrange a half-day guided horseback trip to **Coon Lake** ($25 per person, groups limited to six people) at **Cascade Corrals**, P.O. Box 67, Stehekin, WA 98852, (509) 682-4677, or rent a mountain bike (about $3.50 per hour or $20 all day) at any of several local lodges. It costs $13 to take your own bike along on the ferry.

Information on the numerous hiking trails in the area is available at the North Cascades National Park visitor's center in Stehekin. National Park Service shuttles and independent vans will take you 3 miles to **Rainbow Falls** or, during the warm months, 22 miles to the dead-end of the Stehekin River Road, where the major North Cascades National Park trails start. The 7-mile **Cascade Pass Trail** climbs northwest to an elevation of 5,400 feet to cross the backbone of the Cascade Range, eventually reaching the town of Marblemount on the North Cascades Highway. A 12-mile segment of the **Pacific Crest Trail** goes northeast to intersect Highway 20 at 4,860-foot Rainy Pass. Reservations for the national park shuttles—dropoff, pickup, or both—should be made well in advance of your arrival by calling the visitor's center, (509) 856-5703. The cost is $5 per person each way.

FOOD

The **Campbell House** restaurant in Campbell's Resort, 104 West Woodin Avenue in Chelan, lives up to its long-standing reputation as Chelan's finest restaurant. Dinners start at about $10. For reservations, call (509) 682-4250.

Chelan has other restaurants in abundance, mostly predictable family restaurants and fast-food places. Anywhere in town, you won't have to search far for fried chicken, pizza, or hamburgers. **Goochi's**, 104 East Woodin Avenue, (509) 682-2436, serves steaks and hamburgers in a pub atmosphere and features an impressive selection of designer beers from microbreweries around Washington. Open for lunch and dinner.

There are no full-service public restaurants in Stehekin, but the **Stehekin Pastry Company**, a mile from the boat landing, sells cinnamon rolls, pies, croissants, pastries, and frozen yogurt from 7:00 a.m. to 8:00 p.m. Visitors who spend the night dine at their place of lodging.

LODGING

Chelan has plenty of motels, none of them low priced: the going rates are $45 to $70. With luck, budget travelers may be able to land one of the few $49 rooms (as low as $30 off-season) at the **Apple Inn Motel**, 1002 East Woodin, (509) 682-4044, which has an outdoor swimming pool and a year-round hot tub.

Campbell's Resort, the town's historic lakefront lodge (circa 1901) at 104 West Woodin, (509) 682-2561, has main lodge rooms,

CHELAN

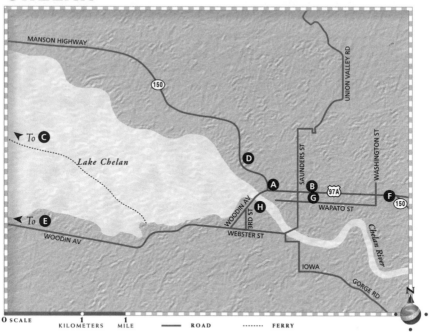

Food

A Campbell House

B Goochi's

C Stehekin Pastry Company

Camping

D Chelan Municipal Campground

E Lake Chelan State Park

Lodging

F Apple Inn Motel

A Campbell's Resort

G Em's Bed & Breakfast Inn

H Mary Kay's Whaley Mansion

C North Cascades Lodge

C Silver Bay Inn Bed & Breakfast

Note: Items with the same letter are located in the same town or area.

modern motel-style units, and private cabins. In 1991 the resort opened a new 40-unit complex to replace some of the housekeeping cabins. Amenities include a beach, a whirlpool spa, and three swimming pools. Rates start at $124 a night during July and August but gradually drop to about half that during the off-season (November to May).

Mary Kay's Whaley Mansion, at 415 Third Street, is Chelan's showpiece bed and breakfast, a big Edwardian house festooned with "gingerbread" and packed with antiques and elaborate interior decor. Rates start at $115. Reservations are essential. Call (509) 682-5735. More affordable B&B accommodations can be found at **Em's Bed & Breakfast Inn**, 304 E. Wapato, (509) 682-4149, about $70.

Condominium resorts and private owners frequently rent units by the night (sometimes requiring three-night minimum stays) for about twice the price of an ordinary motel room. Kitchen facilities make them a reasonable alternative for several people traveling together. Contact the **Lake Chelan Chamber of Commerce**, P.O. Box 216, Chelan, WA 98816, (800) 4CHELAN, for current condominium rental information.

If one of your vacation priorities is to "get away from it all" (and I mean all of it), consider spending the night—or a week—in Stehekin. The main accommodations are at the 26-unit **North Cascades Lodge**, which has a restaurant and small grocery store. Rates for doubles are under $50 off-season, rising to about $75 between July 1 and October 15. For information and reservations, write North Cascades Lodge, P.O. Box 275, Stehekin, WA 98852, or call (509) 682-4711.

Also in Stehekin, the **Silver Bay Inn Bed and Breakfast**, Box 43, Stehekin, WA 98852, (call 509-682-2212 Monday through Friday 8:00 a.m. to 5:00 p.m.) offers a suite or guest cabin for $95 a night. Breakfast is included in the main B&B facility, while the cabins have complete kitchens including microwave and dishwasher. The Silver Bay Inn provides canoes and bikes free to guests.

CAMPING

Chelan has a big **municipal campground**—essentially a city-run RV park—right in the middle of town, with showers and a lakefront beach. The camping fee is $11. Except for a handful of unappealing tent sites, the campground is for RVs only.

A more pleasant lakeside campground is at **Lake Chelan State Park**, 4 miles west of town on U.S. 97 and then 5 miles northwest on

Shore Drive. Standard sites cost $8, with a few higher-priced sites that have hookups. The only drawback to this campground is that the distance from town means you'll have to rise and shine earlier to break camp and be at the boat dock for an 8:30 a.m. departure. Campground reservations are required at Lake Chelan State Park between Memorial Day and Labor Day. Request a reservation form from the **Washington State Parks and Recreation Commission**, 7150 Clearwater Lane, KY-11, Olympia, WA 98504, (360) 753-2027. (See Chapter 4's "Camping" section for more information on reservation procedures.) The reservation address for Lake Chelan State Park is Route 1, Box 90, Chelan, WA 98816.

12
APPLE COUNTRY

One of the images that probably comes to mind when you think of Washington State is apples. Big, bright, red, juicy, delicious ones. Apples are the state's largest agricultural crop, and Washington grows more than half of all the apples sold in the United States and Mexico. Driving through the heart of apple-growing country, the valleys that make their way from the ponderosa pine forests on the dry side of the Cascades down through the foothills and overflow like cornucopias with fruit orchards, you will discover a number of friendly little communities, each with its own unique character.

Astonishing amounts of apple juice and applesauce pour out of factories in the no-nonsense industrial town of Wenatchee. A little way up the road, apple candy is the only factory product in Cashmere, a small town with a big open-air museum of pioneer buildings and a main street refurbished in Early American gingerbread style. Continue a little farther up the highway, and you'll come to the most improbable town of all, Leavenworth, a once-ordinary little place that remade itself into a Bavarian village in the hope of attracting tourists.

For sheer beauty, the time to visit apple country is spring, when the apple and cherry orchards that line both sides of the highway are filled with blossoms. Harvest season in early fall also makes for a memorable experience. In summer the magnificent and relatively uncrowded mountains that lie beyond Leavenworth invite hikers and horseback riders to explore deep into the wilderness and discover pristine alpine lakes. ◼

APPLE COUNTRY

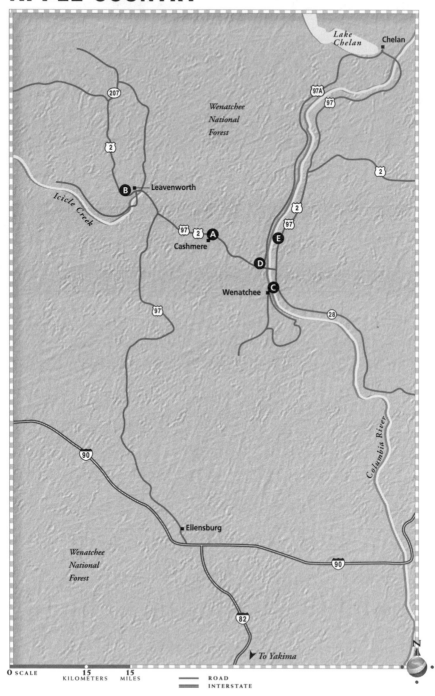

Sightseeing Highlights

Ⓐ Chelan County Museum and Pioneer Village

Ⓑ Leavenworth

Ⓐ Liberty Orchards Company Aplets Factory

Ⓒ North Central Washington Museum

Ⓓ Ohme Gardens County Park

Ⓔ Rocky Reach Dam

Ⓖ Washington Apple Commission Visitor's Center

Note: Items with the same letter are located in the same town or area.

A PERFECT DAY IN APPLE COUNTRY

From Chelan, take U.S. 97 south, through desert country along the banks of the Columbia River, for 35 miles to the highway intersection on the outskirts of Wenatchee. Along the way you'll pass Rocky Reach Dam and 4 miles farther along, Ohme Gardens. The intersection of U.S. 97 and U.S. 2 on the outskirts of Wenatchee is complicated. Follow the signs closely to stay on U.S. 97 in the direction of Cashmere and Leavenworth. If you find yourself in downtown Wenatchee, you took a wrong turn.

From Wenatchee, stay on U.S. 2/97 for about 5 miles west to Cashmere, where you'll see Chelan County Museum and Pioneer Village on your left. Follow U.S. 2/97 west for 10 more miles through the fruit orchards. When U.S. 97 turns off to the south, unless you're in a hurry, keep going straight on U.S. 2 for 4 miles to Leavenworth.

SIGHTSEEING HIGHLIGHTS

✪✪✪ **Leavenworth**—This self-styled "Bavarian village" used to be just another dry-side small town, half-deserted since the lumber mill closed down. Then, in 1965, residents noticed the similarity of the Bavarian Alps to their own alpine scenery and decided to refurbish their town in German style in a desperate attempt to attract tourists. I have to admit that when I first heard about this pseudo-Oberammergau on the American frontier, I thought it sounded like just another tacky tourist trap—but upon visiting, I discovered that I was wrong. It all works! From the main street's Disneyesque charm, to the view of the surrounding mountains from the idyllic riverside park, to the excellent pastry shops and restaurants with European-trained chefs, even to the gift shops bursting with Hummel figurines, souvenir beer steins, and fine wood carvings by German immigrant craftsmen, a single-minded identity and remarkable attention to detail have made Leavenworth a wonderful little one-of-a-kind Fantasyland. Okay, sometimes the Old World look clashes with mainstream America—just down the street from the world's only Tyrolean-style supermarket is a Thai restaurant behind a Bavarian facade. But it's all part of the fun. Leavenworth is jam-packed with oompah bands, beer, and tourist crowds for the Mai Fest in mid-May and the Autumn Leaf Festival (Oktoberfest) from the last weekend in September through the first weekend in October. (3 hours)

✪✪ **Chelan County Museum and Pioneer Village**—At the edge of the town of Cashmere, this outstanding assemblage of rustic buildings from throughout Chelan County presents a vivid picture of what nineteenth-century life was like in central Washington. The "jail" was originally a cabin inhabited by an escaped convict from the federal penitentiary in Leavenworth, Kansas—who settled down in Leavenworth, Washington. Strange are the workings of the criminal mind. Inside the museum is a good collection of Indian artifacts from central Washington and elsewhere. Admission is $3 for adults, $1 for children under 12, maximum $5 per family. Hours: The museum is open April through October, Monday through Saturday 10:00 a.m. to 4:30 p.m., Sunday 1:00 to 4:30 p.m. The pioneer village can be seen any time during daylight hours. Phone: (509) 782-3230. (1 hour)

★★ **Liberty Orchards Company Aplets Factory**—While in pretty little Cashmere, with its refurbished turn-of-the-century storefronts, you might want to take the 15-minute free tour through the small family-run factory where they make Aplets and Cotlets. These all-natural fruit candies, sold throughout Washington and in gourmet shops elsewhere in the west, were invented by an Armenian immigrant who went into the candy business here after his Seattle restaurant failed in the 1920s. Besides the small-town success story, you'll get free samples and an irresistible opportunity to buy more. Tours are free. Hours: Open May through December, Monday through Friday 8:00 a.m. to 5:00 p.m., Saturday and Sunday 10:00 a.m. to 4:00 p.m.; January through April, Monday through Friday, 8:00 a.m. to 12:00 noon and 1:00 to 5:00 p.m. Address: 117 Mission Street. Phone: (509) 782-2191. (1 hour)

★ **Apple Commission Visitor's Center**—Here you can learn all about apple growing and processing in a 15-minute video, then sample three kinds of apples and cold apple cider. Admission is free. Hours: Open daily from 8:00 a.m. to 5:00 p.m. during the spring months, with shorter weekend hours the rest of the year. Address: 2900 Euclid Avenue, Wenatchee. Phone: (509) 663-9600. (15 minutes)

★ **North Central Washington Museum**—Wenatchee is the heart of Washington's apple-growing country, and this museum can tell you everything you ever wanted to know about apples. A complete antique apple-processing factory is in a separate building connected to the main museum by a skybridge. There is also a film and an exhibit about the first trans-Pacific airplane flight, in 1931, which started from Japan and ended, improbably, in Wenatchee. Admission is $2 for adults, $1 for children ages 8 to 12. Hours: Open Monday through Friday from 10:00 a.m. to 4:00 p.m., Saturday and Sunday from 1:00 p.m. to 4:00 p.m. Address: 127 South Mission Street. Phone: (509) 664-5989. (1 hour)

★ **Ohme Gardens County Park**—This 9-acre formal garden, on a rocky point overlooking the Wenatchee Valley and the Columbia River, has been landscaped using native mountain plants. Stone pathways among rugged basalt formations connect various levels of the garden, which features evergreen trees, fern grotto pools, and a wishing well. Admission is $5 for adults, $3 for children ages 7 to 17. Hours: Open mid-April to mid-October, 9:00 a.m. to dusk. Phone: (509) 662-5785. (1 hour)

✿ **Rocky Reach Dam**—Like all dams on the Columbia, this one has a fish ladder with an underwater viewing area where you can watch adult salmon swim up the river to spawn and fingerlings swim down to the sea. This is a less crowded place to watch the Columbia salmon run than Bonneville Dam. The visitor's center's Gallery of Electricity traces developments from Ben Franklin's kite to microchips. Admission is free. Hours: Open daily from 8:00 a.m. to 8:00 p.m. Memorial Day to Labor Day, 8:00 a.m. to 5:00 p.m. the rest of the year, closed January 1 to February 15. Phone: (509) 663-9600. (½ hour)

FITNESS AND RECREATION

Near Leavenworth, the **Wenatchee River Trail** runs along the opposite bank of the river from Highway 2 for about 2 miles, beginning 2 miles west of town and leading into Tumwater Canyon. More suitable for hiking than biking, the otherwise easy trail has a jumbled expanse of scree that must be crossed with the aid of rebar hand holds placed there by the Forest Service. In the mountains west of Leavenworth (follow Icicle Road), the 22-mile-long Icicle Valley is a major backpacking destination in the Alpine Lakes Wilderness. A fairly steep 3½-mile hike from the trailhead on a side road from Bridge Creek Campground leads to **Eight Mile Lake,** and somewhat longer trails branch off to **Stuart Lake** and **Lake Caroline**. A spectacular day hike is the **Icicle Gorge Trail**, a 6-mile loop trail from the end of Icicle Road that leads up one side of the Icicle River and back down the other side.

A popular road bike tour from Leavenworth is the 7½-mile **Leavenworth Loop**, a flat road through the countryside around the confluence of the Wenatchee and Icicle Rivers. The clockwise-only route follows East Leavenworth south from the east side of town and returns via Icicle Road to the west side of town, where a ride through Riverfront Park closes the loop. A more adventurous mountain bike ride is the 5-mile trip through the ponderosa forest on **Mountain Home Road** to the top of Boundary Butte. Along the way are great views of Leavenworth and the Wenatchee River area. Visitors planning cycling trips in the Leavenworth area should bring their own bikes, rent them before leaving Seattle, or stay in a bed and breakfast inn that has bikes for guest use. At this writing there are no bike rentals in town.

Guided horseback rides ranging from a few hours to three-day pack trips can be arranged through **Icicle Outfitters and Guides**, P.O. Box 322, Leavenworth, WA 98826; (509) 784-1145.

FOOD

In Wenatchee, the moderately priced **John Horan House**, 2 Horan Road, (509) 663-0018, serves steak and seafood dinners and Sunday brunch in one of the oldest pioneer homes in town, dating back to 1899. Prices are moderate.

For lunch or dinner in Leavenworth, there is an impressive array of possibilities. Not surprisingly, most feature German food. My nomination for the best in town is **Reiner's Gasthaus** at 829 Front Street, (509) 548-5111. Prices are moderate. If sausage, sauerkraut, and spaetzel don't appeal, you'll find just plain American food—lots of it, at very reasonable prices—at the **Big Y Café**, (509) 548-4012, on the main highway between Cashmere and Leavenworth. If you're traveling during the harvest season, after leaving Leavenworth and turning onto U.S. 97, keep your eyes peeled for **Mom's First and Frank's Last Stand**, which has the edge over the area's many other fruit stands because of the home-baked fruit pies Mom sells there.

LODGING

For low-priced standard motel accommodations in apple country, your best bet is Wenatchee, where motels line north Wenatchee Avenue. Try the 3-story, 108-room **Orchard Inn**, 720 North Wenatchee Avenue, (509) 663-7161, which has a swimming pool and spa. The rooms are recently refurbished in soft hues and floral patterns, and some have microwaves, refrigerators, and bathtubs. Rates start at $53 in the summer, slightly lower off-season.

The **Cashmere Country Inn**, 5801 Pioneer Avenue, Cashmere, (509) 782-4212, is a four-room (two with shared bath) bed and breakfast in a nineteenth-century farmhouse. Rates are in the $60 range.

In Leavenworth, the **Run of the River Bed & Breakfast**, 9308 East Leavenworth Road, (509) 548-7171 or (800) 288-6491, has six rooms and suites in a modern log lodge. Situated on a wooded river bank surrounded by wildflower meadows and mountain peaks a mile out of town, this outdoors-oriented bed and breakfast provides such amenities as binoculars in your room for birdwatching and complimentary mountain bikes. There is a two-night minimum stay on weekends. Rates start at $90.

If you want to immerse yourself in Leavenworth's Bavarian ambience, a good bed and breakfast pick is **Pension Anna**, 926 Commercial

APPLE COUNTRY

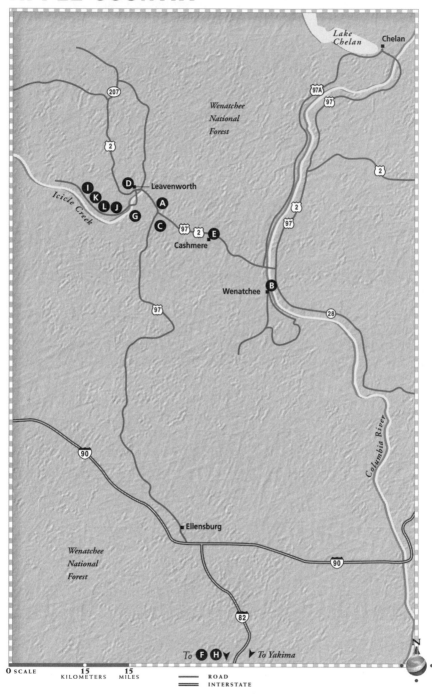

Food

Ⓐ Big Y Café

Ⓑ John Horan House

Ⓒ Mom's First and Frank's Last Stand

Ⓓ Reiner's Gasthaus

Lodging

Ⓔ Cashmere Country Inn

Ⓕ Cavenaugh's at Yakima Center

Ⓑ Orchard Inn

Ⓓ Pension Anna

Ⓖ Run of the River Bed & Breakfast

Ⓗ Toppenish Inn

Camping

Ⓘ Chatter Creek Campground

Ⓙ Eight Mile Campground

Ⓚ Ida Creek Campground

Ⓛ Johnny Creek Campground

Note: Items with the same letter are located in the same town or area.

Street, (509) 548-6273, a country-style 15-room inn furnished and decorated with family heirlooms from Austria. Rates start at $75.

CAMPING

There is a series of national forest campgrounds outside of Leavenworth in the Icicle Valley. **Eight Mile Campground, Johnny Creek Campground, Ida Creek Campground,** and **Chatter Creek Campground** have a total of 132 tent and RV sites without hookups. Fees are $5 a night.

13

MOUNT RAINIER

M ount Rainier is close enough to Seattle that on a clear day
Seattlites can see the volcano in all its icy, solitary splendor from
downtown. But they don't get the magnificent view of the mountain
that you will if you enter Mount Rainier National Park by way of the
less-used east entrance, heading from the Leavenworth area to the wet
side of the Cascades.

Established in 1899 as the United States' fifth national park,
Mount Rainier National Park encompasses the whole mountain. One
mountain may not sound like much, especially if you've spent the last
few days in the Cascades, but Mount Rainier is no ordinary mountain.
Rising 14,410 feet above sea level, Mount Rainier is the tallest of the
great Cascade Range volcanoes—3,600 feet taller than Mount Baker,
3,200 feet taller than Mount Hood, and 7,000 feet higher than Mount
St. Helens. Not only is Mount Rainier taller, but because it stands
away from the main part of the mountain range and rises more than 2
miles high from just 1,760 feet above sea level, its forested base spreads
across an area of almost 400 square miles. There are road entrances at
all four corners of the park, but to circle the mountain and view it from
every side would involve more than 150 miles of mountain driving.
The hiking trail around the central cone is 93 miles long and takes
more than a week. ◨

MOUNT RAINIER

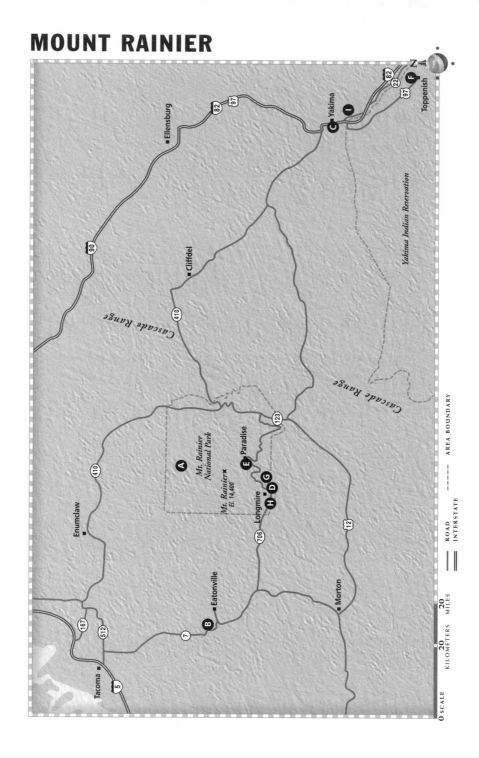

Sightseeing Highlights

Ⓐ Mount Rainier National Park

Ⓑ Northwest Trek

Food

Ⓒ Gasperetti's

Ⓓ Longmire Country Store

Ⓔ Paradise Inn

Ⓒ Santiago's

Ⓕ Yakima Indian Nation Cultural Heritage Center

Lodging

Ⓒ Cavenaugh's at Yakima Center

Ⓓ National Park Inn

Ⓔ Paradise Inn

Ⓕ Toppenish Inn

Camping

Ⓖ Cougar Rock Campground

Ⓗ Sunshine Point Campground

Ⓘ Yakima Sportsman State Park

Note: Items with the same letter are located in the same town or area.

A PERFECT DAY AT MOUNT RAINIER

If you spent the night in the Leavenworth area, leave by mid-morning and you'll arrive at Mount Rainier National Park in early afternoon. (Leave two hours earlier if you plan to take a side trip to the Yakima Indian Cultural Center, 15 miles south of Yakima.)

To drive from Leavenworth to Mount Rainier National Park, backtrack 4 miles from Leavenworth to where U.S. 97 turns south, and take that turn. Highway 97 climbs over the Wenatchee Mountains and descends to Ellensburg on the other side, a 51-mile trip. At Ellensburg, get on Interstate 90 eastbound and drive to the second exit, Interstate 82 southbound. It's 31 miles on I-82 to Yakima. If you wish to visit the Yakima Indian Cultural Center in Toppenish, take four-lane U.S. 97, which parallels I-82, south for 15 miles and, after visiting the center, return by the same route to Yakima.

From Yakima, follow U.S. 12 west for 18 miles to where Highway 410 forks off to the north. From there, it is 51 miles on Highway 410 through Mount Baker-Snoqualmie National Forest to the eastern boundary of Mount Rainier National Park at Cayuse Pass. An hour's drive through the most spectacular scenery in the Pacific Northwest lies between you and Paradise, where the main park lodge is located. Plan to arrive in time for a late afternoon walk on the side of Mount Rainier, with the promise of more to come in the morning.

SIGHTSEEING HIGHLIGHTS

✮✮✮ **Mount Rainier National Park**—Indians called this mountain *Tahoma*, meaning "the mountain that is God." Mount Rainier is not dead but sleeping. It feels peaceful and timeless but smolders with hidden power. Steam hisses from fumaroles high on the glacier-clad cone, where stranded climbers have survived by huddling around the steam vents for warmth.

The main visitor facilities in the park—an inn, an endless parking lot, and a huge visitor's center with historical and natural history exhibits, an always busy cafeteria, and a warm viewing area where you can look out at the mountain's glaciers and meadows through giant windows—are located at **Paradise**, 5,400 feet above sea level on the south face of the mountain. The visitor's center and surrounding area are crowded virtually all the time. Foot trails cross and climb every side of Mount Rainier, but only Paradise lets you start hiking so high up the mountainside.

If you enter the park from the east at Chinook Pass, take time for a side trip north to the White River park entrance, where a winding road leads to the **Sunrise Visitors Center**. Higher than Paradise at an elevation of 6,600 feet, Sunshine has less tourist traffic and an even more awe-inspiring view of Mount Rainier. It is especially impressive in the morning; unfortunately, there's nowhere to spend the night anywhere near it.

Heading south from Chinook Pass, you pay the park fee at the Stevens Canyon entrance, near the **Ohanapecosh Visitor Center**, which has exhibits on ancient forest diversity and tree and plant identification, as well as a 1½-mile interpretive trail that leads among thousand-year-old trees to a secluded hot spring. From there, heading west toward the turnoff to Paradise, the park road crosses the Cowlitz Divide and follows Stevens Canyon toward Mount Rainier itself, an area of deep forests and waterfalls with scenic stops at Reflection Lake and Box Canyon. (The Stevens Canyon road is closed during the winter months.)

Continuing west on the main park road past the turnoff to Paradise, you'll come to **Longmire**, built in the 1880s and 1990s by homesteader James Longmire, who hoped to develop a hot-springs spa at the site. The Longmire Museum has historical exhibits about human exploration and development of Mount Rainier, from early Indian times to the present day.

Geologists predict that the volcano will erupt again—but probably not today. The bigger worry is mudflows, which can happen when the snowcap suddenly melts from the volcanic heat or heavy rain. Near Longmire, you'll see the aftermath of the 1947 Kautz Creek mudflow, which was up to 50 feet deep. About 5,800 years ago (only an eye blink in geologic time), such a mudflow buried the site of present-day Enumclaw 70 feet deep and reached almost as far as the suburbs of Tacoma.

Admission to Mount Rainier National Park is $5 per vehicle. There is no additional charge at visitor's centers or museums. Hours: Paradise Visitor Center is open daily from 9:00 a.m. to 7:00 p.m. in the summer months, 9:00 a.m. to 6:00 p.m. daily in May, September, and October, and weekends only from 10:00 a.m. to 5:00 p.m. the rest of the year. The Sunrise and Ohanapecosh visitor's centers are open daily from 9:00 a.m. to 6:00 p.m. July through mid-September only. The Longmire Museum is open daily from 9:00 a.m. to 5:00 p.m. during the summer months, weekends only from 9:00 a.m. to 4:30 p.m. the rest of the year. Phone: (360) 569-2211. (full day)

✸✸✸ **Northwest Trek**—If you drive to Mount Rainier from Seattle, this place located near the town of Eatonville is right on your route. If you're following this book chapter by chapter, you can visit Northwest Trek on a short detour off the route between Mount Rainier and Mount St. Helens. Animal lovers and anyone traveling with children will want to allow several extra hours in their itinerary to visit this outstanding wildlife park. A division of Tacoma's Metropolitan Park District, it offers a close-up look at native Northwestern wildlife roaming free in 435 acres of meadows and forest. A 45-minute tram tour runs hourly through the park. Sit on the left-hand side for the best view of mountain goats, bighorn sheep, bison, Roosevelt elk, caribou, and, if you're lucky, a moose. See predators such as bears, wolves, mountain lions, and eagles in their separate enclosures while you're waiting for the tour.

Northwest Trek's most numerous residents, Pennsylvania wild turkeys, are not native to this region. They were brought here by state government as a pilot project to see whether they could be introduced in the wilds of Washington as a game bird. They flourished and practically overran the park. With the decision to set their turkeys free in other areas, the park staff drew media snickers because they couldn't catch the birds. The final solution was alcohol-spiked grain, on the theory that turkeys are easier to catch when they're drunk. It worked, and you stand a good chance of seeing the immigrant fowl elsewhere in western Washington during this tour.

Admission is $7.75 for adults, $6.75 for senior citizens, $5.25 for students ages 5 to 17, and $3.25 for children ages 3 and 4. Hours: Opens at 9:30 a.m. daily from mid-February through October 31, Friday through Sunday only the rest of the year. Closing times vary. Phone: (360) 832-6117 or (800) 433-8735 (Washington and Oregon only). (3 hours)

FITNESS AND RECREATION

Hiking to the summit of Mount Rainier takes three days. Climbers need ice-climbing gear and an experienced guide on the steep glacier slopes. (Guided summit climbs and instruction can be arranged through Rainier Mountaineering Inc., 201 St. Helens, Tacoma, WA 98402, 360-627-6242.)

Independent backpackers can hike *around* Mount Rainier on the 93-mile **Wonderland Trail**. Starting from Longmire, the trail leads through every life zone from ancient forests of 250-foot-tall trees to alpine meadows and glaciers. The hike around the mountain is both longer and more strenuous than the climb to the top; the changes in elevation along this trail total the equivalent of climbing and descending 20,000 feet.

There are day hikes up the mountainside from Paradise for everyone from the intrepid to those who consider mountaineering a spectator sport. Easiest are the 1¼-mile **Nisqually Vista Trail**, commanding a view of the full length of Nisqually Glacier, and the 1½-mile **Alta Vista Trail**, through meadows of wildflowers to views of the Paradise River and distant snowcapped volcanoes to the south (Mount St. Helens and Mount Adams). Each of these walks begins at the visitor's center and takes about an hour. The most ambitious and rewarding day hike from Paradise is the 6-mile, five-hour **Ice Caves Trail**. It leads from the visitor's center to the foot of Paradise Glaciers, where the summer melt flows in rivers under the ice, hollowing out caves big enough to walk into. For information on these and other hikes on Mount Rainier's 300 miles of foot trails, talk to the ranger at the hikers' desk in the visitor's center.

Paradise receives a 30-foot snow accumulation in the winter, and snow stays on the ground until June. It's an equally popular playground all year. In the snowy months, cross-country skis and snowshoes are available for rental at the Ski Shop near the National Park Inn at Longmire, between Paradise and the west entrance gate.

FOOD

In Yakima, **Gasperetti's** at 1013 North First Street, (509) 248-0628, is probably the best Italian restaurant on the dry side of the Cascades. Similarly, **Santiago's** at 111 East Yakima Avenue, (509) 453-1644, may be the best Mexican restaurant. I heartily recommend the restaurant at the **Yakima Indian Nation Cultural Heritage Center** in Toppenish, where entrées include the best buffalo burgers in the Northwest.

In Mount Rainier National Park, the **Longmire Country Store** beside the National Park Inn has a limited selection of picnic items, but campers would be wise to stock up on groceries in Leavenworth or Yakima.

The dining room at **Paradise Inn** serves breakfast from 7:00 to 9:00 a.m., lunch from 12:00 noon to 2:00 p.m., and dinner from 5:30 to 8:00 p.m. Sunday brunch hours are 11:00 a.m. to 2:30 p.m., during the months when the inn is open. (See "Lodging," below.) Food service is also available at the National Park Inn at Longmire, as well as at the huge cafeteria in the Paradise Visitors Center (May through September and weekends in April and October), which can be crowded enough to keep you waiting an hour in line for a Coke.

LODGING

Accommodations in Yakima tend to be business-oriented motor inns, such as the 152-room **Cavenaugh's at Yakima Center**, 607 East Yakima Avenue, (509) 248-5900, a conference center with large, modern rooms, many with private balconies. Rates start at $67 a night. A budget alternative that is convenient to the Yakima Indian Cultural Center is the **Toppenish Inn**, 515 South Elm Street, (509) 865-7444, in the Indian town of Toppenish south of Yakima.

Paradise Inn, a historic 1917 lodge with massive stone fireplaces in the lobby, rents rooms at surprisingly reasonable rates: single or double for $90 with a private bath, $60 with a shared bath. The catch is that you need to make reservations far in advance. Prepayment for one night's lodgings is required to guarantee your reservation; then they'll send you a confirmation. (Hint: cancellations often make rooms available at the last minute. If you don't have a reservation, ask at the desk when you arrive at Paradise, and again around 4:00 p.m.) Paradise Inn only operates from the last week of May through the last week of September. Partway up the road to Paradise, at Longmire, is the smaller, cozier, recently renovated, and still rustic National Park Inn. Rates are a few dollars lower than at Paradise Inn. The reservation address is the same as for Paradise Inn. For information and reservations at either inn, call or write Mount Rainier Guest Services, P.O. Box 108, Ashford, WA 98304, (360) 569-2275.

CAMPING

Near Yakima, you'll find a lakeside campground with electric, water, and sewer hookups at Yakima Sportsman State Park. Fees range from $7.50 to $10.50.

The top campground choice in Mount Rainier National Park is Cougar Rock Campground, 2½ miles north of Longmire. At an elevation of 3,180 feet, this 200-site campground is open from late May through mid-October. You can camp year-round at the 18-site Sunshine Point Campground a short distance past the Nisqually entrance gate. Both campgrounds operate on a first-come, first-served basis, and neither has hookups, though Cougar Rock has a central dumping station. Camping fees are $6 per night at Cougar Rock, $5 at Sunshine Point.

SIDE TRIP: YAKIMA INDIAN NATION

This detour from the main route is unquestionably worthwhile for travelers who are interested in the native cultures of the Northwest. One's first impression of the Yakima tribe from the most populated part of the reservation, the 15-mile strip of U.S. 97 between Yakima and Toppenish, is of total assimilation: the Yakima people's homes, cars, commercial districts, and apple orchards look pretty much like everybody else's in this part of the state. But the Yakimas' cultural center is one of the finest Indian centers anywhere. The main visitors' attraction is the Yakima Nation Museum, where exhibits include wildlife dioramas; a full-size winter house made entirely of tule grass mats, where several Indian families might have lived during the cold months; a copy of the tribe's handwritten treaty with the United States; and talking rocks. Notice the diorama that depicts tribal ancestors fishing the salmon run at Celilo Falls on the Columbia River. Photographs of Indians fishing at the falls in more modern times are common in gift shops and visitor's centers all along the Columbia. The falls themselves vanished forever in 1957 with the completion of The Dalles Dam. Besides the museum, the center has an extensive library on Native American subjects, a theater, and local handcrafts for sale. Admission to the museum is $2 per adult, $1 for children ages 5 to 18 and persons over the age of 54, with a maximum family rate of $10. Hours: Open daily from 9:00 a.m. to 6:00 p.m. June through September, 10:00 a.m. to 5:00 p.m. the rest of the year. Address: U.S. 97, Toppenish. Phone: (509) 865-2800. (1 hour)

YAKIMA INDIAN NATION

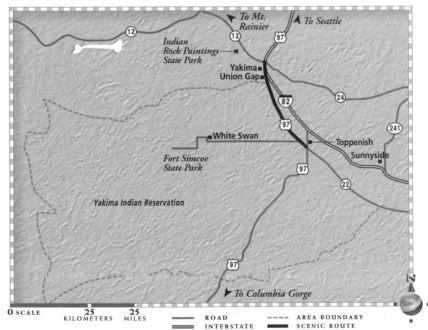

14
MOUNT ST. HELENS

In startling contrast to the glaciers and alpine meadows of Mount Rainier, Mount St. Helens' barren, blasted slopes are ample proof of the awesome power sleeping within the Cascade Mountains. While Mount Rainier is the tallest of the great volcanoes in the Cascade Range, Mount St. Helens attained equal fame on May 18, 1980, by becoming the shortest (8,365 feet). On that date, practically without warning, the mountain blew off 1,300 feet of its summit, sending up a 15-mile-high plume of rock, ash, and smoke that darkened the sky over much of eastern Washington and portions of Idaho and Montana, devastating 235 square miles of landscape on the east slope of the mountain and claiming 57 human lives along with 221 homes and 17 miles of railroad track. It presented television audiences across the nation with a staggering new image of nature's potential for sudden violence.

Today new life springs from the ash-enriched slopes. The most common vegetation is fireweed, which sets the slopes ablaze in brilliant magenta during the summer months. The once-bare mountainside is also painted seasonally with blue lupine, purple penstemon, and a host of other colorful flowers. Frogs and fish now live in most of the lakes and attract wading birds such as the great blue heron. Here and there, tiny new evergreen seedlings are beginning to sprout from the ashes. National monument status ensures that as the forests slowly return to the mountaintop over the next few generations, they and their animal inhabitants will be safe from lumberjacks' chainsaws forever. ◪

MOUNT ST. HELENS

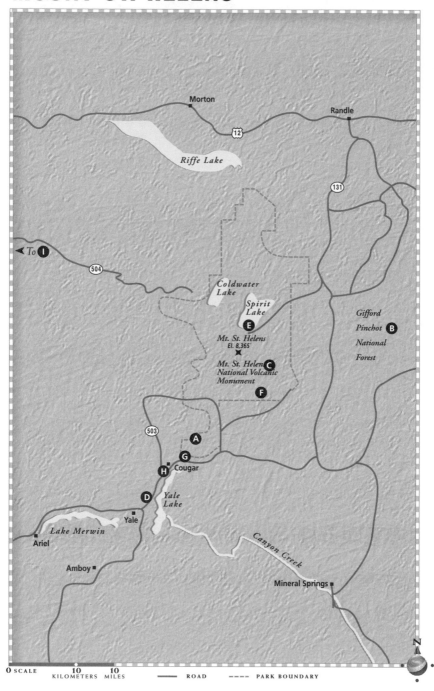

Sightseeing Highlights

Ⓐ Ape Cave Geological Site

Ⓑ Gifford Pinchot
National Forest

Ⓒ Mount St. Helens
National Volcanic Monument

Ⓓ Pine Creek Information Station

Ⓔ Spirit Lake

Ⓕ Windy Ridge

Food and Lodging

Ⓖ Lone Fir Resort

Ⓖ Monfort's Bed & Breakfast

Camping

Ⓖ National Forest
Campground at Cougar

Ⓗ National Forest
Campground at Merrill Lake

Ⓘ Seaquest State Park

Note: Items with the same letter are located in the same town or area.

A PERFECT DAY AT MOUNT ST. HELENS

A three-hour drive will take you from Mount Rainier to Mount St. Helens, a distance of 145 miles. From Paradise, return to the main park road and proceed east for about 15 scenic miles to the intersection with WA 123. Turn right (south), and in 6 more miles, just after leaving the national park, the road merges with U.S. 12. Continue south on U.S. 12 to the small town of Randle, a distance of 26 miles. Turn left (south) at Randle onto paved Forest Road 25. Follow FR 25 south for 20 miles to the junction with paved FR 99.

Depending on how early you left Mount Rainier, you have most of the afternoon to explore Mount St. Helens. FR 99 climbs for 17 steep miles to dead-end at Windy Ridge. Upon leaving Windy Ridge, go back downhill to FR 25 and turn right (south), driving 20 miles to the Pine Creek Information Station. Turn right (west) on WA 503 and proceed 18 more miles to Cougar. Forest roads to other areas of Mount St. Helens National Monument, including Lava Canyon and Ape Cave, leave FR 90 between the Pine Creek Information Station and Cougar.

Upon leaving Mount St. Helens, you can take Interstate 5 to Seattle (144 miles) or follow this Trip Planner south to Portland (57 miles).

SIGHTSEEING HIGHLIGHTS

✹✹✹ **Mount St. Helens National Volcanic Monument**—Formerly an out-of-the-way place with a handful of mountain cabins and small resort ranches, Mount St. Helens now attracts more than 2 million visitors a year. Before the blast, environmentalists had been fighting to save the forest around Mount St. Helens, legendary home of the Sasquatch ("Bigfoot"), from timber operations. In 1982, 110,330 acres of the **Gifford Pinchot National Forest** encompassing the volcano were set aside as Mount St. Helens National Monument. (The trees, of course, had been destroyed more thoroughly than if they had been clear-cut—burned, blown flat, and buried in tons of volcanic ash.)

The main road route around the east side of the mountain, which provides the best access to the blast area at **Windy Ridge**, has been paved. On Windy Ridge, the paved road dead-ends at the top ridgeline, where a long, steep stairway climbs to a hilltop that affords the best view of **Spirit Lake**, a thousand feet below. The lake was there before the eruption, a remote fishing area with a few summer cabins on its shores. After the blast, its surface rose 200 feet as huge amounts of volcanic ash filled it. Today much of the surface is covered with logjams of trees blown down by the eruptions. Forest Road 83, which leaves FR 90 midway between the **Pine Creek Information Station** and Cougar on the south side of the mountain, affords access to a network of unpaved roads and foot trails on the south side of the mountain. **Ape Cave Geological Site**, reached from a turn-off 2 miles up this road, is the longest lava tube in North America—12,810 feet long. It was formed during volcanic activity about 2,000 years ago. Contrary to what you might think, the cave was not named for the Sasquatch that some people claim to have seen in this area, but for the St. Helens Apes, a local hiking club that discovered the cave in the 1940s. (*They* were named for the legendary Sasquatch.) If you want to explore the depths of the cave, wear warm clothes and bring a flashlight. Lights can be rented at the cave entrance during the summer season.

The roads around the south and east sides of Mount St. Helens are snowbound from October to late May or early June. You can get current road and hiking information from the Woods Creek Information Station south of Randle.

Admission to Mount St. Helens National Volcanic Monument is $5 per vehicle. Hours: The visitor's center is open daily from 9:00 a.m.

to 6:00 p.m. April through September, daily 9:00 a.m. to 5:00 p.m. the rest of the year. Phone: (360) 750-3902. (½-day)

Sightseeing flights over Mount St. Helens are available at general aviation airports at Silver Lake and Kelso-Longview. Expensive but worth every penny, the flights range from 30 to 90 minutes and cost from $40 to $100 per person. (1–2 hours)

FITNESS AND RECREATION

The shore of Spirit Lake can be reached by foot on **Harmony Trail**, a strenuous 1-mile hike that descends 600 feet to the lakeshore from the trailhead at Harmony Viewpoint on Windy Ridge Road. From another trailhead nearby, an easy ½-mile paved trail leads to **Meta Lake**, a little "island" of forest that was sheltered from the volcano's blast by a cliff and now provides an oasis of green in the midst of desolation.

The ultimate view of the Mount St. Helens blast area is from the unpaved, hikers- and mountain bikers-only trail that continues beyond the parking area at the top of **Windy Ridge**. The trail continues for 3 miles across the face of the crater, providing a constant view of the St. Helens summit from just 4½ miles away. At the end, it joins the **Boundary Trail**, which goes all the way around the volcano. It's a dry, sun-blasted hike—be sure to take water.

In the area of Ape Cave, several trails connect to the **Loowit Trail** around Mount St. Helens at approximately timberline (4,800 feet). At **Lava Canyon Recreation Area**, a trail leads ½-mile to a waterfall that plunges over an ancient lava flow, then continues another 2½ strenuous miles up a mudflow-scoured canyon, where it sometimes narrows and edges along steep cliffs.

FOOD AND LODGING

Since most visitors come to Mount St. Helens on day trips from Seattle and Portland, the lodging situation around the national monument has not kept pace with the area's burgeoning tourism. Roadside motels, fast-food places, and family restaurants can be found near most exits from Interstate 5. However, if you have not made reservations near Mount St. Helens, it's as easy to drive on into Portland as it is to search for a motel along the interstate.

In the small country community of Cougar, the **Lone Fir Resort** offers motel units and cabins—not luxurious but in a beautiful mountain setting, with rooms starting at $38 a night. The resort is small, so reservations are essential. Call (360) 238-5210. In a slightly higher price range, **Monfort's Bed & Breakfast** offers new, comfortable rooms and a full country breakfast. Call (360) 238-5229.

CAMPING

The public campground most convenient to Mount St. Helens is **Seaquest State Park,** across the road from the Mount St. Helens visitor's center, 5 miles east of the Castle Rock exit from I-5. Sites cost $7 a night, $2.50 more with full hookups. The park has nature trails and a beach on Silver Lake. There is no access to Mount St. Helens itself from this road. There are also small **national forest campgrounds** at **Cougar** and nearby **Merrill Lake.**

15
PORTLAND

O n first impression, Portland may seem like Seattle's kid sister. A little smaller (pop. 366,000), bordered by narrower bodies of water (the Columbia and Willamette Rivers), in the shadow of a somewhat smaller volcano (Mount Hood, 11,239 feet above sea level), Portland surpasses Seattle in at least two respects: first, it's older (founded in 1844, it was the departure point when Seattle's founding fathers started their journey north seven years later); and second, it receives more rainfall (37.6 inches a year).

The largest city in Oregon, Portland is also the third-largest U.S. shipping port on the West Coast and one of America's most beautiful cities. Its setting, on the banks of the Willamette River with Mount Hood and Mount St. Helens on the horizon, and the abundance of public and private rose gardens throughout the city, are among the factors that help make Portland visually stunning—at least on a clear day. Equally important is an environmentally aware city government, which has been a Portland tradition at least since 1905, when the mayor proposed demolishing the buildings on alternate blocks throughout the city and replacing them with shady parks and rose gardens. Although the idea never came to fruition, the sentiment is echoed in Portland's Park Blocks, a grassy 25-block-long promenade with fountains on the west side of downtown, and in Tom McCall Waterfront Park, also 25 blocks long, on the east side along the river. ◪

PORTLAND

Willamette River

BURNSIDE BRIDGE
MORRISON BRIDGE
HAWTHORNE BRIDGE
HAWTHORNE ST

To A

NW 2ND ST
NW 4TH AV
NW COUCH ST
SW FRONT AV
SW 3RD AV
SW 4TH AV
SW 5TH AV
BROADWAY
BURNSIDE ST
SW WASHINGTON ST
SW ALDER ST
MORRISON ST
YAMHILL ST
SALMON ST
MAIN ST
JEFFERSON ST
COLUMBIA ST
CLAY ST
MARKET ST
MADISON ST
HARBOR WAY
SW PARK AV
SW 9TH AV
South Park Blocks
SW 15TH AV
18TH AV
SW CANYON RD
SW VISTA AV
NW 23RD AV
TUNNEL
To C

0 SCALE
3 KILOMETERS
3 MILES

——— ROAD

‑ ‑ ‑ ‑ AREA BOUNDARY

Sightseeing Highlights

🅐 American Advertising Museum

🅑 Governor Tom McCall
Waterfront Park

🅒 International Rose
Test Garden

🅓 Oregon Art Institute

🅔 Pioneer Courthouse Square

🅕 Portland Building

🅖 *Portlandia*

🅓 Portland Museum of Art

🅖 *The Quest*

🅗 Skidmore/Old Town District

🅒 Washington Park

🅒 Washington Park Zoo

🅒 World Forestry Center

🅘 Yamhill District

Note: Items with the same letter are located in the same town or area.

A PERFECT DAY IN PORTLAND

For travelers who are following this Trip Planner step by step, I suggest a day-long "vacation from your vacation" to rest up, replenish your trip provisions, and explore Oregon's largest city before heading off on the second half of your Northwest trip, into the even more remote backcountry.

Downtown Portland is a fine place for a walking tour. An easy-to-find starting point is Governor Tom McCall Waterfront Park, then make your way through the Yamhill and Skidmore/Old Town Historic Districts, continuing west to the Park Blocks and the Oregon Art Institute before returning through the heart of downtown Portland. Later in the afternoon, drive or taxi to Washington Park to see Portland's pride and joy, the International Rose Test Garden.

SIGHTSEEING HIGHLIGHTS

✮✮ **American Advertising Museum**—Ads from early newspaper days to the TV era are immortalized in this unique, highly entertaining museum. Admission is $3, children ages 6 to 12, $1.50. Hours: Open Wednesday through Friday 11:00 a.m. to 5:00 p.m., Saturday and Sunday 12:00 noon to 5:00 p.m. Address: 600 NE Grand Avenue. Phone: (503) 230-1090. (1 hour)

✮✮ **Governor Tom McCall Waterfront Park**—The park is named for Oregon's environmentalist, antigrowth governor of the early 1970s, the late Tom McCall, who launched a publicity campaign inviting tourists to visit Washington, Idaho, Montana—any place but Oregon. The park runs along the banks of the Willamette River for 25 blocks, the entire eastern edge of downtown. Near the south end of the park is the Visitors Information Center pavilion. Stop there for walking tour brochures of the Yamhill and Skidmore/Old Town historic districts, as well as information on performing arts and other entertainment. (½ hour)

✮✮ **Portland Museum of Art**—From downtown, head west to Broadway, then south (left) to Salmon Street. At the corner, under the Jackson Tower Clock decorated with flags and lights, turn right and go 1 block to the north end of the Park Blocks (also called "the Boulevard"). The blocks were an experiment by a turn-of-the-century mayor who had proposed demolishing the buildings on alternating blocks throughout the city to create a checkerboard of open-space "park blocks" like these. (½ hour)

Three blocks south of the walkway is the Oregon Art Institute. Located inside, the Portland Museum of Art has exhibits that include exceptional collections of Oriental and Pacific Northwest Indian art. Admission is $4.50 for adults, $3.50 for seniors, $2.50 for students age 6 and up. No admission fee is charged on the first Thursday of the month after 4:00 p.m. Hours: Open Tuesday through Saturday from 11:00 a.m. to 5:00 p.m. and Sunday from 1:00 to 5:00 p.m., as well as 5:00 to 9:00 p.m. on the first Thursday of each month. Address: 1219 SW Park Avenue. Phone: (503) 226-2811. (2 hours)

✮✮ **Skidmore/Old Town District**—A 7-block walk north through the waterfront park brings you to the Skidmore/Old Town District, where historic buildings similar in style to those in the Yamhill District are scattered between Pine and Davis Streets within 3 blocks of the river. The Skidmore Fountain, on Ankeny Street 1 block from the waterfront past Ankeny Park and Arcade, is a well-known Portland landmark. This 1888 bronze and granite masterpiece was the first of Portland's famous fountains, which now seem to be everywhere. Across the railroad tracks from the Skidmore Fountain is the thoroughly gentrified New Market Block. Formerly the New Market Theater, it was a 1,200-seat center for the city's performing arts—on the second floor of a farmers' market! Also of interest in the Skidmore/Old Town District is the old Erickson's Saloon, where sailors and sophisticates used to rub elbows along a 684-foot bar before Prohibition shut it down.

If you're visiting Portland on the weekend, don't miss the Saturday Market under the Burnside Bridge, a block north of Ankeny Park and the Skidmore Fountain. It's the city's liveliest assemblage of artists, craftspeople, and street musicians. Hours: 10:00 a.m. to 5:00 p.m. Saturday and 11:00 a.m. to 4:30 p.m. Sunday. (½ hour)

★★ **Yamhill District**—Stroll Portland's original commercial area, a 6-square-block area beginning 2 blocks north of the visitor's center, along Taylor, Yamhill, and Morrison Streets between Front and Third Avenues. The Yamhill District's buildings, with their unusual wrought-iron facades, had deteriorated sadly before restoration began in the late 1970s and chic retail establishments moved in. The centerpiece of the district is Yamhill Marketplace, a 1982 building designed to be compatible with the surrounding historic architecture, where a produce market coexists with upscale restaurants, shops, and art galleries. (½ hour)

As you pass the 900 block of Fifth Avenue, you can't help but notice the white marble sculpture entitled *The Quest*, which residents have nicknamed "Three Groins in the Fountain." Controversial public art and architecture have come to characterize Portland in recent years, and several of the best (or worst) examples can be found around **Pioneer Courthouse Square**, to your right, bordered by Sixth Avenue, Broadway, Morrison, and Yamhill. Amid the wrought-iron gates and fences, neoclassical columns (including an intentionally collapsed column with a chessboard on top), and purple-tiled waterfall, 48,000 bricks bear the names of donors who helped make it all possible. The adjoining transit mall between Fifth and Sixth Avenues is a people watcher's paradise. The ultimate offbeat building downtown (or, for that matter, anywhere) is the **Portland Building** at 1120 SW Fifth Avenue.

Designed by Michael Graves, billed as "the first major postmodern structure erected in the United States," it's pink, yellow, blue, and bizarre. On the Fifth Avenue side of the Portland Building is the kneeling statue of *Portlandia*, the largest hammered copper sculpture erected since the Statue of Liberty. (1 hour)

★ **Washington Park**—Portland is famed for its roses, and while they grow in most city parks as well as private yards throughout the city, one of the world's finest rose gardens is the **International Rose Test Garden** in Washington Park, about 2 miles west of downtown off Burnside Road, where over 400 varieties have been cultivated continuously since 1917. Admission is free. Hours: Open at all times during daylight hours. Phone: (503) 823-2223. (½ hour)

Also in the park, the **Washington Park Zoo** replicates animal habitats from all over the globe. The newest exhibit area, a rain forest exhibit that seems to fit right in with the soggy Portland climate, houses pythons, crocodiles, and bats from the Congo. Nearby, antelopes and zebras roam the African veldt. There's even an Arctic exhibit with musk oxen and grizzly bears, and another where penguins cavort around a reproduction of the rocky cliffs of Tierra del Fuego, the tip of South America. This zoo boasts the world's largest captive breeding program for Asian elephants, and most people will never have another chance to see as many elephants at one time. The zoo also has the largest chimpanzee population in the United States. Admission is $5.50 for adults, $4 for children under 12 and seniors over 65. Hours: Open daily from 9:30 a.m. with variable closing hours; weekends only in winter. Address: 4001 SW Canyon Road. Phone: (503) 226-7627. (2 hours)

Next to the zoo is the **World Forestry Center**, where you'll learn everything you may ever want to know about the lumber industry (a looming presence in any Pacific Northwest tour) from exhibits that include a 70-foot talking tree. Admission is $3 for adults, $2 for children ages 6 to 18 and seniors over 65. Hours: Open daily 10:00 a.m. to 5:00 p.m. Address: 4003 SW Canyon Road. Phone: (503) 228-1368. (½ hour)

FITNESS AND RECREATION

The best hiking in the Portland area is west of the city in the Columbia Gorge (see the next chapter). Also on the west side is **Forest Park**, the largest city park in the United States with 5,000 acres of wooded land and more than 50 miles of hiking and biking trails. The main park trail is the 24-mile **Wildwood Trail**.

Both hikers and bikers use the extensive trail network on **Sauvie Island**, a 12,000-acre wildlife refuge 10 miles west of Portland. Bike rentals are available at **Agape Cycle and Sports**, 2610 SE Clinton Street, (503) 230-0317.

FOOD

Perhaps downtown Portland's most popular restaurant (at least the most often recommended) is **Jake's Famous Crawfish** at 401 South 12th. Jake's has been serving local crawfish since 1892 and also offers a large selection of other seafood specialties. Open Monday through Saturday for lunch and dinner, Sunday for dinner only. Prices are moderate. Call (503) 226-1419.

For Japanese cuisine in Portland, try **Zen**, 910 SW Salmon, open Monday through Friday for lunch and Monday through Saturday for dinner, (503) 222-3056; or the popular sushi bar at **Bush Garden**, 900 SW Morrison, open Monday through Friday for lunch and daily for dinner, (503) 226-7181.

Inexpensive and unusual are **Chang's Mongolian Grill**, 1 SW Third, open daily for lunch and dinner, (503) 243-1991; **Saigon Express** (Vietnamese), 309 West Burnside, open Monday for lunch and dinner, (503) 227-7499; and **Alexis** (Greek), 215 West Burnside, open Monday through Friday for lunch and dinner, Saturday and Sunday for dinner only, (503) 224-8577. For a good, really low-priced breakfast or lunch downtown (breakfast served all day), stop at the **Bijou Café**, 132 SW Third Avenue, open for breakfast and lunch, (503) 222-3187.

LODGING

The perfect location in downtown Portland is the **Riverside Inn** at Morrison and Front Avenue, facing Governor Tom McCall Waterfront Park on the edge of Old Town. Rates are in the $72 to $87 range. For reservations, call (503) 221-0711, toll-free (800) 648-6440.

The longtime lap of luxury in downtown Portland is the **Heathman Hotel**, a National Historic Landmark at SW Broadway and Salmon Street, next door to the Center for the Performing Arts and a short stroll from the art museum. This hotel has everything—24-hour concierge service; a video library; a grand piano and fireplace in the

PORTLAND

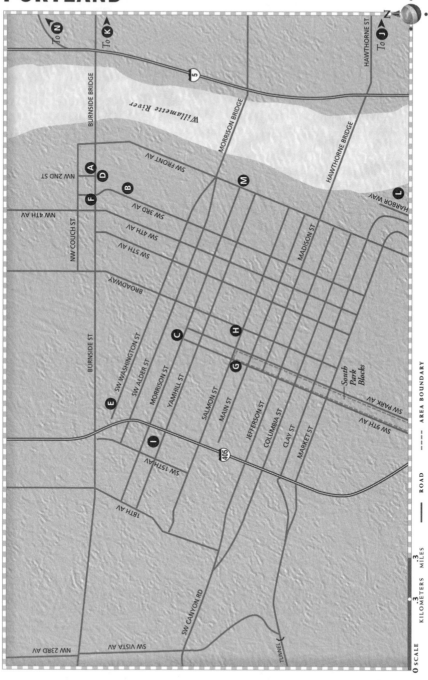

Food

A Alexis

B Bijou Café

C Bush Garden

D Chang's Mongolian Grill

E Jake's Famous Crawfish

F Saigon Express

G Zen

Lodging

H Heathman Hotel

I Mallory Hotel

J Portland International Hostel

K Portland's White House

L RiverPlace Hotel

M Riverside Inn

Camping

N Ainsworth State Park

lobby; guest rooms furnished in Ming, Regency, or Biedermeier style; and one of Portland's finest restaurants. Rates start at $175 double. For reservations, call (503) 241-4100 or (800) 551-0011 nationwide.

For more contemporary upscale accommodations, the place to go is the **RiverPlace Hotel**, a modern luxury hotel with rooms overlooking the waterfront promenade, 1510 SW Harbor Way, (503) 228-3233. Room rates start at $175 a night.

More affordable elegance is to be found at **Portland's White House**, a bed and breakfast across the river at 1914 NE 22nd Avenue, (503) 287-7131. This restored turn-of-the-century mansion has Greek columns, a circular driveway with a fountain, and an uncanny resemblance to the President's house in Washington. Surprisingly reasonable rates, in the $80 range, include a gourmet breakfast. There are only six guest rooms, so make reservations well in advance.

Close to downtown and in a lower price range, the **Mallory Hotel** at SW 15th and Yamhill offers rooms starting at $65 a night. Call (503) 226-2970, toll-free (800) 228-8657.

Portland International Hostel, 3031 SE Hawthorne Boulevard, provides easy access to downtown on the #14 Tri-Met bus line. Dormitory beds cost under $10 for AYH members. Desk hours are 8:00 to 9:30 a.m.; 5:00 to 10:00 p.m. Reservations are a good idea. Call (503) 236-3380.

CAMPING

The best public campground in the Portland area is **Ainsworth State Park** at the western end of the Columbia Gorge Scenic Highway. There are 63 campsites, all but five with full hookups. Camping fees are $10 during the summer season, $7 off-season. The park also has a trailhead for a portion of the Columbia Gorge Trail.

NIGHTLIFE

Portland's top comedy club is **The Last Laugh Comedy Club** at 426 NW Sixth Avenue, (503) 295-2844, serving up nationally known comedy acts along with dinner and cocktails nightly. Prices are reasonable. Other intriguing clubs include the tropical-style **Key Largo** at 31 NW First Avenue, (503) 223-9919 and the nearby **Starry Night**, 8 NW Sixth Avenue. Downtown art galleries are open late on the first Thursday of each month, and many host wine-and-cheese artist receptions.

16

COLUMBIA GORGE

U.S. Army Captains Meriwether Lewis and William Clark were commissioned by Thomas Jefferson to explore the newly purchased Louisiana Territory. Starting near St. Louis on May 14, 1804, they traveled across what would become Missouri, Iowa, Nebraska, South and North Dakota, Montana, Idaho, and eastern Washington before reaching the Columbia River in October 1805. They found the Pacific Ocean a month later and started back the following spring. Their 8,000-mile round-trip took 861 days. Today history buffs can find historical markers commemorating Lewis and Clark's progress at Horsethief Lake State Park, The Dalles, Beacon Rock State Park, and Lewis and Clark State Park, as well as exhibits on the expedition at the Bonneville Dam visitor's center. More Lewis and Clark memorabilia are at the High Desert Museum near Bend and at Ecola State Park, Seaside, Fort Clatsop, and Fort Canby.

The Columbia River Gorge is also filled with reminders of a more recent, less familiar historical figure—Sam Hill. A pioneer at reproducing classic Old World architecture in concrete, Hill created Maryhill and Stonehenge on the Washington side of the river 100 miles east of Portland. He also envisioned and built the first highway up the Columbia Gorge. Today part of his original road has been preserved as the Columbia Gorge Scenic Highway. Sam wanted to build his road on the Washington side but couldn't convince state congressmen that the idea had merit. That's why all the traffic is on the Oregon side of the river today; for a more relaxing trip, switch to the Washington side at the first opportunity. ◣

COLUMBIA GORGE

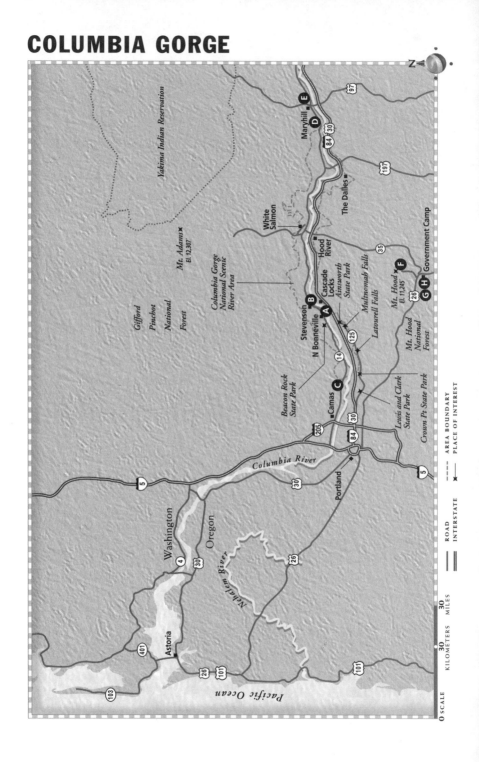

Sightseeing Highlights

Ⓐ Bonneville Dam

Ⓑ Bridge of the Gods

Ⓒ Lewis and Clark Trail

Ⓓ Maryhill Art Museum

Ⓔ Stonehenge

Food and Lodging

Ⓓ Maryhill Art Museum

Ⓕ Timberline Lodge

Note: Items with the same letter are located in the same town or area.

Camping

Ⓖ Still Creek Campground

Ⓗ Trillium Lake Campground

A PERFECT DAY ALONG THE COLUMBIA RIVER

From Portland, follow Interstate 84 (which meets I-5 just across the river from downtown) east for 16 miles to the second Troutdale exit. This is the beginning of the Columbia Gorge Scenic Highway. Several scenic stops and 22 relaxing miles later, you'll rejoin the interstate. Just 5 miles on, you'll come to Bonneville Dam (exit 40).

Four miles east of the dam, at Cascade Locks, cross the river into Washington on the Bridge of the Gods. Washington State Highway 14, slower but quieter, follows the north bank of the Columbia River for 60 miles to Maryhill. It is known as the Lewis and Clark Trail.

After visiting Maryhill, cross the river back into Oregon and take Interstate 84 west for 40 fast miles to Hood River. Turn south there on Highway 35 and drive 47 miles, climbing along the west side of Mount Hood, to Government Camp and Timberline Lodge.

SIGHTSEEING HIGHLIGHTS

★★ **Bonneville Dam**—The dam, built between 1933 and 1937 at a cost of nearly $89 million, impounds a 48-mile-long reservoir on the Columbia and produces 1,084,900 kilowatts of electricity. You can ride an elevator down to see the hydropower generators. The five-level Bradford Island Visitor Center in the middle of the dam is the largest visitor's center on the river. Even if the dam itself holds no interest for you, other exhibits here will. They range from ancient Indian rock effigies and Lewis and Clark memorabilia to underwater fish-viewing windows. Admission is free. Hours: This visitor's center, as well as a second, smaller one on the Washington shore, is open daily from 8:00 a.m. to 6:00 p.m. Memorial Day to July 3, 8:00 a.m. to 8:00 p.m. July 4 to Labor Day, and 9:00 a.m. to 5:00 p.m. the rest of the year. Phone: (541) 374-8820.

Also of interest during your Bonneville Dam visit are the methods they've devised to let both people and fish travel the river despite the massive wall of concrete. Watch the operation of the navigation locks that allow barges and other craft, as well as log floats, through the dam. When salmon are running, the sight of myriad fish climbing over the dam on the four fish ladders (pools arranged like staircases to let the fish leap from one to the next) attracts hordes of spectators. Steelhead run from July through October; chinook have three separate runs between mid-April and October. Between 700,000 and 1 million adult fish climb the ladders each year as they travel upriver to spawn and die. From 30 million to 50 million young fish travel down the fish ladders each year on their journey to the ocean. Besides being tourist attractions, the fish ladders and fish counters are vital parts of a 1980 federal plan to halt and reverse the massive depletion of salmon caused by this and other dams in previous decades. The same plan is likely to halt at least 200 proposed hydroelectric projects in the Northwest. (1 hour)

★★ **Maryhill Museum of Art**—This classically French, concrete château in the middle of nowhere, where peacocks stroll on acres of landscaped lawn amid barren hills overlooking the Columbia River, was the creation of turn-of-the-century visionary capitalist Sam Hill (as in, "What in the name of Sam Hill is he up to now?"). Hill was an assistant to railroad baron James J. Hill—no relation until Sam married James' daughter, Mary Hill, for whom the estate was named. Sam bought

7,000 acres here with plans to start a town. In 1914, he began building this mansion to preside over the new community, but when his real estate scheme collapsed, Sam lost interest in his unfinished home.

Sam traveled to Europe 50 times selling railroad bonds to royalty. During these trips he befriended Loie Fuller, the Chicago-born Folies Bergere star and pioneer of modern dance. Loie convinced Sam that he should turn his white-elephant mansion into an art museum. She sold Sam a large number of works by her friend Auguste Rodin (often called the greatest sculptor since Michelangelo), while Sam prevailed on his friend, Queen Marie of Romania, to travel to the high desert of southern Washington to dedicate the museum.

Maryhill Museum displays the results of this unlikely quartet's efforts in three floors of well-focused and fascinating exhibits that would do credit to any art museum, anywhere. Rodin bronzes and plasters (including a study for his familiar *The Thinker*) fill most of the upper floor, while the ground-floor main hall contains the Romanian royal furniture and memorabilia. Other galleries feature Sam's excellent Indian basketry collection, chess sets from around the world, and an array of small, powerful paintings and prints that depict the destruction of Europe in World War I. Admission is $4 for adults, $3.50 for seniors, $1.50 for students ages 6 to 16, children age 5 and under free. Hours: Open daily from March 15 through November 15, 9:00 a.m. to 5:00 p.m. Phone: (509) 773-3733. (2 hours)

As a pioneer road builder, Sam Hill loved concrete. And the horrifying World War I paintings on the lower level of his art museum attest that he also hated war. The two passions united in this huge, strange artifact—a full-sized exact replica of **Stonehenge**, constructed entirely of cast concrete, which sits on a hilltop overlooking the Columbia River as a memorial to the World War I dead of Klickitat County. Hill's tomb is here. The road up to Stonehenge starts right next to the campground entrance at Maryhill State Park. (½ hour)

✦ **Bridge of the Gods**—This toll bridge takes its name from an Indian legend that says a vast natural bridge, built by gods, once spanned the river (though not at this site). If true, it was by far the largest natural bridge on earth. As the story goes, the legendary bridge collapsed to create Celilo Falls, the falls depicted in the salmon-fishing diorama at the Yakima Nation Museum; you can see photographs and postcards of Indians fishing there at any gift shop along the Columbia. Don't look for the falls themselves, though. Like the original Bridge of the Gods, they have vanished forever into legend, flooded by the completion of The Dalles Dam in 1957. The toll is 50 cents; towed vehicles, 25 cents per axle.

✩ **Lewis and Clark Trail**—Washington State Highway 14, along the north bank of the Columbia River, is known as the Lewis and Clark Trail. While the explorers traveled down the Columbia in dugout canoes, paddling back upstream proved such hard work that they traded their canoes to Indians at The Dalles for horses and rode up the route this road follows today. (3 hours)

FITNESS AND RECREATION

Justly famous and next door to Portland, the waterfalls along the Columbia Gorge Scenic Highway can be crowded beyond belief in July and August, as well as on any weekend when the weather is fair. Here's a secret for escaping the mob: hike. A trail parallels the highway, a few hundred feet uphill where it's peaceful and quiet. For a fine two- to three-hour hike, park at Horsetail Falls and clamber up the short, steep trail to the top of the falls, where you'll join the main gorge trail. Cross the creek and hike west, skirting the rim of Oneonta Gorge, and continue until you reach Multnomah Falls. Descend there and walk back up the road to where you parked. The trail is a little more than 3 miles long, and the road distance back from Multnomah Falls to Horsetail Falls is 2½ miles. If you want a longer hike, deeper into the dense wilderness above the gorge, first stop at the Multnomah Falls gift shop to buy the $1.25 "Forest Trails of the Columbia Gorge" map published by the U.S. Forest Service. It describes 36 trails in the area—a total of 166 miles of hiking, along most of which you'll never meet another human being.

FOOD AND LODGING

While there are plenty of freeway eateries in Cascade Locks, Hood River, and The Dalles, there's not much in the way of food along the Lewis and Clark Trail until you reach the **Maryhill Art Museum**, which has a gourmet snack bar on the lower level.

Timberline Lodge, a 1937 National Historic Landmark lodge at 6,000 feet elevation on the slope of Mount Hood, 6 miles up a well-marked road near Government Camp, is noteworthy for the

Northwestern artwork on display as well as the craftsmanship of the decor and furnishings, products of a Depression-era WPA program to support artists. Today it serves primarily as a ski lodge but is open—and popular—year-round. Rates range from $86 to $101 a night, and reservations are essential. Call (503) 231-7979, or toll-free 231-5400 in Portland, (800) 452-1335 within Oregon, or (800) 547-1406 nationwide. A cafeteria nearby offers a quicker and less costly alternative to dining at the lodge.

CAMPING

There are two public campgrounds at the small resort community of Government Camp. **Trillium Lake Campground**, 2¼ miles southeast of the highway intersection on U.S. 26 and then 1¼ miles south on Forest Road 2656, offers swimming and sites for larger RVs and charges $6 to $8 per night. **Still Creek Campground**, 1¼ miles southeast on U.S. 26 and ½-mile south on Forest Road 2650, is limited to tents and RVs 16 feet in length or less. The camping fee is $8 a night. Both are open from Memorial Day to Labor Day only.

Scenic Route: Columbia Gorge Scenic Highway

In 1913, when Sam Hill started building his highway up the Columbia, he paved this stretch first. The spectacular roadside beauty generated enough excitement to convince politicians to finance the rest of the road. When the highway was widened to become Interstate 84, this stretch was bypassed and preserved as a scenic detour. The best scenery is along the first few miles from the eastern end of the highway, in **Mount Hood National Forest**. Farther down toward Troutdale, where most land is under private ownership, some local residents chafe under tight restrictions on development imposed to prevent, as a recent letter to the editor in a Portland newspaper put it, "wall-to-wall bed and breakfasts."

First take the 1-mile side road up to **Vista House** at Crown Point, a hilltop overlook that commands a 30-mile view up the river and gorge, where you can look down at the scenic highway you're about to travel. At Latourell Falls, a short hiking trail lets you walk close enough to the 224-foot cataract to feel the spray and even climb behind it. **Wahkeenee Falls**

derives its name from an Indian word meaning "most beautiful." **Multnomah Falls**, at 620 feet one of the highest waterfalls in the United States, is the most developed stop on the route, with a visitors center, a gift shop, and a paved walkway to a footbridge midway up the falls. Next comes **Oneonta Gorge**, a stop that many sightseers bypass because there's no waterfall—but don't miss it. The fantastic assortment of plant life to be seen along the short nature trail between the sheer cliffs includes subspecies that exist no place else on earth. **Horsetail Falls** is a good place to access the east end of the Columbia Gorge hiking trail system.
(2 hours). ◩

COLUMBIA GORGE SCENIC HIGHWAY

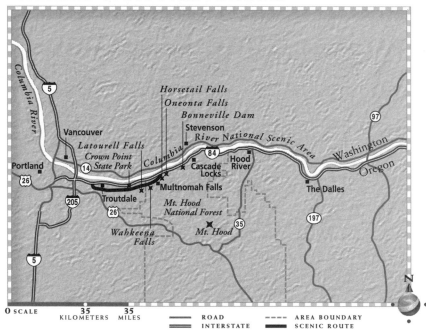

17

JOHN DAY COUNTRY

Prehistoric rhinoceroses and guru Bhagwan Sri Rajneesh both used to live in central Oregon, but they don't anymore. Hardly anybody else does either, as you'll discover while traveling the stark labyrinth of John Day Country.

Seems like they haven't had many people in these parts to name things after. Practically everything in this part of the state—referred to as John Day Country—is called John Day (except for the town of Mount Vernon, which was named after a horse). John Day Fossil Beds and the towns of John Day and Dayville were so named because they were on the John Day River. John Day himself was a hunter on a John Jacob Astor expedition that came west in 1811. He was separated from his party, and Indians robbed him of his "possibles." He was rescued, but later, when he returned to the site where he'd been found, Day's mind snapped and he went mad. So his companions named the river after him. From Blue Basin it's a short drive to the John Day Fossil Beds Visitor Center at Cant Ranch.

The trip back westward to Bend passes through some thoroughly logged parts of Ochoco National Forest. Chief Ochoco and his band of about 50 followers, who had never signed a treaty with the United States, lived in the forest during the 1880s until the chief was shot and killed by members of a notorious Prineville vigilante group known as the Izee Sheepshooters Association. So the government named the forest after him. ◣

JOHN DAY COUNTRY

N

Government Camp ▪

▲ To Portland

Maupin ▪

197

197

216

216

97

G ▪ **Shaniko**

A **Antelope**

E 218

B ▪ **Fossil**

J

19

I
207

Umatilla National Forest

Spray

19 207

Kimberly ▪

19

C
D

Dayville ▪

H

26

207

John Day River

F

Mitchell ▪

John Day Fossil Beds National Monument

Ochoco National Forest

26

26

Madras ▪

26

97

Redmond ▪

126

Prineville ▪

Bend ▪

Warm Springs Indian Reservation

Deschutes National Forest

Cascade Range

0 SCALE

25 KILOMETERS

25 MILES

―――― ROAD

- - - - AREA BOUNDARY

Sightseeing Highlights

Ⓐ Antelope

Ⓑ Fossil Museum

**John Day Fossil Beds
National Monument**
    Ⓒ Sheep Rock Unit
    Ⓓ Cant Ranch Visitor Center
    Ⓔ Clarno Unit
    Ⓕ Painted Hills Unit

Ⓖ Shaniko

Food and Lodging

Ⓗ Best Western

Ⓖ Shaniko Hotel

Camping

Ⓘ Bull Prairie Campground

Ⓘ Fairview Campground

Ⓙ Shelton Wayside

Note: Items with the same letter are located in the same town or area.

A PERFECT DAY IN JOHN DAY COUNTRY

This 290-mile route is the longest and loneliest single-day drive I suggest in this book. You could easily skip it and follow U.S. Highways 26 and 97 directly from Government Camp to Bend, a 163-mile, three-hour drive. But by doing so, you would miss experiencing the rugged beauty of the Oregon desert.

Instead drive 13 miles southeast of Government Camp on U.S. 26 and watch for Highway 216, which forks off to the left. Follow Highway 216 for 29 miles to Maupin. From Maupin, take the two-lane highway that leaves town to the north and then, in less than a mile, forks east toward Shaniko, 26 miles away, where you'll briefly intersect U.S. 97.

From Shaniko, follow U.S. 218, which leaves town to the south, 8 miles to Antelope and 11 more miles to the Clarno Unit of John Day Fossil Beds. Both stretches of road—from Shaniko to Antelope and Antelope to Clarno—appear straight on the map, but don't be fooled into thinking it's a short drive. This is rugged country with extreme altitude changes. Especially in a motor home, the road will seem much longer than its actual mileage. It's your introduction to the roads of John Day Country—empty, fun to drive, but not for those in a hurry.

From the remote Clarno Unit, it's another 20 miles to Fossil, the biggest town in these parts (which is to say, there are buildings on both sides of the street). Be sure to fill the gas tank in Fossil. You won't see another service station for 140 miles.

From Fossil, follow Highway 19 south for about 60 miles to Blue Basin. If you camped at Shelton Wayside last night, it's all downhill to the John Day River; the last 40 miles along the riverbank are easier and faster than the roads you've been on. Watch for the Blue Basin parking area on your left. A short distance south from the ranch is the junction with U.S. 26. Turn right (west), and 28 miles will bring you to the turnoff on the right to the Painted Hills Unit of John Day Fossil Beds. It's 6 miles in to the painted hills themselves.

Returning to U.S. 26, continue west for another 71 miles to Redmond. Turn south on busy U.S. 97, and 16 more miles will bring you to Bend.

SIGHTSEEING HIGHLIGHTS

☆☆☆ **John Day Fossil Beds National Monument**—From 65 million to 25 million years ago, the John Day region was subtropical forest inhabited by a wide variety of prehistoric mammals. Massive volcanic eruptions buried vast areas in ash, and torrential rains turned the ash to mud, preserving the remains of animals and plants for thousands of millennia—until the late nineteenth century.

In the 1860s this colorful but hostile desert, which remains largely uninhabited, gained international fame. Charles Darwin's recently published *On the Origin of Species* had stirred up the biggest scientific controversy since the notion that the earth might not be flat, and evolution advocates desperately needed fossil evidence to prove their case. When a cavalry troop passing through this desolate area found some fossilized bones and teeth in the sand, the news touched off the academic equivalent of a gold rush, as expeditions from Yale, the University of Pennsylvania, Princeton, and the University of California raced by wagon to scour the desert for signs of prehistoric wildlife. Enduring a harsh climate and harassment by unfriendly Indians, as well as theft and sabotage by competing scientific teams, early paleontologists shipped hundreds of crates of fossils back to eastern museums and changed forever humanity's understanding of the world.

Today the ancestry of modern flora and fauna is well known. Most of us, when we were schoolchildren, stared in wonder at museum exhibits or picture books depicting strange jungle beasts such as saber-toothed tigers, tiny horses, and giant pigs. Yet pictures are one thing; seeing the physical proof, still in the spots where it has lain hidden since long before the dawn of humanity, is quite another. Take time to explore the various units of John Day Fossil Beds, and open your mind to a strange lost world surpassing any in science fiction.

Blue Basin—Although it doesn't appear on most road maps, this small area just north of the **Sheep Rock Unit** is the most fascinating of the John Day Fossil Beds districts open to the public. The ground here is entirely turquoise blue, and minerals stain the creek water bright green. (1½ hours)

Cant Ranch Visitor Center—The main John Day Fossil Beds Visitor Center is in a 1920s ranch house on the Sheep Rock Unit of the national monument, a few miles south of Blue Basin. (There is a second visitor's center in the town of John Day, 38 miles to the east and not included in this itinerary.) The first floor of the main ranch house contains two rooms of interpretive exhibits, an information desk, and an antique-filled living room from the days when it was a private residence. The second floor is where the park rangers live. They divide their time between answering tourist questions, checking out reports of new fossil finds, feeding the livestock, and fixing the roof. Some of the ranch outbuildings house historical exhibits about early paleontologists and a laboratory where you can sometimes watch technicians preparing fossils for display. Other outbuildings shelter sheep. (½ hour)

Painted Hills Unit—Fossils found here are of tree leaves, not animals. You can see some along the ¼-mile Leaf Fossil Hills Trail, though you get a better look at more of them at the Cant Ranch Visitor Center. The real reason to take this side trip 6 miles from the main highway is the scenery: the bold yellow and red striped hills are the brightest-colored bit of painted desert I've seen anywhere in the American West. Admission to John Day Fossil Beds National Monument is free. Hours: The visitor's center at Cant Ranch is open daily from 9:00 a.m. to 5:00 p.m. Phone: (541) 575-0721. (1½ hours)

Clarno Unit—The least-known of three widely scattered units that comprise John Day Fossil Beds National Monument, Clarno is also the oldest. Found here are fossils from 40 million years ago, when the Cascade Mountains had not yet formed and this area was a subtropical rain forest. Animals whose petrified skeletons have been unearthed at Clarno include tapirs, ancestral horses, primitive rhinoceroses, and other massive vegetarians that have no modern counterparts. While early mammals are more fascinating to laymen, Clarno holds special interest for paleontologists because of the many fossilized nuts, fruits, and seeds that have been discovered here, including prehistoric coconuts and avocados. Admission to this unit of the national monument is free. (1 hour)

★ **Antelope**—Here's a different kind of ghost town. This tiny ranching village (pop. 45) gained national notoriety in the early 1980s when Bhagwan Sri Rajneesh moved here. The guru originally picked the location, about as far as one can live from modern mainstream civilization, for the peace, quiet, and spiritual freedom he hoped to find there, but soon his 100-square-mile ranch about 18 miles outside town was occupied by thousands of his followers. What's more, 100,000 visitors a year were flocking to see the social and agricultural miracles he had worked there, as well as new boutiques, restaurants, and even a disco. Hopelessly outnumbered, longtime Antelope residents shouted their outrage far and wide. The final indignity came when "Rajneeshees" overwhelmingly voted to change the town's name from Antelope to Rajneesh. The uproar attracted the attention of the federal government, which sent the IRS (rather than the cavalry) galloping to the rescue upon discovering that the guru hadn't paid taxes on Rajneeshpuram's tourist income. Bhagwan Sri Rajneesh was deported to India, his followers scattered, the town's old name was restored, and once again its residents are only outnumbered by pronghorn antelope. *Sic transit gloria mundi.*

★ **Fossil Museum**—The town of Fossil has a free local museum of curiosities gathered from around Wheeler County. Like a big, cluttered, slightly dingy antique store without price tags, this museum has eccentric, down-home charm. On display are many items you won't find elsewhere, such as saloon gambling tables, an albino porcupine, a two-headed lamb, a petrified turtle, the only wolverine ever seen (and shot) in the county, and the original city limits sign from Rajneesh, Oregon. Donations are welcome. Hours are usually about 10:00 a.m. to 4:00 or 4:30 p.m. more or less, most days. (1 hour)

★ **Shaniko**—With a population of 25, Shaniko is Oregon's best-known ghost town. Its name is an Indianization of the surname of its founder,

August Scherneckau. In 1900 the arrival of a railroad spur line caused Shaniko to boom as "The Wool Shipping Capital of the World" for ten years before a new railroad route bypassed it. Today Shaniko's Old West buildings wear fresh coats of paint, and its past glories have been augmented by a church, which was actually a schoolhouse moved here from another ghost town, and a fictitious "Boot Hill" (Shaniko had neither a church nor a cemetery of its own). Several old buildings house museum displays, and a large collection of carriages and buckboards covers a vacant lot near the town center. (½ hour)

FITNESS AND RECREATION

In John Day Fossil Beds National Monument's Clarno Unit, two walking trails that begin at the base of the eroded palisades lead you past plant fossil exhibits. Each trail is only ¼-mile long, and you can walk them both in under an hour.

A ½-mile walk into Blue Basin on the **Island in Time Trail**, through a landscape so unfamiliar it feels like another planet, takes you past fossilized turtles, saber-toothed cats, oreodonts, and miniature horses. The original fossils are now in museums, but cast reproductions have been placed where they were found. For a longer hike, take the 2-mile **Blue Basin Overlook Trail** to the top of the ridge for a spectacular view of the area. As you can see, fossils are only exposed when the steep banks erode with rain and wind, so a new one might appear at any time. If you spot one, do not touch it! These fossil skeletons are very fragile and of great scientific value. Immediately report any finds to the rangers at Cant Ranch.

The best views of the Painted Hills Unit are from the 1-mile **Carroll Rim Trail** and the ½-mile **Painted Hills Overlook Trail**.

FOOD AND LODGING

The historic **Shaniko Hotel** rents rooms for about $60 a night. Very limited motel accommodations and a small café can be found in the town of Fossil. For a good food and lodging selection in the John Day region, though, the only option is to head east from Cant Ranch on U.S. 26 for 38 miles to John Day—by far the largest town in this part of Oregon, with a population of over 2,000—where you'll find a number of roadside motels including a **Best Western** (315 West Main Street, (541) 575-1700, $55 a night). The drive from Fossil to John Day takes about three hours and may keep you on the road well after dark. Don't worry—"No Vacancy" signs are highly unlikely out here.

CAMPING

Ten miles south of Fossil is **Shelton Wayside**, a small state park campground with 36 primitive campsites and no hookups. At 4,000 feet, the campground is only open from mid-April to the end of October. The fee is $6.

On the off-chance that this campground may be full, there are two national forest campgrounds 39 miles farther on, **Bull Prairie Campground** and **Fairview Campground**, both open May through October. To find them, turn onto Highway 207, 3 miles past the town of Spray, and go north about 12 miles.

18
BEND

The largest Oregon "dry side" town, Bend is the ideal base camp for outdoor activities on the eastern slope of the Cascades. Though the town got its start as a logging camp and ranching center, today Bend's economy turns almost entirely on recreation.

The towering ponderosa pine stands of Deschutes National Forest come right up to the edge of town, offering a year-round array of adventures such as hiking, mountain biking, whitewater rafting, fishing, canoeing, snowmobiling, and dogsledding. A 20-minute drive takes travelers to the Mount Bachelor Ski Area in the heart of the high Cascades, and further explorations reach the spectacular scenery of the Cascade Lakes and the Three Sisters volcanic peaks.

To the south lies a cluster of scenic areas that includes volcanic cones, lava caves, lava fields, and a unique lava cast forest. Formerly a national forest scenic area called Lava Lands, the volcano field was recently transferred to National Park Service jurisdiction to become Newberry Crater National Volcanic Monument, one of only two national volcanic monuments in the United States (the other is Mount St. Helens). ◼

NEWBERRY CRATER NATIONAL VOLCANIC MONUMENT

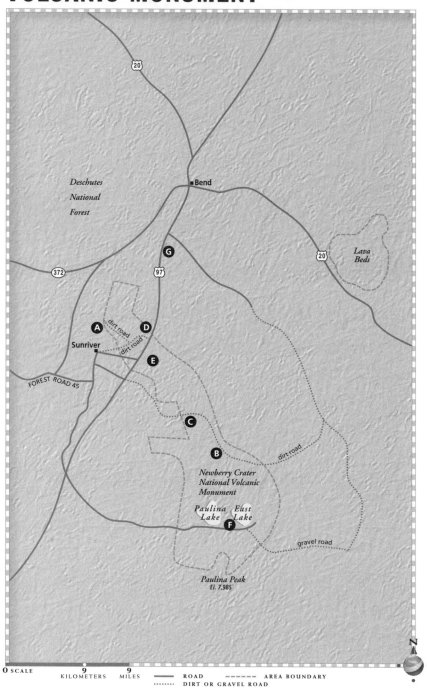

Sightseeing Highlights

Ⓐ Benham Falls

Ⓑ Newberry Crater National Volcanic Monument

Ⓒ Lava Cast Forest

Ⓓ Lava Lands Visitors Center/Lava Butte

Ⓔ Lava River Cave

Ⓕ Newberry Crater

Ⓖ Oregon High Desert Museum

A PERFECT DAY IN THE BEND AREA

The Oregon High Desert Museum and the various Lava Lands points of interest are all near U.S. 97 south of Bend. Drive 11 miles south of town to reach Lava Lands Visitor Center, on your right, where the road up Lava Butte begins. One mile farther south on the opposite side of the road is Lava River Cave. Two more miles on U.S. 97 will bring you to the turnoff on your left to the Lava Cast Forest. I suggest visiting the Oregon High Desert Museum (7 miles south of Bend) on your way back from Lava Lands to Bend. The museum does not open until 9:00 a.m.

After lunch in Bend, follow Highway 46 south as far as you can go, and you'll reach a T-intersection. Turn left (east), and another 8 miles will bring you back to U.S. 97. Proceed south on U.S. 97 for 28 miles and turn right (west) on Highway 138. Fifteen more miles will bring you to the north gate of Crater Lake National Park.

Off-season alternate route: Both the Cascade Lakes Highway and Crater Lake's north gate are closed by snow until late spring. Early-season travelers can get from Bend to Crater Lake only by driving directly south on U.S. 97 for 110 miles, then turning back northwest on Highway 62 for 29 miles to the Crater Lake south gate. This route is much faster than the Cascade Lakes Highway but not nearly as scenic.

SIGHTSEEING HIGHLIGHTS

★★★ **Newberry Crater National Volcanic Monument**—This cluster of volcanic sights south of Bend includes:

Lava Lands Visitors Center/Lava Butte—The visitor's center, at the foot of Lava Butte, features several large, automated dioramas showing the volcanic and human history of the area, including one where you can watch a model of Mount Mazama explode and collapse to become Crater Lake. Two short nature trails leave from the visitor's center, taking you across a lava flow and through a pine forest. Drive up the dizzying spiral road to the summit of Lava Butte, a small, perfectly cone-shaped volcano, where a ¼-mile trail leads around the crater, commanding panoramic views of the Lava Lands area, the Three Sisters, Mount Bachelor, and more distant peaks of the Cascades. (1 hour)

Lava River Cave—A self-guided, one-hour, 1½-mile walk takes you through the longest known uncollapsed lava tube in Oregon (about 6,700 feet, the last 1,500 feet of which are closed to the public because of dangerous loose rocks). The tunnel is as much as 58 feet high and 50 feet wide in some places, while elsewhere the ceiling is as low as 5½ feet. The sand that covers most of the cave floor is from the Mount Mazama (Crater Lake) eruption. There is no electric lighting; bring a flashlight, or in summer months only, rent a lantern at the cave entrance. (1½ hours)

Lava Cast Forest—During an eruption from Newberry Volcano about 6,000 years ago, molten lava oozed slowly through a ponderosa pine forest, forming a hard coating around each tree. Standing trees and fallen logs, some in piles, left the unique molded impressions you see today along the 1-mile trail. (1 hour)

Newberry Crater—Less than an hour's drive south of Bend, camp and explore this collapsed crater of the largest ice-age volcano in Oregon. Newberry Crater is larger than Crater Lake at 25 miles across, though not as deep, and contains two lakes separated by an area of recent eruptions. The crater's most unusual feature is a massive flow of obsidian (shiny black volcanic glass) that extends from the main road nearly to the south rim. For many centuries Indians came here to gather obsidian for tools and weapons, and they left chipped fragments that are often found along the shores of both lakes. To reach Newberry Crater, continue for 22 miles south of Bend on U.S. 97 and turn left on the paved road that takes you 15 miles east to the crater. (1½ hours)

Admission to most areas of Newberry Crater National Volcanic

Monument is free. There is an admission charge of $4 for adults, $1.50 for teens ages 13 to 17, and 75 cents for seniors at Lava River Cave. Hours: The Lava Lands Visitor Center is open daily from 10:00 a.m. to 4:00 p.m.; the visitor's center at Newberry crater is open the same hours, but only during the summer months. Phone: (541) 593-2421.

★★ **Oregon High Desert Museum**—The assortment of exhibits at this indoor-outdoor museum ranges from Lewis and Clark memorabilia and forestry displays to a settler's cabin, an Indian wickiup shelter, and a chuckwagon where frontier cooking is demonstrated. Live animal exhibits, including otters and birds of prey, are enlivened as human handlers give frequent presentations. This could be your chance of a lifetime to watch someone cuddle a porcupine. Admission is $5.50 for adults, $5 for senior citizens, $2.75 for children ages 6 to 12. Hours: Open daily from 9:00 a.m. to 5:00 p.m. (2 hours)

★ **Benham Falls**—Six miles west on the wide unpaved forest road that starts near the Lava Lands Visitors Center is a day-use fishing and picnic area with the biggest trees in the woods. The local lumber company, which logged the forest around Bend so thoroughly from 1916 to the 1940s that they finally declared it worthless and donated the land to the forest service for rehabilitation, left this stand of tall ponderosa intact because it was the site of their annual company picnic. They used to bring 2,000 employees and their families out here from Bend each year on railroad flatcars for the picnic. Cross the bridge and take an easy walk along the old railroad bed, now trackless and blocked from vehicle traffic, to the falls overlook. As you stroll beside the lazy Deschutes River, imagine what it would be like to glide gently along in a canoe. Minutes later your daydream will turn into a classic movie heart-stopper: you'll feel like Hepburn and Bogart in *The African Queen*, or Monroe and Mitchum in *River of No Return*, as the placid river rounds a bend and suddenly plunges into a spectacular series of whitewater cataracts. (½ hour)

FITNESS AND RECREATION

Within Newberry Crater are 68 miles of hiking trails, including the **Newberry Crater Rim Loop**, which is also open to mountain bikers. Shorter hikes are found at **Lava River Cave** and **Lava Cast Forest**, each with a trail about a mile long.

Along the Cascade Lakes Highway are a number of trailheads that provide access to the Three Sisters Wilderness. One of the best is the 4½-mile **Green Lakes Trail**, a sometimes steep scramble that passes several waterfalls on its way to a pretty alpine lake.

Bike rentals are available in Bend at **Skjersaa's**, 130 SW Century Drive, (541) 382-2154, or **High Cascade Descent**, 333 Riverfront Street, (541) 389-0562. Hundreds of miles of unpaved forest roads make Deschutes National Forest a mountain biker's dream. For high-altitude thrills, in the summer the chairlift at the **Mount Bachelor Ski Area** west of Bend carries mountain bikers and their bikes to the mountain's 9,065-foot summit and a network of ridgeline trails.

Bend is a big river rafting area. Whitewater trips on the McKenzie, Deschutes, and Umpqua Rivers can be arranged in Bend at **Hunter Expeditions**, Highway 97, (541) 389-8370, and **Rapid River Rafts**, 60107 Cinder Butte Road, (541) 382-1514.

FOOD

Restaurants in Bend outnumber the motels. Virtually every famous-name fast-food franchise has a location here. **Le Bistro**, in Bend at 1203 NE Third, (541) 389-7274, is a very good and accordingly high-priced French restaurant in a converted church. Hours are 5:30 to 10:00 p.m., closed Monday. More moderately priced is **Giuseppe's Ristorante**, downtown at 932 NW Bond Street, (541) 389-8899. Outstanding Italian dishes include 17 pasta entrées; open daily for dinner only. Also affordable is **Mexicali Rose**, 301 NW Franklin, (541) 389-0149, serving traditional Mexican food for lunch (weekdays only) and dinner (nightly). Last but not least, **Jake's Truck Stop** at the south end of town serves big, inexpensive breakfasts.

LODGING

Motels seem to be the main industry in Bend. You won't need reservations. In general, well-furnished, attractive, modern motels in the $50 to $60 price range are along the highway on the north side of town, while older ma-and-pa motels on the south side of town have suffered from the booming competition, resulting in lower rates—typically in the $40 range—for adequate roadside accommodations. Two small (two-unit) bed and breakfasts, for which you need reservations, are near Drake Park and Mirror Pond on the east side of town, in much quieter and more natural

settings than any of the motels. They are **Lara House** at 640 NW
Congress, (541) 388-4604, about $60; and **Mirror Pond House**, 1054
NW Harmon, (541) 389-1680, about $75. In addition, there are many
ski lodge and dude ranch resorts within an hour's drive of Bend—not
worth the price if all you want is a place to sleep tonight but interesting
options if you plan to spend enough extra time in the area to take advan-
tage of the fishing, boating, and horseback riding possibilities. A complete listing is available from the Bend Chamber of Commerce, 164 NW
Hawthorne Avenue, Bend, OR 97701, (541) 382-3221

At Newberry Crater, **Pauline Lake Resort** has a rustic lodge
and log cabins with kitchens. Rates vary from $40 to $100, depending
on the unit and the time of year. Call (541) 536-2240 for details and
reservations.

CAMPING

The most accessible of the many campgrounds in the Bend area is
Tumalo State Park, 5 miles northwest of town on U.S. 20 where the
highway crosses the Deschutes River, with 68 tent sites and 20 RV sites
with hookups, open mid-April through October. Fees are $6 for most
sites, $8 for sites with hookups.

The national forest west and south of Bend is full of campgrounds. The best are found at Newberry Crater, a little under an
hour's drive south of Bend. Along the way are two other small campgrounds you might check out: **Bessen Camp** (about 18 miles south of
town on U.S. 97, turn right on Forest Road 40 and go about 2 miles);
and **Big River Campground** (2 miles farther south on U.S. 97, take
Forest Road 42 on your right). About 2 more miles south on U.S. 97
(22 miles from Bend) is the turnoff on the left to Newberry Crater.
Fifteen miles east on this road, you'll enter the crater and find six road-
accessible campgrounds totaling more than 300 units, as well as two
small hikers-only lakeshore campgrounds.

West of Bend on the Cascade Lakes Highway, within about 30
miles of town, are lakeside campgrounds at **Todd Lake**, **Devil's Lake**,
Soda Creek, and **Elk Lake**. None have RV hookups or drinking water.

These are only a sampling of the approximately 80 national forest
campgrounds in the area (many of which are far off the highway on
unpaved roads). You can get a complete list from the Deschutes
National Forest ranger station at 1230 NE Third Street (U.S. 97),
Bend, OR 97701, (541) 388-5664.

BEND REGION

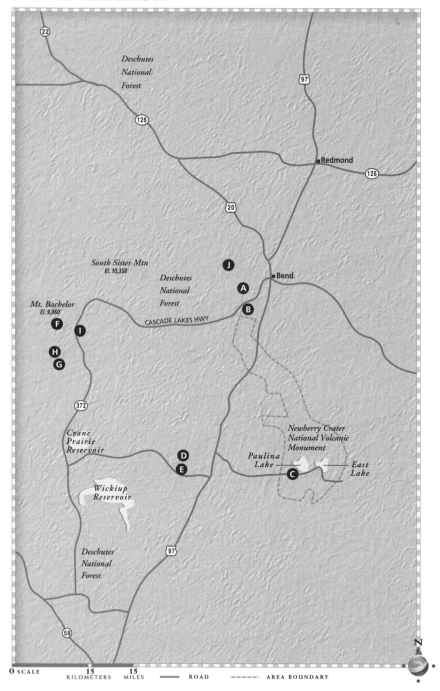

Deschutes
National
Forest

22

97

126

Redmond

126

20

South Sister Mtn
El. 10,358'

J

Deschutes
National
Forest

A

Bend

Mt. Bachelor
El. 9,060'

B

CASCADE LAKES HWY

F

I

H

G

372

Crane
Prairie
Reservoir

D

E

Newberry Crater
National Volcanic
Monument

Paulina
Lake

C

East
Lake

Wickiup
Reservoir

Deschutes
National
Forest

97

58

N

0 SCALE   15   15   ——— ROAD   ▬ ▬ ▬ ▬ AREA BOUNDARY
       KILOMETERS   MILES

Food

Ⓐ Giuseppe's Ristorante

Ⓑ Jake's Truck Stop

Ⓐ Le Bistro

Ⓐ Mexicali Rose

Lodging

Ⓐ Lara House

Ⓐ Mirror Pond House

Ⓒ Pauline Lake Resort

Camping

Ⓓ Bessen Camp

Ⓔ Big River Campground

Ⓕ Devil's Lake Campground

Ⓖ Elk Lake Campground

Ⓗ Soda Creek Campground

Ⓘ Todd Lake Campground

Ⓙ Tumalo State Park

Note: Items with the same letter are located in the same town or area.

Scenic Route: Cascade Lakes Highway

Follow Highway 372 west from Bend. After 25 miles, you'll come to a wayside on the slope of **Bachelor Butte**, affording a magnificent view of the Three Sisters volcanoes. Just beyond is Dutchman Flat, a small expanse of pumice desert. The next 50 miles, perhaps the most scenic stretch of road on the east side of the Cascades, provide access to a dozen beautiful lakes. **Devil's Lake** and **Elk Lake** are right by the roadside. Pause for a look at **Devil's Rock Pile**, near Devil's Lake: astronaut James Irwin carried a rock from here to the moon in the late 1960s.

From the main highway, well-marked side roads take you back to **Hosmer Lake** (shallow, crystal-clear, and stocked with Atlantic salmon), **Little Lava Lake** (the spring-fed headwaters of the Deschutes River), or **Cultus Lake** (the best for swimming). **Osprey Point**, on Crane Prairie Reservoir, is reached by an easy nature trail from the parking area. The eaglelike American osprey (fishhawk), once a vanishing species in the U.S., is now quite common around this reservoir. If you visit between April and October you may see one diving from hundreds of feet in the air to grab a fish in its razor-sharp talons. (3 hours) ◥

CASCADE LAKES HIGHWAY

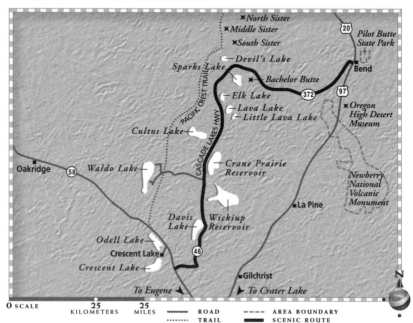

19
CRATER LAKE

As early as the tenth century B.C., ancestors of the Klamath Indians lived in the shadow of 12,000-foot Mount Mazama, the southernmost major volcano in the Cascade Range, then about the same height as Mount Adams is today. According to legends that have survived into historical times, the Indians believed that Mazama's fiery eruptions were battles between two gods. In 4860 B.C., the gods' "war" reached a climax, when the mountain exploded with a force 42 times that of Mount St. Helens' 1980 eruption, hurling rock and ash over 5,000 square miles of what are now eight states and three Canadian provinces. The volcano collapsed, leaving a crater 6 miles across, which filled with water to a depth of 1,932 feet and created the deepest lake in the United States.

So sacred was Crater Lake to American Indians that shamans forbade their people from going there. Indians never mentioned the place to white pioneers, who explored the area for 50 years before "discovering" it in 1853. Theodore Roosevelt declared Crater Lake the United States' sixth national park 49 years later.

The volcano under Crater Lake has been dormant for about a thousand years. However, in August 1987, scientists discovered an active thermal vent on the lake bottom, which they are now studying with minisubmarines and remote-control underwater video cameras. ◧

CRATER LAKE

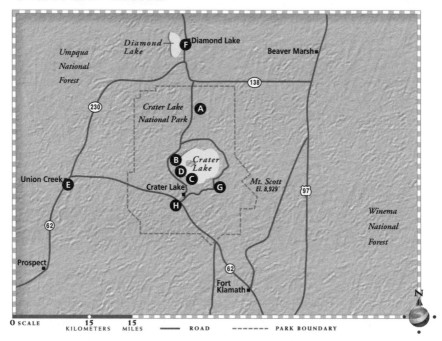

Sightseeing Highlights

- **A** Crater Lake National Park
- **B** Cleetwood Trail
- **C** Rim Village

Food and Lodging

- **D** Crater Lake Lodge
- **E** Union Creek Resort

Camping

- **F** Diamond Lake
- **G** Lost Creek
- **H** Mazama Campground

A PERFECT DAY AT CRATER LAKE

Shadows settle early on Crater Lake, so the best plan is to spend a night in the area and rise soon after dawn to explore the lake and its surroundings. Start with the visitor's center, then drive the Rim Road, hike down to the lakeshore, or take a tour boat to Wizard Island and explore the island on foot.

If you leave Crater Lake by 4:00 this afternoon, you can arrive in Ashland in time to check into a bed and breakfast, eat dinner, and catch the Shakespeare performance.

SIGHTSEEING HIGHLIGHT

✯✯✯ **Crater Lake National Park**—Deep snow keeps most roads in the park closed until July and closes them again in October. If you are visiting at any time except July, August, and September, the only road you can drive will be the one from the south entrance to park head-quarters at **Rim Village**. The other park roads are used off-season for cross-country skiing, and rangers lead snowshoe trips on weekend afternoons from December through May. A complete circuit of the rim on skis takes about three days.

During the short summer season, the 33-mile drive around the **Crater Rim Road** lets you view the lake from every angle. The longest segment of the road, along the east side of the lake, is one-way from the north gate road to Rim Village and the visitor's center at the south gate road—so no matter where you start, drive in a clockwise direction. The park is open 24 hours a day, but the north entrance is only open from June through September, and the Rim Drive is open from July through September.

The only way to hike down to the lake is on **Cleetwood Trail**, a steep 1-mile descent from the picnic area above Cleetwood Cove to the boat landing. From there, a narrated boat tour (daily, between 9:00 a.m. and 3:00 p.m., July and August only, $10 for adults, $5.50 for children 12 and under) takes you counterclockwise along the shore to Wizard Island, the volcanic cone that rises out of the lake near the west shore. The tour takes two hours, including a short stop on the island; catch a morning trip and you can stay on the island to hike the mile-long trail that spirals to the top of the cone, then board a midafternoon tour boat for the return trip. Admission to the park is $5 per vehicle. Hours: Visitor's centers open daily 9:00 a.m. to 5:00 p.m. Phone: (541) 594-2211. (full day)

FITNESS AND RECREATION

There are 90 miles of trails within Crater Lake National Park. Most of them are short except for the **Pacific Crest Trail**, which intersects the north gate road and crosses the Pumice Desert before making its way through the forest on the west side of the crater.

Short hikes in the park include not only the abovementioned **Cleetwood Trail** from the rim to the lake shore but also the easy ½-mile Castle Crest Wildflower Trail, which starts near the park headquarters, the 1½-mile **Godfrey Glen Trail** 2 miles down the south gate road, and the 1¾-mile **Annie Spring Canyon Trail** from Mazama Canyon near the south gate.

The Rim Road is groomed for cross-country skiing during the snowy months (which last through late June). There are ski rentals at Rim Village, where the lodge and visitor's center are located.

FOOD AND LODGING

Originally built in 1915 and now one of the oldest lodges in the national park system, **Crater Lake Lodge** on the south rim at Rim Village reopened in 1995 after being closed for renovation for five years. The lodge has 75 guest rooms and four luxury suites with lofts. There are no phones or TVs on the premises. Rates start at $89. The lodge is open from early June through September 15. Make reservations far in advance by writing to Crater Lake Lodge Company, P.O. Box 97, Crater Lake, OR 97604, or by calling (541) 594-2511. The lodge has a restaurant and a cafeteria.

Lower cost accommodations are available at **Union Creek Resort**, 16 miles west of the Crater Lake south entrance gate on Highway 230. It's smaller and friendlier, and reservations are usually easier to get on short notice, and it's open all year. Rustic cabins start at about $60 a night, rooms in the lodge (all with shared bath) about $45. This early-1900s "resort," on the National Register of Historic Places, doesn't have any of the usual resort amenities like a swimming pool, a golf course, or tennis courts. It does have a game room with a big stone fireplace, a country grocery store, a little café that's famous for its homemade huckleberry pies, a creek running through the yard, and nothing but forest all around for miles and miles and miles. Write to Union Creek Resort, Prospect, OR 97536, or call (541) 560-3565.

CAMPING

At Crater Lake National Park, **Mazama Campground** near the south entrance gate has 198 campsites at $8 each. The only other camping in the park is at **Lost Creek** on the road to the Pinnacles, with 12 primitive sites, tents only, free. Both campgrounds are only open from the 4th of July through September.

If you can't find a campsite in the national park, national forest campgrounds are small but numerous to the west of the park. From the north entrance gate, drive 7 miles north to **Diamond Lake** and look for campsites around the lake; if you don't find one to your liking there, follow Highway 230 west from the south end of the lake, and after about 12 miles you'll see the first of a half-dozen campgrounds between there and Union Creek. If you're leaving the park by the south entrance, drive 16 miles west to Union Creek and check out the three campgrounds nearby; turn north on Highway 30 toward Diamond Lake and you'll find more. Some of these national forest campgrounds open in late May, others not until July; some close by mid-September, others stay open through October.

20
ASHLAND

"Men are merriest when they are from home" (Henry V, Act I).

The mountains of southwestern Oregon are farther from Merry Old England than were dreamt of in Shakespeare's philosophy. Yet in this graceful little creekside community at the base of 7,533-foot Ashland Peak, you'll find the nation's finest performances of his plays. The Oregon Shakespeare Festival dates back to 1935 and plays to 300,000 people each year.

Shakespeare came to Ashland thanks to an odd coincidence: an abandoned Chautauqua building that had been used for concerts and lectures in the early years of the century was condemned and in the process of being torn down when it came to the attention of Elizabethan buff Angus Bowmer. Bowmer noticed that, with its original roof removed, the structure's architecture was almost identical to London's Fortune Theater (c. 1600), where many of Shakespeare's plays premiered. Ashlanders refurbished the building into a replica of the original open-air Shakespearean theater, and the rest, as they say, is history.

Especially during the busy summer months, tickets and lodging reservations can be hard to get, and the art galleries, boutiques, bookstores, and cafés that occupy Ashland's Tudor-style buildings bustle with activity. The town empties at the end of the festival season in late October, and in winter the most elegant bed and breakfast accommodations can be had at bargain basement rates. Why go to Ashland in winter? Nearby Mount Ashland offers the finest skiing in southern Oregon, with 23 ski runs and 100 miles of cross-country trails. ◨

A PERFECT DAY IN ASHLAND

The plays at the Elizabethan Stage and other theaters that host the Oregon Shakespeare Festival are presented in the evening, so you may wish to arrive in Ashland late after spending the day at Crater Lake. From the south gate of Crater Lake, take Highway 62 westbound for 72 miles to Medford, where you join Interstate 5. Take the interstate southbound for 17 miles to Ashland. Before leaving Ashland, set aside a morning for the Backstage Tour.

SIGHTSEEING HIGHLIGHTS

★★★ **Oregon Shakespeare Festival**—This is the oldest and largest Shakespeare Festival in the United States. In 1983 the festival won a Tony Award, the theater equivalent of the Oscar. The festival runs from mid-February through the end of October, with performances daily except Mondays. However, the Elizabethan Stage (an exact reproduction of London's circa 1600 Fortune Theatre), where Shakespeare's plays are presented outdoors, as when they were first performed, only operates from mid-June through September. The festival also includes indoor performances at the nearby Angus Bowmer Theatre and the more intimate Black Swan Theater, but most of the plays performed in the indoor theaters are not Shakespearean. Instead, they range from modern classics by Ibsen, O'Neill, and Pirandello to premieres of works by contemporary playwrights.

Performances on the Elizabethan Stage begin at 8:30 p.m. Old English dances are performed outside the theater before the play. Ticket prices range from $16 to $24. For the current season's schedule and ticket ordering information, write: Oregon Shakespeare Festival, Box 158, Ashland, OR 97520. To be on the safe side, you should order tickets several months in advance. If you didn't, call the box office at (541) 482-4331 to inquire about last-minute ticket availability.

★★ **Shakespeare Festival Backstage Tour**—This two-hour tour is almost better than the plays themselves. A guide brimming with historical information and gossip will meet you at the Black Swan and lead you behind the scenes of the Elizabethan Stage to show you stagehands at work, dressing rooms, and the green room, where actors relax when they're not on stage. You can also see and handle costumes and props such as broadswords and severed heads. The tour costs $7.50. It starts

ASHLAND

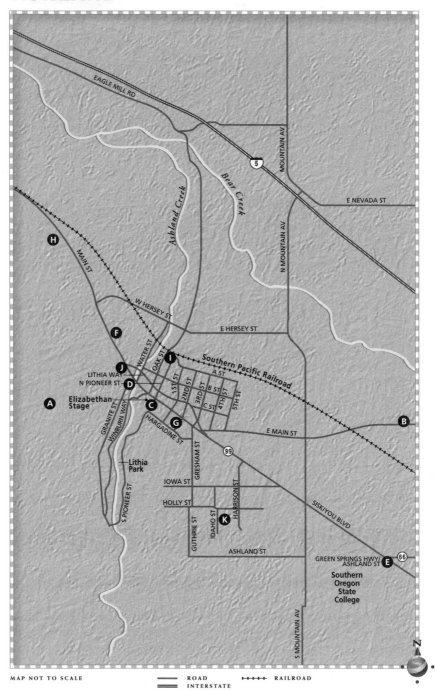

MAP NOT TO SCALE

ROAD
INTERSTATE

RAILROAD

Sightseeing Highlights

Ⓐ Oregon Shakespeare Festival

Ⓑ Pacific Northwest Museum of
Natural History

Ⓐ Shakespeare Festival
Backstage Tour

Food

Ⓒ Chateaulin

Ⓓ Greenleaf Delicatessen

Ⓔ Omar's

Lodging

Ⓕ Ashland Hostel

Ⓖ Columbia Hotel

Ⓗ The Morical House

Ⓘ Oak Street Station
Bed & Breakfast

Ⓙ Queen Anne

Ⓚ Romeo Inn

Note: Items with the same letter are located in the same town or area.

promptly at 10:00 a.m. Reservations are required; call (541) 482-4331. There are no tours on Mondays. (2 hours)

☆ **Pacific Northwest Museum of Natural History**—You can interact with computers and walk through a simulated lava tube in this new Ashland museum full of excellent exhibits on the various ecosystems of the Pacific Northwest, from rain forests to desert. Admission is $6 for adults, $5.50 for seniors, and $4.50 for students ages 5 to 15. Hours: Open daily 11:00 a.m. to 6:00 p.m. in the summer months, 11:00 a.m. to 5:00 p.m. the rest of the year, closed Monday through Wednesday in March, April, May, and October. Address: 1500 East Main Street. Phone: (541) 488-1084. (1½ hours)

FITNESS AND RECREATION

The **Bicentennial Bikepath**, which runs along Bear Creek for 10 miles from Ashland to Medford, is one of several beautiful bike tour routes in the Ashland area. You can rent mountain bikes at **The Adventure Center**, 40 North Main Street, (541) 488-2819.

Raft trips on the Rogue River, the most popular whitewater rafting river in Oregon, can be arranged in Ashland at **Noah's World of Water**, 53 North Main Street, (541) 488-2811.

FOOD

My favorite Ashland restaurant is **Omar's** at the intersection of Siskiyou Boulevard and Highway 66; call (541) 482-1281 for reservations. Since it opened in 1946, Omar's has been known for its reasonably priced outstanding steak and seafood selections. Try the "Toad in the Hole" (sounds ghastly but tastes great and doesn't actually involve eating an amphibian), or, if you are less adventurous, the Dijon chicken.

Also in Ashland, an intimate, uncompromisingly romantic French restaurant is the **Chateaulin** at 50 East Main, open daily, hours vary seasonally, expensive, reservations required, (541) 482-2264. You'll find inexpensive fare and a deck overlooking the creek at the **Greenleaf Delicatessen**, 49 North Main, open Monday 9:00 a.m. to 3:00 p.m., Tuesday through Sunday 9:00 a.m. to 8:00 p.m., (541) 482-2808. For an Ashland dining experience as outrageous as its name, check out the **Bushes Rock & Roll Burger Bar** (no relation to George) at 1474 Siskiyou Boulevard, where amid the din of video games you can sink your teeth into what they claim is the largest flame-broiled hamburger in the world.

LODGING

Ashland has more bed and breakfast inns per capita than any other town in Oregon, including Portland. A few of the nearly three dozen possibilities are **The Morical House**, an elegantly restored 1880s home at 668 North Main, Ashland, OR 97520, $80 to $112; **Oak Street Station Bed & Breakfast**, a Queen Anne home at 239 Oak Street, (541) 482-1726, $75 to $85; the **Queen Anne**, 125 North Main Street, (541) 482-0220, $75 to $90; and the quietly luxurious **Romeo Inn**, 295 Idaho, (541) 488-0884, starting at $115. For a complete listing of Ashland B&Bs, contact the Ashland Chamber of Commerce, P.O. Box 606, Ashland, OR 97520, (541) 482-3486.

The **Columbia Hotel**, 262 E. Main, (541) 482-3726, is a small European-style historic hotel just a block from the theaters. Rates start under $50. **The Ashland Hostel** at 150 North Main, (541) 482-9217, offers dormitory beds at just $9.50 a night for AYH members.

Two miles north of town on Highway 99, you can rent a rustic cabin with kitchen facilities for as little as $40 a night and enjoy the 50-by-100-foot hot mineral pool at **Jackson Hot Springs**, 2235 Highway 99 North, (541) 482-3776.

En route from Ashland to the Coast, Crescent City has a reasonable selection of motels. **Curley Redwood Lodge**, a motel that the owners boast was built entirely from a single redwood tree, is at 701 Redwood Highway South, (707) 464-2137. Rates start around $60 a night.

A more interesting alternative is to spend the night in **Oregon Caves Château** at the national monument. Rooms at this rustic 1934 lodge cost $66. A creek runs right through the dining room. For reservations, write Oregon Caves Château, P.O. Box 128, Cave Junction, OR 97523, or call (541) 592-3400. Open from Memorial Day to Labor Day only. Near Oregon Caves, at 250 Robinson in Cave Junction, dormitory accommodations are available in the AYH-affiliated **Fordson Home Hostel**. Reservations are essential; call (541) 592-3203.

ASHLAND REGION

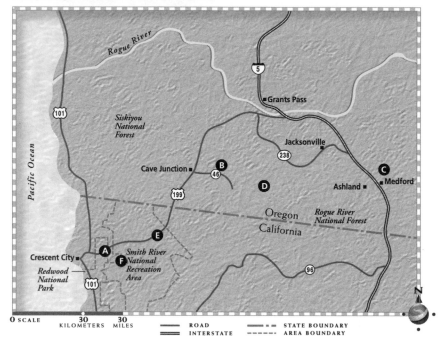

Lodging

Ⓐ Curley Redwood Lodge

Ⓑ Fordson Home Hostel

Ⓒ Jackson Hot Springs

Ⓓ Oregon Caves Chateau

Camping

Ⓔ Cedar Rustic National Forest Campground

Ⓔ Grassy Flat National Forest Campground

Ⓒ Jackson Hot Springs

Ⓔ Panther Flat National Forest Campground

Ⓔ Patrick National Forest Campground

Ⓕ Jedediah Smith Redwoods State Park Campground

Note: Items with the same letter are located in the same town or area.

CAMPING

Near Ashland, there's camping at **Jackson Hot Springs**, 2235 Highway 99 North, (541) 482-3776. Rates are $18 a night.

On the way from Ashland to the coast, you'll find a 108-site campground at **Jedediah Smith Redwoods State Park**, $10, open all year. Reservations are accepted; call (800) 444-7275 in California. California state park reservations can be a problem on short notice. First-come, first-served camping can be found along U.S. 199 at several national forest campgrounds—**Cedar Rustic, Patrick Creek, Grassy Flat**, and **Panther Flat**, all within 10 miles east of Gasquet.

Scenic Route: Ashland to the Coast

From Ashland, go north on Interstate 5 for 48 miles to the second Grants Pass exit. Follow US 199 for 31 miles to the turnoff at Cave Junction for **Oregon Caves National Monument**. This cave (there's only one, despite its name) is Oregon's largest. At the end of a winding, 20 mile paved road, at 4,020 feet in elevation, the cave penetrates an outcropping of solid marble to a series of large rooms dripping with stalactites, flowstone curtains, and columns. Visitors 6 and older can enter the cave only on 75-minute guided tours offered by the Oregon Caves Company (503-592-3400).

Returning to US 199, drive south 50 miles to **Jedediah Smith Redwoods State Park**, which preserves 18 memorial redwood stands along the Smith River, including the 5,000-acre National Tribute Grove. The park's tallest tree is 20 feet in diameter and 340 feet tall. Trees like these once grew throughout Oregon's southern coastal forest, but now they're nearly all gone. (1 hour) ◙

ASHLAND TO THE COAST

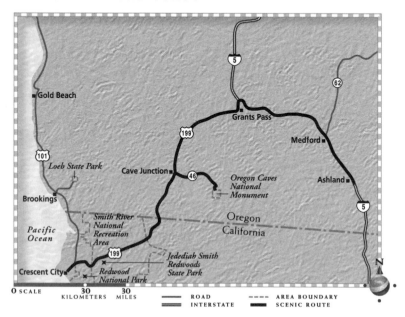

21

SOUTHERN OREGON COAST

U.S. 101 parallels the coast for 1,556 miles from Los Angeles, California, north to Port Angeles, Washington, and then swings south again to Olympia. Following this and the next three chapters, you can take a 346-mile drive up the Oregon coast and another 286 miles around the Olympic Peninsula to return to the Seattle area. That's an average of less than 160 miles per day for the next four days, but the many breathtaking view points and inviting beaches will make you long for twice as much time to explore.

Oregon's coast is 350 miles of practically continuous parks. A state law makes all seashore below the mean high tide mark public land, and 67 state parks and waysides along U.S. 101, as well as a 45-mile-long national recreation area, give access to the beaches and rocky shores practically everywhere. I've pared the list of Oregon coast scenic spots down to the "must-sees" plus a few less-known personal favorites. Despite such ruthless selectivity, the "Sightseeing Highlights" in this and the next chapter include more spectacular scenery and special places than any traveler could hope to visit in just two days. Here they are. Take your pick. ◼

SOUTHERN OREGON COAST

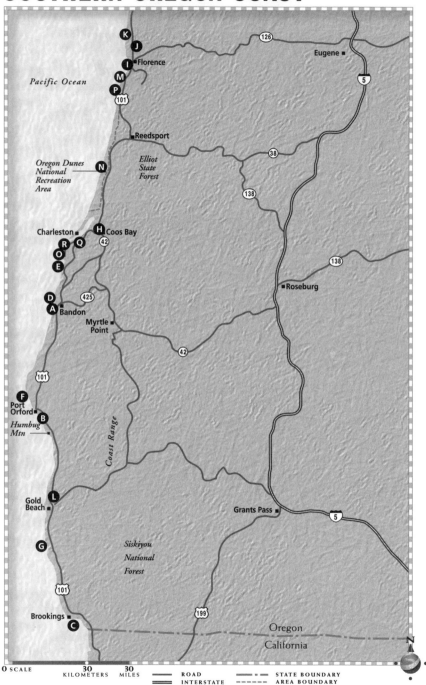

Pacific Ocean

K
J
Florence
I
M
P
101

Reedsport

Oregon Dunes
National
Recreation
Area

N

Elliot
State
Forest

Charleston
R
Q
H
Coos Bay
O
42
E

D
425
A
Bandon

Myrtle
Point

42

F
Port
Orford

B

Humbug
Mtn

101

Coast Range

Gold
Beach
L

G

Brookings
C

Siskiyou
National
Forest

126

Eugene

5

38

138

138

Roseburg

Grants Pass

5

199

Oregon

California

N

0 SCALE
30
KILOMETERS
30
MILES
ROAD
INTERSTATE
STATE BOUNDARY
AREA BOUNDARY

Sightseeing Highlights

Ⓐ Bandon

Ⓑ Battle Rock State Park

Ⓒ Brookings

Ⓓ Bullard Beach State Park

Ⓔ Cape Arago State Park

Ⓕ Cape Blanco State Park

Ⓖ Cape Sebastian

Ⓗ Coos Bay

Ⓘ Florence

Ⓙ Darlingtonia Wayside

Ⓚ Heceta Head Lighthouse

Ⓚ Sea Lion Caves

Ⓛ Gold Beach

Ⓜ Jessie M. Honeyman State Park

Ⓝ Oregon Dunes National Recreation Area

Ⓞ Shore Acres State Park

Ⓟ Siltcoos Lake, Dunes, and Beach

Ⓠ South Slough Estuarine Sanctuary

Ⓡ Sunset Bay State Park

Note: Items with the same letter are located in the same town or area.

A PERFECT DAY ON THE SOUTHERN OREGON COAST

Heading north on U.S. 101 from Crescent City, you will drive 51 miles to Gold Beach. Another 55 miles, and you'll be in Bandon. The driving distance on U.S. 101 from Bandon north to the campgrounds at Siltcoos Lake, Dunes, and Beach is 64 miles, and you have all afternoon to get there. Take the scenic route. Either of two turnoffs to the left, about 5 miles and 10 miles north of Bandon, will take you past the South Slough Estuarine Sanctuary, then to the village of Charleston, where a dead-end road takes you to Sunset Bay, Shore Acres, and Cape Arago.

Returning through Charleston, keep going straight into Coos Bay, where you'll find your way back onto U.S. 101. From there north to the campgrounds, the Oregon Dunes National Recreation Area lies between you and the ocean on your left, while on your right is a series of lakes.

SIGHTSEEING HIGHLIGHTS

★★★ **Florence**—Adjoined by Oregon Dunes National Recreation Area to the south and Siuslaw National Forest to the north, within an hour's drive of more than half of Oregon's coastal parks, this is the premier resort town of the central coast. Like Bandon, Florence has a recently gentrified waterfront Old Town. The main local holiday is the Rhododendron Festival, held annually for more than 80 years on the third weekend of May. Besides the usual small-town events, such as a parade, carnival, queen coronation, pancake breakfast, and soap box derby—and, of course, a rhododendron show—the festival features the Sunday afternoon Silver Trails Slug Race. (If you don't own a slug, you can rent one of these slimy little critters from local entrepreneurs.) (½ hour)

If you find bizarre flora intriguing, stroll the half-mile nature trail at **Darlingtonia Botanical Wayside**, 6 miles north of Florence, for a close-up look at carnivorous cobra lilies. Don't worry—they only eat insects. Admission is free. (½ hour)

Sea Lion Caves, the Oregon coast's most famous commercial tourist attraction, is 12 miles north of Florence. When the weather is lousy, the sea lions huddle inside the large cave, the only known year-round sea lion rookery on the U.S. mainland. On warm sunny days, the sea lions bask on rocky islands outside, and you can save the admission fee by watching them through binoculars from the overlook just around the next curve in the highway. The $6 elevator ride ($4 for children ages 6 to 15) down to the cave is well worth the price. Hours: 8:00 a.m. to sunset during the summer months, 9:00 a.m. to sunset the rest of the year. Phone: (541) 547-3111. (2 hours)

A short distance north of the Sea Lion Caves, **Heceta Head Lighthouse** is probably the most-photographed lighthouse on the Pacific coast. You may experience a sense of déjà vu as you pause at the overlook to snap your own shot of it. (1½ hours)

★★★ **Jessie M. Honeyman State Park**—About 6 miles north of the Siltcoos turnoff on U.S. 101 is the pride of the Oregon State Parks system. A truly vast campground and meticulous landscaping surround picture-perfect little Cleawox Lake, flanked by high sand dunes that create a big, steeply slanted beach for sunbathers. The lakeshore is usually crowded, and some nature lovers find the carefully shaped shrubbery flanking paved trails a bit too perfect; nevertheless, many Northwesterners cite this as their favorite park on the Oregon coast.

The campers' grocery store here has a low-priced snack bar. Popular trails lead from the park to the dunes and ocean beach. Admission is free. (1½ hours)

☆☆☆ Oregon Dunes National Recreation Area—The Oregon Dunes extend north from Coos Bay 45 miles to Florence. Coastal rocks in this area are sandstone, so over millennia, erosion from ocean waves has deposited prodigious quantities of sand on the beach. At low tide, winds blow the sand inland to create the dunes. Some of the sandpiles are over 500 feet high—taller than those of the Sahara Desert. Neither the ocean nor the largest expanses of open sand are visible from the highway for most of the drive, but short hiking trails can take you across the sand from several waysides along U.S. 101. Take your pick—any of them makes for an ideal one- to two-hour hike. While exploring the dunes, wrap your camera in a plastic bag to protect the mechanism from sand. Admission is free. Phone: (541)271-3611. (2 hours)

Siltcoos Lake, Dunes, and Beach, adjoining the National Recreation Area on the north, offer the most varied hiking in the Oregon Dunes area. An estuary creates wetlands among the dunes from the ocean to Siltcoos Lake, Oregon's largest coastal lake, on the east side of U.S. 101. Admission is free. (1½ hours)

☆☆ Coos Bay—Coos Bay is the largest town on the Oregon coast and the second-largest U.S. lumber shipping port. The principal sightseeing highlight in town is the Weyerhaeuser Lumber Mill, U.S. 101 at Newmark Street, (541) 756-5121, which offers free 90-minute tours Monday through Friday, between 10:30 a.m. and 1:30 p.m., mid-June through August. The lumber industry will be a gut-wrenching presence for the next few days as you drive up the Olympic Peninsula. The Coos Bay Sawmill alone churned out 20 billion board-feet of lumber last year. This plant tour will overwhelm you with the harsh reality of where forest products, from your furniture to the pages these words are printed on, actually come from. (Keep reminding yourself, "it's only a renewable resource." If you care about the natural environment, it's okay to cry.) (½ hour)

A less traumatic Coos Bay stop is the **Coos Art Museum**, where work by Oregon Coast artists is exhibited. Suggested donation is $2 for adults, $1 for children. Hours: Open Tuesday through Friday 11:00 a.m. to 5:00 p.m., Saturday and Sunday 1:00 to 4:00 p.m. Address: 235 Anderson Avenue. Phone: (541) 267-3901. (½ hour)

✮✮ **Sunset Bay, Shore Acres, and Cape Arago State Parks**—**Sunset Bay** is the first of three quite different parks on the Cape Arago Highway. From Seven Devils Road, turn left at Winchester; it's 5 miles to the end of the "highway." This small, round, secluded bay framed by forests of Douglas fir takes its name from the fact that it is most beautiful at sunset. The beach is peaceful and picture-perfect any time of day. Admission is free. Hours: Open daily during daylight hours.

Just down the road from Sunset Bay, the formal gardens at **Shore Acres State Park** were the legacy of lumber baron Louis J. Simpson, who used profits from cutting forests to landscape over 100 acres of rose gardens, Japanese gardens, rhododendrons, and azaleas. His mansion burned to the ground more than 50 years ago, but his gardens remain spectacular under the care of the state park service. Admission is $3 per vehicle. Hours: Open daily during daylight hours. Phone: (541) 888-3723.

Buy your picnic lunch in Bandon and eat at **Cape Arago State Park.** Secluded picnic tables overlook the sea. Sea lions often bask on the rocks offshore. At low tide, explore the tide pools at any of three coves below. North Cove, the best, largest, and easiest to reach, is a good spot to see sea anemones. Admission is free. Hours: Open daily during daylight hours.

The return trip along the Cape Arago Highway will bring you into the heart of Coos Bay.

✮✮ **South Slough Estuarine Sanctuary**—There's more to the Northwest Coast than beaches, dunes, and rocky headlands. Here you can explore coastal wetlands where fresh water flows into the ocean—or, when the tide is rising, where salt water flows into the estuary. This buffer zone supports abundant and varied wildlife. Thanks to the perseverance of local environmentalists, the 4,400-acre sanctuary at South Slough was the first of 20 wild coastal wetlands to be preserved in its natural state under the federal Coastal Zone Management Act.

It is a rookery for great blue herons and also attracts birds that migrate along the Pacific Coast Flyway. Beavers, bald eagles, black-tailed deer, and fish, including trout, salmon, steelhead, sea bass, and shellfish, make their homes here. You can see the whole estuary from the Interpretive Center. A 3-mile Estuary Study Trail descends by loops through the forest, past an abandoned pioneer homestead, to salt marshes, tide flats, and open water. The round-trip takes about two hours. Admission is free. Hours: Open daily from 8:00 a.m. to 4:00 p.m. during the summer months, closed on weekends the rest of the year. Address: Seven Devils Road, Charleston. Phone: (541) 888-5558. (1½ hours)

✴ **Bandon**—The self-proclaimed "Storm-Watching Capital of the World," Bandon has done an admirable job of rebuilding its town center, which was destroyed by fire in the 1930s and long-neglected afterward. The mostly new Old Town boasts outstanding gourmet and gift shops. Cranberries and myrtlewood products are local specialties. The biggest local holiday is the Cranberry Festival on the second weekend in September, but the year's most intriguing event is the sand castle sculpture contest held annually on Memorial Day, with stiff competition for cash prizes. If you'd like to participate, call the Bandon Chamber of Commerce at (541) 347-9616, and they'll send you an entry form. (1 hour)

✴ **Battle Rock State Park**—At the south end of Port Orford is the rock where, in 1851, nine would-be settlers retreated from unfriendly Indians. On top of the rock, they awaited a chance to move their colony farther up the coast. Climb to the cluster of pines on top of Battle Rock for the view, and bring binoculars. Sea otters, once nearly extinct, are making a comeback and can sometimes be spotted among the rocks to the south. (½ hour)

✴ **Brookings**—Horticulture is a major industry in Brookings, where 90 percent of all the lilies sold commercially in the United States are grown. **Azalea State Park**, in town, is a botanical wonderland—and a must-see if you're passing through in May when the azaleas bloom. In April Brookings' annual Driftwood Show brings together serious beachcombers.

North of town, **Harris Beach State Park** and **Samuel H. Boardman State Park** (the latter named after the "Father of the Oregon State Park System") provide access to miles of coastline where you can collect your own souvenir driftwood. Particularly attractive stops include Whalehead Beach, less than a ¼-mile from the turnoff 6 miles north of Brookings, where an offshore rock appears to spout like a whale; Indian Sands Trail, about a mile north of Whalehead Beach, a short, steep hike through forests and fields of flowers to the sea; Natural Bridge, 2 miles north of Indian Sands, a fascinating, photogenic view point of an island linked to the mainland by a rock span; and Arch Rock, about a ½-mile from the turnoff 3 miles north of the Natural Bridge Viewpoint, an unusual formation in a sheer cliff seascape. Admission is free to state parks in the area. Hours: The state parks are open daily during daylight hours. Phone: (541) 469-3181. (1 hour)

✷ **Bullard Beach State Park**—This long, broad beach 3 miles north of Bandon is an ideal place to get sand between your toes and hunt for pretty pebbles. Watch out for equestrians and off-road vehicles, though. Admission is free. Hours: Open daily during daylight hours. Phone: (541) 347-2209. (1 hour)

✷ **Cape Blanco State Park**—The 1870 lighthouse at the westernmost point in Oregon is typical of lighthouses found all along the Oregon coast. It is still in use, and the Coast Guard conducts free tours. Here you'll also find a rare stretch of black sand beach. (½ hour)

✷ **Cape Sebastian**—About 23 miles north of Brookings and 6 miles south of Gold Beach, turn off on a steep road up to the top of a 700-foot cliff that commands perhaps the finest view to be found on the southern Oregon coast. (½ hour)

✷ **Gold Beach**—This resort community's main attraction is jet-boat touring on the Rogue River, one of only 13 federally designated Wild and Scenic Rivers in the United States. The hydrojet boats carry up to 49 passengers, shoulder-to-shoulder, upriver through virgin forests and rugged canyons teeming with wildlife. You may see black bears, river otters, bald eagles, and beavers. Two-hour, 36-mile round-trips leave at 8:00 or 8:30 a.m. and 2:30 p.m. and cost $20 for adults and $10 for children ages 4 to 11. Longer jetboat trips are also available, as well as one- to three-day raft trips. Trips run daily, May through October; inquire about occasional winter trips. Reservations are recommended; in July and August they are essential. For complete information, contact Rogue River Mail Boats, P.O. Box 1165, Gold Beach, OR 97444, (541) 247-7033; Court's at Jot's Resort, P.O. Box J, Gold Beach, OR 97444, (541) 247-6676; or Jerry's Rogue River Jet Boats, P.O. Box 1011, Gold Beach, OR 97444, (541) 247-4571. (1 hour)

FITNESS AND RECREATION

Twenty-one miles north of Gold Beach, **Humbug Mountain State Park** offers the best hiking on the southern Oregon coast—a 3-mile climb to the summit of 1,756-foot Humbug Mountain overlooking the seashore. This is an ambitious half-day hike. For an easier stroll, the beach here—several miles long—is one of the best for beachcombing. Look for agate, driftwood, unusual seashells, and the rarest of seashore treasures, Japanese glass floats.

In **Oregon Dunes National Recreation Area, Eel Creek Trail**, and **Umpqua Dunes Scenic Area Trail** (each ¼-mile to open sand, another 2 miles to the beach) start at Eel Creek Campground, about 13 miles north of Coos Bay. About 11 miles north of the town of Reedsport, where the Oregon Dunes National Recreation Area Headquarters and Information Center is located, Tahkenitch Campground is the trailhead for **Tahkenitch Trail** (¾-mile through coastal forest to open sand, another mile to the beach). About a mile north of Tahkenitch Campground, at Oregon Dunes Overlook, the **Overlook Trail** starts at the south viewing platform (1 mile to the beach). Just north of there, the **Carter Dunes Trail** starts at Carter Lake Campground (¼-mile to open sand, 1¼ miles farther to the beach). On open sand the footpaths are invisible; follow the wooden posts to find your way.

Across U.S. 101 from the main beach access road at **Siltcoos Lake, Dunes, and Beach**, the **Siltcoos Lake Trail**, 2 miles through lush 50-year-old second-growth forest to the lakeshore, is a favorite spot of mushroom hunters; the trail is presently being extended to 3.3 miles. On the west side of the highway along the beach access road, walk the **River of No Return Nature Trail** (easy ½-mile loop from Lagoon Campground), the **Chief Tsiltcoos Trail** (1 mile to the beach from the trailhead by the main beach access road west of the Waxmyrtle Campground turnoff), or the **Fisherman's Trail** (1½ miles along the river from Waxmyrtle Campground to the beach). You can usually see wildlife in the wetlands areas along these trails, especially at sunset. Recently on an after-dinner walk on the Chief Tsiltcoos Trail, I watched for half an hour as five fearless beavers swam around the pond, sometimes approaching within 5 feet of where I stood. Speaking of wildlife, when exploring these trails be sure to wear insect repellent.

FOOD

Both Bandon and Florence have numerous regional and specialty food shops in their Old Town areas. Besides buying picnic food for today, now is a good time to start stocking up on gourmet groceries for the remainder of your trip. If you plan to cross back into the state of

SOUTHERN OREGON COAST

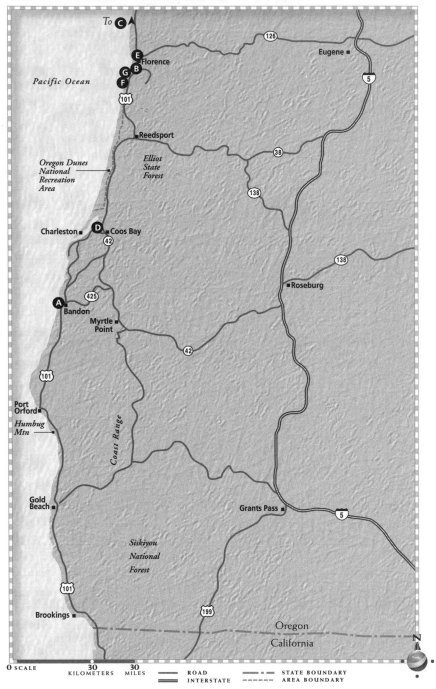

Pacific Ocean

To **C** A

E ■Florence

G **B**

F

101

■Reedsport

126

Eugene ■

5

*Elliot
State
Forest*

38

138

*Oregon Dunes
National
Recreation
Area*

Charleston ■ **D** ■Coos Bay

42

138

A ■
■Bandon

425

Myrtle
Point ■

■Roseburg

42

Port
Orford■

101

*Humbug
Mtn*

Coast Range

Gold
Beach ■

Grants Pass ■

5

*Siskiyou
National
Forest*

101

Brookings ■

199

Oregon

California

N

0 SCALE			ROAD	STATE BOUNDARY
30	**30**		INTERSTATE	AREA BOUNDARY
KILOMETERS	MILES			

Food

A Bandon's Cheddar Cheese

B Bridgewater Seafood Restaurant

A Cranberry Sweets Company

A Fish Market

B Incredible Edible Oregon

B Morgan's Country Kitchen

B Old Sarajevo Bakery

B Windward Inn

Lodging

B Driftwood Shores Surfside Resort

B Johnson House

B Money Saver Motel

D Newport Hostel

B Park Motel

C Sea Gull Hostel

A Sea Star Hostel

Camping

E Carter Lake

F Jessie M. Honeyman State Park

G Siltcoos Lake, Dunes, and Beach

Note: Items with the same letter are located in the same town or area.

Washington, fine dining or even grocery shopping opportunities will be quite limited for the rest of your trip.

In Bandon the **Fish Market** on First Street at the boat basin sells seafood from the local catch, as well as canned and smoked fish. Also on First Street, the **Cranberry Sweets Company** sells various types of candy made from the region's major fruit product. **Bandon's Cheddar Cheese** not only sells the cheese but makes it in public view.

In Florence **Incredible Edible Oregon** at 1336 Bay Street has a wide array of regional specialty foods from all over Oregon. The **Old Sarajevo Bakery** at 185 Maple Street is a fine little European-style pastry shop.

In Florence you'll find outstanding seafood, especially shellfish, at the **Bridgewater Seafood Restaurant**, 1297 Bay Street, open daily for lunch and dinner, (541) 997-9405. Meals here are fairly expensive. More moderately priced seafood, along with fabulous baked goods, can be found at the large but tasteful **Windward Inn**, 3757 U.S. 101, open Tuesday through Sunday for breakfast, lunch, and dinner, (541) 997-8243. Just-plain-good food at very reasonable prices is served for breakfast and lunch at **Morgan's Country Kitchen**, 85020 Highway 101 South, (541) 997-6991.

LODGING

The Florence area's largest hotel, and the only one on the ocean, is **Driftwood Shores Surfside Resort**, at 88416 First Avenue, about 4 miles north of town via Heceta Beach Road, (541) 997-8263. The resort has a beach, spa, and indoor pool, and rooms have balconies overlooking the ocean. Rates run $95 June through September, slightly less off-season. Another outstanding lodging choice is the **Johnson House**, a Victorian bed and breakfast downtown at the corner of First and Maple Streets, just a block from the bayfront. Rates range from $70 to $95 in season (mid-June through September), slightly less off-season. For reservations, write to the Johnson House, P.O. Box 1892, Florence, OR 97439, or call (541) 997-8000.

The Money Saver Motel, ¾-mile south of Florence at 170 Highway 101, (541) 997-7131, offers rooms starting at $50 in season (June through September), $14 less off-season. You can save more money on one of the small, rustic rooms starting at $47 ($13 less off-season) at the **Park Motel**, 85034 Highway 101, (541) 997-2634.

Florence has no hostel accommodations. You'll find them elsewhere along the coast at the **Sea Star Hostel** in Bandon, (541) 347-9533; the **Sea Gull Hostel** in Coos Bay, (541) 267-6114 (open Memorial Day through Labor Day only); and the **Newport Hostel** in Newport, (541) 265-9816.

CAMPING

Jessie M. Honeyman State Park is generally known as the finest campground in Oregon. It's certainly one of the biggest (382 campsites, second only to the campground at Fort Stevens). Despite its size, reservations are required here between Memorial Day weekend and Labor Day weekend but are not necessary at other times of year. To make a reservation, you must write for a campsite reservation application to Honeyman, 84505 Highway 101, Florence, OR 97439, or call the State Campsite Information Center at (800) 452-5687 within Oregon or (541) 238-7488. When you receive the application, fill it out and enclose a check for $10 ($7 deposit toward the first night's camping fee plus $3 nonrefundable reservation fee). Mail it directly to Honeyman State Park at the above address. Reservations can't be made by phone; cancellations can. If you cancel before 6:00 p.m. on the reservation date, you'll receive by mail a $7 "rain check" good for camping fees at any Oregon State Park.

In other words, reserving a campsite at Honeyman or any of the 12 other Oregon state parks that require reservations is a big hassle. If you don't have a reservation, you might be able to get a campsite anyway. Campsites that have not been reserved or for which cancellations have been received are assigned on a first-come, first-served basis.

The national forest campgrounds at **Siltcoos Lake**, **Dunes, and Beach**, and nearby **Carter Lake** don't have a reservation system, though they can also fill up early, especially on summer weekends and holidays.

NORTHERN OREGON COAST

The Oregon coast is a kaleidoscope of booming tourist resorts, quaint old fishing villages, lighthouses, tide pools, broad beaches, sea-swept headlands, sea lions, sea anemones, seafood, and Seaside. Evening will find you at the mouth of the Columbia River. (Lewis and Clark slept here.)

After you pass through big, busy Lincoln City, U.S. 101 narrows and winds as you wonder what happened to all the traffic. Resort development seems to have bypassed the stretch of coast highway from here north almost to Seaside. Along this, the low-rent district of the Oregon coast, quiet little towns that could stand a fresh coat of paint suggest what life on the rest of the Oregon coast must have been like 40 years ago. ◣

NORTHERN OREGON COAST

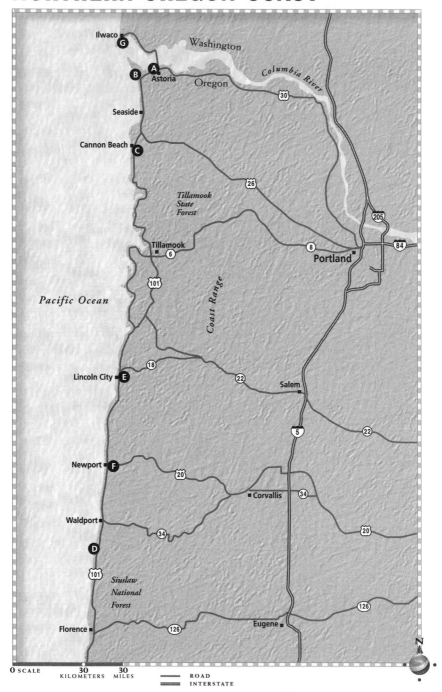

Ilwaco
G

Washington

Columbia River

A

B
Astoria

Oregon

30

Seaside

Cannon Beach
C

26

Tillamook
State
Forest

Tillamook
6

8
Portland

205

84

101

Coast Range

Pacific Ocean

18

Lincoln City
E

22

Salem

5

22

Newport
F

20

Corvallis

34

Waldport

34

20

D

101

Siuslaw
National
Forest

126

Florence

126

Eugene

126

N

0 SCALE
KILOMETERS   MILES
30   30

ROAD
INTERSTATE

Sightseeing Highlights

Ⓐ Astoria

Captain Flavel House

Columbia River
Maritime Museum

Fort Clatsop
National Memorial

Fort Stevens State Park

Heritage Center Museum

Ⓑ Beach Drive

Ⓒ Cannon Beach

Ⓓ Cape Perpetua

Ⓔ The "D" River

Ⓔ Lincoln City

Ⓕ Newport

Agate Beach Wayside

Mark O. Hatfield
Marine Science Center

Oregon Coast Aquarium

Ⓑ Seaside

Food

Ⓐ Café Uniontown

Ⓐ Maxine's Produce

Ⓒ Osburn's "World Famous"
Grocery Store and Delicatessen

Ⓐ Ships Inn

Lodging

Ⓐ Crest Motel

Ⓐ Franklin St. Station B&B Inn

Ⓐ Red Lion Inn

Camping

Ⓖ Fort Canby State Park

Ⓐ Fort Stevens State Park

Note: Items with the same letter are located in the same town or area.

A PERFECT DAY ON THE NORTHERN OREGON COAST

Follow U.S. 101 north all the way to the Washington state line, a distance of 186 miles. The first part of the trip, between Florence and Newport, contains the coast's most-photographed lighthouses and rocky seascapes as well as easily accessible tide pools. The area around Lincoln City, within easy reach of Portland, has the most commercial development. North of there the towns are older, quainter, and less prosperous.

After visiting Astoria, unless you plan to spend tonight there, cross the mouth of the Columbia River on the high arch of the 4-mile-long Astoria Bridge ($1.50 toll), and you're in Washington. Completed in 1966, this bridge was the last link in U.S. 101 up the entire Pacific coast from Mexico to Canada. Ten miles farther up the highway, take Highway 103 west (left) to Ilwaco and follow the signs to Fort Canby State Park.

SIGHTSEEING HIGHLIGHTS

★★★ **Cape Perpetua**—This is my favorite spot on the Oregon coast. Captain James Cook, the British explorer who later was the first white man to discover both New Zealand and the Hawaiian Islands, apparently didn't share my opinion. While searching for the Northwest Passage and naming practically every point of land along the coast for one saint or another, Cook designated this headland for St. Perpetua, an obscure third-century Carthaginian, after a March storm had held his ship here—"perpetually," it seemed—until he and his crew grew sick of the sight of it. From the visitor's center, 12 miles north of the Sea Lion Caves, a short hike across lava flows takes you down to a wonderful series of tide pools where you may discover sea anemones, starfish, sea urchins, hermit crabs, mussels, barnacles, limpets, and whelks. Look, touch, but please don't remove (or eat) them. On the way you'll see a shell mound, the only remaining trace of Indian habitation along the coast. Very little is known about these Indians—except that over the centuries they ate a lot of clams. Some of these piles of discarded shells are more than 40 feet high. Other trails from the visitor's center go uphill through old-growth forest with giant spruce trees. The longest, 4½-mile **Cook's Ridge Trail,** takes you to the top of the 800-foot headland for magnificent views of the coast. During whale-watching season, mid-December through May, wait patiently in the visitor's center hoping to glimpse a cetacean through the high-powered telescope. (1 hour)

★★ **Astoria**—In 1811, fur trader John Astor founded the first permanent settlement in the Pacific Northwest here. A replica of his small blockhouse fort is at 15th and Exchange Streets. The premier attraction in town, however, is the 123-foot Astoria Column atop Coxcomb Hill. Climb the stairway to the observation deck for an incomparable view of the town and the river mouth. (½ hour)

Murals on the column depict the city's history. To get there, drive—or, better yet, walk—along Eighth Street and turn left up Franklin Avenue, lined with nineteenth-century mansions; return down Grand Avenue, paralleling Franklin 1 block uphill, with equally magnificent historic homes. For a look inside one of these residences, stop at the **Captain Flavel House**. The high point among the museum exhibits is its collection of photographs showing the wreckage of ships that didn't quite make the treacherous passage from the ocean around the sandbars at the mouth of the river. Admission is $4 for adults, $2 for senior citizens, $2 for children ages 6 to 12. Hours: Open from 10:00 a.m. to 5:00 p.m. daily, May through October, and 11:00 a.m. to 4:00 p.m. the rest of the year. Address: 441 Eighth Street. Phone: (503) 323-2203. The admission charge also covers the **Heritage Center Museum** in the restored former city hall at 1618 Exchange Street, open the same hours as the Flavel House. The phone number is the same for both places. (½ hour)

Nearby, the **Columbia River Maritime Museum** is the best museum of its kind in the Pacific Northwest. See the Columbia lightship (an old seagoing lighthouse that guided ships into the mouth of the Columbia) anchored beside the museum. Admission is $5 for adults, $4 for senior citizens, $2 for children ages 6 to 18. Hours: The ship and maritime museum are open from 9:30 a.m. to 5:00 p.m. daily. Address: 1793 Marine Drive. Phone: (503) 325-2323. (½ hour)

Fort Clatsop National Memorial is a reconstruction of Lewis and Clark's end-of-the-trail fortress, where their party shivered and grumbled through the gloomy, stormy winter of 1805. "Winds violent Trees falling in every direction, whorl winds, with gusts of Hail & Thunder," wrote Clark (never much of a speller). "Oh how disagreeable our Situation during this dreadful winter." The visitor's center has audiovisual and museum exhibits on the expedition, and rangers in frontier costume demonstrate pioneer skills during the summer months. Admission $2 per adult, free for children 12 and under and seniors 61 and up. Hours: Open 8:00 a.m. to 6:00 p.m. mid-June through Labor Day, until 5:00 p.m. the rest of the year. Phone: (503) 861-2471. (½ hour)

Take a short detour north from U.S. 101 at Skipanon, around the peninsula that shelters Astoria, to **Fort Stevens State Park** to see what's left of military fortifications built during the Civil War to protect the Columbia River. As it turned out, the South never invaded Oregon, but in World War II Fort Stevens was fired on by a Japanese submarine. The most interesting sight here is the 1906 wreckage of the 287-foot British schooner *Peter Iredale* on the beach. Admission is free. Open daily during daylight hours. (1 hour)

✮✮ **Cannon Beach**—Traveling about 40 miles beyond Tillamook along the coast on U.S. 101 will bring you to this artists' colony. Take time to browse in the art and craft galleries. The local landmark, just offshore, is Haystack Rock. Around the base of the rock, tide pools contain a particularly colorful assortment of sea life. The year's biggest local event is Sandcastle Day, the third Saturday in June, which draws 1,000 contestants and up to 35,000 spectators each year. This sand sculpture competition has achieved such renown that the local chamber of commerce has been asked to help organize similar contests in North Carolina, California, and Australia. (1 hour)

✮✮ **Newport**—In the town of Newport (exit U.S. 101 just south of the art deco Yaquina Bay Bridge), the **Mark O. Hatfield Marine Science Center** houses a public aquarium where exhibits include more than a dozen large tanks containing native fish and other Oregon coast sea life, including many varieties of brightly colored anemones and sea pens, as well as a huge octopus. Another display, showing how beach trash cripples and kills sea creatures, is gruesome enough to haunt you whenever you start to toss aside a pop-top or plastic six-pack holder. Admission is free. Hours: Open 10:00 a.m. to 4:00 p.m., May through September until 6:00 p.m. Address: Marine Science Drive. Phone: (541) 867-0226. (1½ hours)

Oregon Coast Aquarium, a new aquarium in Newport, has indoor displays and a touch tank as well as an outdoor nature trail that leads among habitat exhibits with seabirds, sea otters, sea lions, and an octopus that lives in a glass-walled grotto. Admission is $7.75 for adults, $5.50 for students ages 13 to 18, and $3.30 for children ages 4 to 12. Hours: Open daily from 9:00 a.m. top 6:00 p.m. April through October, 10:00 a.m. to 4:30 p.m. the rest of the year. Address: 2820 SE Ferry Slip Road. Phone: (541) 867-3474. (2 hours)

About 2½ miles north of Newport, **Agate Beach Wayside** is a promising spot to beachcomb for semiprecious beach pebbles. The Newport Chamber of Commerce distributes a pamphlet, *Agates: Their Formation and How to Hunt for Them.* (1 hour)

✴ **Lincoln City**—Strategically located where the main route from Portland joins the coast highway, Lincoln City is the Oregon coast's boomtown. This "city" was formerly five separate towns, collectively known as the "Twenty Miracle Miles." Though it has a year-round population of only 6,000, driving through it on U.S. 101 seems to take forever. To find the town's namesake, turn left 1 block past the turnoff to Devil's Lake State Park and look for *Lincoln on the Prairie*, a 14-foot bronze sculpture depicting Honest Abe as a young lawyer on horseback reading a book. Maybe it's a guidebook; he's a long way from home. (Why Lincoln, you ask? In 1848, Honest Abe was appointed to serve as the first territorial governor of Oregon, but his wife objected to the idea of such a long journey to such a remote place, so Lincoln turned down the appointment and never set foot in Oregon.) (1 hour)

The **"D" River**. Short name. Short river. World's shortest, they claim. Flows 440 feet from Devil's Lake to the ocean. Lincoln City's major tourist attraction. If it weren't advertised, you'd never notice it. (2 minutes)

✴ **Tillamook Area**—Follow the coastline road through Pacific City, past **Cape Kiwanda** and **Cape Lookout state parks** (two more world-class seascape views), through the village of Oceanside, which looks out on **Three Arches National Wildlife Refuge**, one of North America's largest seabird nesting grounds in the spring and year-round home to a large sea lion colony, to **Cape Meares**, where you'll find an abandoned lighthouse and a giant, ancient Sitka spruce known as the Octopus Tree. This relaxed drive, which takes about half an hour longer than the main highway, not counting stops, brings you back to U.S. 101 at Tillamook, a dairy farming town that bills itself as "The Cheese Capital of Oregon." Stop to sample the local products at the **Blue Heron French Cheese Factory**. You can tour the Tillamook Cheese Factory, about a mile farther up the road, where you'll also find freshly made ice cream. (½-day)

✴ **Seaside**—The oldest resort town on the Oregon coast, Seaside has been a tourist mecca since the 1870s. Even earlier, this site was the end of Lewis and Clark's trek to the Pacific, as a reconstruction of the salt cairn where members of their party boiled seawater into salt attests. It's near the south end of the promenade. Recent big resort and convention developments have obscured some of Seaside's old-fashioned tourist town quaintness, and the decades-old Fun Zone amusement park seems in danger of being overwhelmed by video games. In midsummer, however, the high-energy crush of fun seekers on the 2-mile beachfront promenade is as exciting as ever. (1 hour)

At low tide you can drive your car or camper along the hard-surface beach for 10 miles from Gearhart to Fort Stevens State Park. The **Beach Drive** begins at Marion and Tenth Street in Gearhart, just north of Seaside. Free. Open daily during daylight hours. (1 hour)

FITNESS AND RECREATION

One of the best among the many hiking trails on the north coast, the 6-mile **Tillamook Head Trail**, an ancient Indian path believed to have been followed by Lewis and Clark, starts near Seaside and climbs to 1,200 feet above the ocean as it crosses Tillamook Head to Ecola State Park. Both Fort Canby and Fort Stevens state parks near Astoria also have hiking trails.

For bike touring, try the spectacular, physically demanding 40-mile **Three Capes Loop** between Tillamook and Pacific City. Bike rentals are available at **Mike's Bikes**, 248 North Spruce Street, Cannon Beach, (541) 436-1266.

FOOD

Stock up on picnic supplies in downtown Cannon Beach at **Osburn's "World Famous" Grocery Store and Delicatessen**, a "thrifty gourmet" grocery store in one of the town's oldest buildings. Cannon Beach also has numerous small specialty food shops that sell seafood, baked goods, candy, and wine. If **Maxine's Produce** is selling strawberry shortcake at its stand just south of Astoria, buy some. It's the biggest shortcake bargain I've ever seen, and the berries are fresh.

In Astoria, the **Ships Inn**, 1 Second Street, (541) 325-0033, is the best fish 'n' chips place I've found in the Northwest. All the locals go there. Try it and find out why. Lovely decor, a view of the mouth of the Columbia River, and a menu that runs the gamut from seafood tempura to Italian pasta make the **Café Uniontown**, 218 West Marine Drive, (541) 325-8708, a special place to dine.

LODGING

One of Astoria's grand Victorian mansions rents rooms. It's the **Franklin St. Station B&B Inn** at 1140 Franklin Street, Astoria, OR 97103, (541) 325-4314. There are only four guest rooms and suites, in the $60 range, so make reservations well in advance. Astoria also has less extraordinary, but perfectly acceptable, accommodations, such as the **Red Lion Inn**, 400 Industry Street, at the junction of U.S. 101 and U.S. 30, (541) 325-7373, with a view of the marina and river. Rates are $83 to $88 in the summer, $70 to $79 off-season. The **Crest Motel**, 533 Leif Erickson Drive, east of town on Highway 30, (541) 325-3141, also overlooks the Columbia River. Rates for a double room start around $46.

CAMPING

Fort Stevens State Park has Oregon's largest campground—605 sites, many with full hookups. Reservations are required from Memorial Day weekend through Labor Day weekend. The reservation procedure is the same as that for Honeyman State Park, described in Chapter 19. The address is: Fort Stevens, Hammond, OR 97121.

What's that? You're not sure you want to stay in Oregon's largest campground? Well, okay . . . drive across the river and over to the southern end of Long Beach Peninsula, where you'll find **Fort Canby State Park**. This park is the site of another Civil War era fort and another Lewis and Clark "end of the trail." (Clark described in his journal standing where Cape Disappointment Lighthouse is now and "beholding with estonishment this emence Ocian.") There are a total of 250 campsites in several campgrounds scattered through the 1,700-acre park. Fort Canby State Park also operates on a reservation system during the summer months. The reservation system is the same as that described in Chapter 4 for Moran State Park. The address is: Fort Canby State Park, Box 488, Ilwaco, WA 98642. The park also has a Lewis and Clark Interpretive Center, hiking trails, and beaches. For beachcombers, Waikiki Beach (which bears no resemblance to its Hawaiian namesake) has impressive piles of driftwood.

APPENDIX

METRIC CONVERSION CHART

1 U.S. gallon = approximately 4 liters
1 liter = about 1 quart
1 Canadian gallon = approximately 4.5 liters

1 pound = approximately $\frac{1}{2}$ kilogram
1 kilogram = about 2 pounds

1 foot = approximately $\frac{1}{3}$ meter
1 meter = about 1 yard
1 yard = a little less than a meter
1 mile = approximately 1.6 kilometers
1 kilometer = about $\frac{2}{3}$ mile

90°F = about 30°C
20°C = approximately 70°F

Planning Map: Pacific Northwest

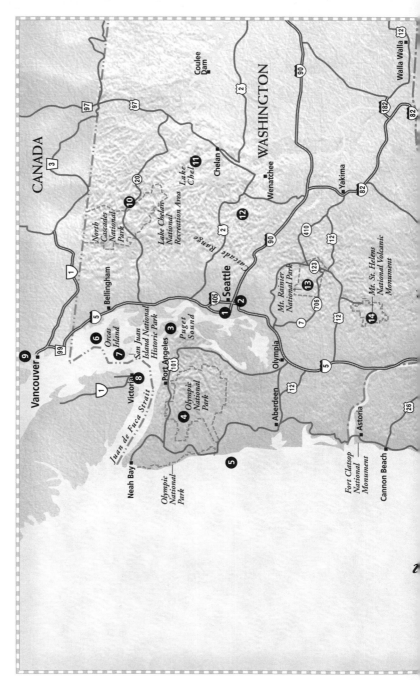

You have permission to photocopy this map.

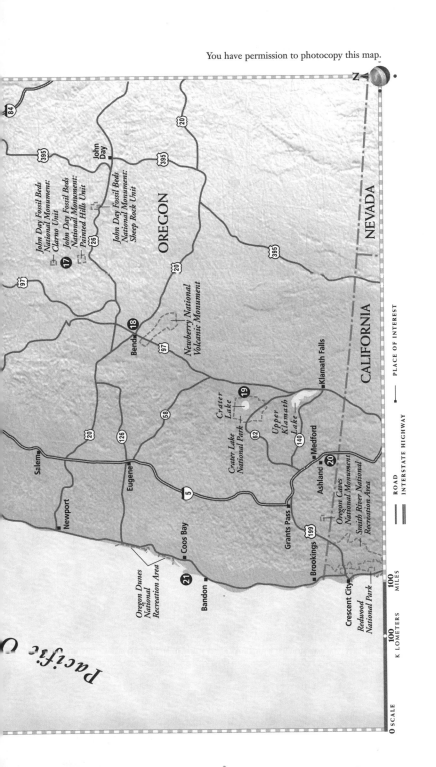

N

Pacific O

OREGON

NEVADA

CALIFORNIA

84

395

395

97

20

20

20

126

395

John Day

John Day Fossil Beds
National Monument:
Clarno Unit

John Day Fossil Beds
National Monument:
Painted Hills Unit

John Day Fossil Beds
National Monument:
Sheep Rock Unit

17

26

Bend 18

Newberry National
Volcanic Monument

97

58

Salem

Newport

Eugene

Coos Bay

Bandon

Oregon Dunes
National
Recreation Area

21

5

Crater
Lake

Crater Lake
National Park

62

Upper
Klamath
Lake

140

Klamath Falls

19

Medford

Ashland

20

Grants Pass

Brookings

199

Oregon Caves
National Monument

Smith River National
Recreation Area

Crescent City

Redwood
National Park

ROAD

INTERSTATE HIGHWAY

PLACE OF INTEREST

0 SCALE

100

K LOMETERS

100

MILES

INDEX

Map Index

Other Books from John Muir Publications

Rick Steves' Books

Asia Through the Back Door, 400 pp., $17.95
Europe 101: History and Art for the Traveler, 352 pp., $17.95
Mona Winks: Self-Guided Tours of Europe's Top Museums, 432 pp., $18.95
Rick Steves' Baltics & Russia, 144 pp., $9.95
Rick Steves' Europe, 528 pp., $17.95
Rick Steves' France, Belgium & the Netherlands, 256 pp., $13.95
Rick Steves' Germany, Austria & Switzerland, 256 pp., $13.95
Rick Steves' Great Britain, 240 pp., $13.95
Rick Steves' Italy, 224 pp., $13.95
Rick Steves' Scandinavia, 192 pp., $13.95
Rick Steves' Spain & Portugal, 208 pp., $13.95
Rick Steves' Europe Through the Back Door, 480 pp., $18.95
Rick Steves' French Phrase Book, 176 pp., $5.95
Rick Steves' German Phrase Book, 176 pp., $5.95
Rick Steves' Italian Phrase Book, 176 pp., $5.95
Rick Steves' Spanish & Portugese Phrase Book, 304 pp., $6.95
Rick Steves' French/German/Italian Phrase Book, 320 pp., $7.95

A Natural Destination Series

Belize: A Natural Destination, 344 pp., $16.95
Costa Rica: A Natural Destination, 380 pp., $18.95
Guatemala: A Natural Destination, 360 pp., $16.95

City·Smart Guidebook Series

City·Smart™ Guidebook: Denver, 224 pp., $14.95 (avail. 9/96)
City·Smart™ Guidebook: Minneapolis/St. Paul, 224 pp., $14.95 (avail. 10/96)
City·Smart™ Guidebook: Portland, 224 pp., $14.95 (avail. 8/96)

Unique Travel Series

All are 112 pages and $10.95 paperback, except Georgia and Oregon.
Unique Arizona
Unique California
Unique Colorado
Unique Florida
Unique Georgia ($11.95)
Unique New England
Unique New Mexico
Unique Oregon ($9.95)
Unique Texas
Unique Washington

Travel+Smart™ Trip Planners

All are 256 pages and $14.95 paperback.
American Southwest Travel+Smart™ Trip Planner
Colorado Travel+Smart™ Trip Planner (avail. 9/96)
Eastern Canada Travel+Smart™ Trip Planner
Hawaii Travel+Smart™ Trip Planner
Kentucky/Tennessee Travel+Smart™ Trip Planner (avail. 9/96)
Minnesota/Wisconsin Travel+Smart™ Trip Planner (avail. 10/96)
New England Travel+Smart™ Trip Planner
Pacific Northwest Travel+Smart™ Trip Planner (avail. 8/96)

Other Terrific Travel Titles

The 100 Best Small Art Towns in America, 256 pp., $15.95
The Big Book of Adventure Travel, 384 pp., $17.95
Indian America: A Traveler's Companion, 480 pp., $18.95
The People's Guide to Mexico, 608 pp., $19.95
Ranch Vacations: The Complete Guide to Guest and Resort, Fly-Fishing, and Cross-Country Skiing Ranches, 528 pp., $19.95
Understanding Europeans, 272 pp., $14.95
Undiscovered Islands of the Caribbean, 336 pp., $16.95
Watch It Made in the U.S.A.: A Visitor's Guide to the Companies that Make Your Favorite Products, 328 pp., $16.95
The World Awaits, 280 pp., $16.95
The Birder's Guide to Bed and Breakfasts: U.S. and Canada, 416 pp., $17.95

Automotive Titles

The Greaseless Guide to Car Care, 272 pp., $19.95
How to Keep Your Subaru Alive, 480 pp., $21.95
How to Keep Your Toyota Pickup Alive, 392 pp., $21.95
How to Keep Your VW Alive, 464 pp., $25

Ordering Information

Please check your local bookstore for our books, or call **1-800-888-7504** to order direct and to receive a complete catalog. A shipping charge will be added to your order total.

Send all inquiries to:
John Muir Publications
P.O. Box 613
Santa Fe, NM 87504